Reinventing an Urban Ve

With increasing population and its associated demand on our limited resources, we need to rethink our current strategies for construction of multifamily buildings in urban areas. *Reinventing an Urban Vernacular* addresses these new demands for smaller and more efficient housing units adapted to local climate.

In order to find solutions and to promote better urban communities with an overall environmentally responsible lifestyle, this book examines a wide variety of vernacular building precedents, as they relate to the unique characteristics and demands of six distinctly different regions of the United States. Terry Moor addresses the unique landscape, climate, physical, and social development by analyzing vernacular precedents, and proposing new suggestions for modern needs and expectations.

Written for students and architects, planners, and urban designers, *Reinventing an Urban Vernacular* marries the urban vernacular with ongoing sustainability efforts to produce a unique solution to the housing needs of the changing urban environment.

Terry M. Moor obtained a Bachelor of Architecture from the University of Texas and a Masters in Studio Arts from Harvard University. He served in the Peace Corps in Tunisia for two years. Upon returning to the U.S., he established his own architectural firm near Boston, and taught and served as department head and dean in the Department of Architecture at Wentworth Institute of Technology before retiring.

Reinventing an Urban Vernacular

Developing Sustainable Housing
Prototypes for Cities Based on
Traditional Strategies

Terry M. Moor

Routledge
Taylor & Francis Group

NEW YORK AND LONDON

First published 2017
by Routledge
711 Third Avenue, New York, NY, 10017

and by Routledge
2 Park Square, Milton Park, Abingdon, Oxon, OX14 4RN

Routledge is an imprint of the Taylor & Francis Group, an informa business

Library of Congress Cataloging in Publication Data
Names: Moor, Terry M., author.
Title: Reinventing An Urban Vernacular / by Terry M. Moor.
Description: New York, NY : Routledge is an imprint of the Taylor & Francis
Group, an Informa Business, [2017]
Identifiers: LCCN 2016041767| ISBN 9781138682528 (pbk) | ISBN 9781315545097 (ebk)
Subjects: LCSH: Housing—United States. | Vernacular architecture—United
States. | Sustainable urban development—United States. | City planning—
United States.
Classification: LCC HD7293 .M647 2017 | DDC 307.1/4160973—dc23
LC record available at https://lccn.loc.gov/2016041767

ISBN: 978-1-138-68252-8 (pbk)
ISBN: 978-1-315-54509-7 (ebk)

Typeset in Avenir
by Florence Production Ltd, Stoodleigh, Devon, UK

Printed and bound in the United States of America by Sheridan

"Through custom people cling to old traditions and try to perpetuate them by adapting them to new conditions, but necessity argues the case on its merits without much regard for precedent. Out of conflict comes a compromise in which the old is modified and adapted."

Walter Prescott Webb from *The Great Plains*

"The true basis for any serious study of the art of Architecture still lies in those indigenous, more humble buildings everywhere that are to architecture what folklore is to literature or folk song to music and with which academic architects were seldom concerned . . . These many folk structures are of the soil, natural. Though often slight, their virtue is intimately related to environment and to the heart-life of the people. Functions are usually truthfully conceived and rendered invariably with natural feeling. Results are often beautiful and always instructive."

Frank Lloyd Wright from *The Sovereignty of the Individual* (1910)

"I like to work on direct, honest solutions, avoiding exotic materials, using indigenous things so that there is no affectation and the best is obtained for the money."

William Wurster (1936) regarding the Gregory farmhouse

To Susan, my steady companion, my inspiration, and my joy everyday

Contents

Figures

Image Credits

With exception of the credits listed below, the author is responsible for all of the images presented in this book.

1.1   Library of Congress Reproduction Number: LC-USZ 62–16068
1.2   Library of Congress Reproduction Number: LC-DIG-pga-05780
1.3   Courtesy of the National Park Service Frederick Law Olmsted National Historic Site
1.4   Library of Congress Reproduction Number: LC-DIG-highsm-22775, Carol M. Highsmith Archives
1.5   Library of Congress Reproduction Number: LC-DIG-highsm-21694, Carol M. Highsmith Archives
1.6   Courtesy of the Regional Planning Association
2.2   Base map of the U.S. courtesy of the Department of Geography of the University of Alabama
3.1   Library of Congress Reproduction Number: LC-DIG-highsm-13007, Carol M. Highsmith Archives
3.2   Photo by author with the consent of Plimoth Plantation
3.3a   Courtesy of the University of Texas Libraries, The University of Texas at Austin: Perry-Castañeda Library Map Collection
3.3b   Image is located in Independence Hall Philadelphia, Pennsylvania
3.4   Photo by author with the consent of Plimoth Plantation
3.11   Library of Congress Reproduction Number: LC-DIG-nclc-04208
4.1   Library of Congress Reproduction Number: LC-HS503-749, Carol M. Highsmith Archives
4.9   Dr. Deanna Schmidt
4.10   Image taken from an Aladdin Company catalogue
5.1   Library of Congress Reproduction Number: LC-DIG-highsm-28028, Carol M. Highsmith Archives
5.2   Courtesy of the University of Texas Libraries, The University of Texas at Austin: Perry-Castañeda Library Map Collection
5.15   Library of Congress Reproduction Number: LC-DIG-highsm-12618, Carol M. Highsmith Archives
6.1   Library of Congress Reproduction Number: LC-DIG-highsm-33063, Carol M. Highsmith Archives
6.2   George Catlin; Smithsonian American Art Museum
6.4   Library of Congress, Geography and Map Division
6.6   Library of Congress, Prints and Photographs Division, Edward S. Curtis Collection, [reproduction number, LC-USZ 62–1145820]
6.8   Nebraska State Historical Society, [Digital ID: RG 2608–000000–002023–0]
6.10   Nebraska State Historical Society, [Digital ID: RG 2608–000000–003116–0]
6.12   Environmental Protection Agency
6.13   Library of Congress Reproduction Number: LC-DIG-highsm-04523, Carol M. Highsmith Archives

Acknowledgments

There are many people who graciously gave their time to make this book possible. I owe them all a debt of gratitude and wish to thank them for their kind help.

First, I wish to thank several members of my family who through their enthusiasm, encouragement, and thoughtful comments made the book a much better work than it would have been otherwise. To my wife, Susan, who in addition to her dogged efforts at editing my poor grammar and spelling gave her unrelenting moral support, which was needed especially in those times of doubt; no words can properly express my gratitude. To my son, Ben, who challenged concepts and gave sage advice when and where it was most necessary. Finally, to my brother, Ted, who supported me in so many ways, but most of all through his unfailing good humor and love of a good story.

My thanks to Marc Neveu, who helped me understand more clearly how I should approach the topic in general and then put it together in a consistent manner.

Steve Diamond, an old friend and colleague, for his interest and willingness to support my efforts in every way. To my colleagues, Troy Peters and Anne-Catrin Schultz, who were willing to read and comment on some very rough drafts. Their thoughts were invaluable. Chelsea Gazaille, my student research assistant, who saved me a great deal of time and effort through her love of architecture and research into it.

To three very kind and helpful women at the Historic Charleston Foundation—April Wood, Katherine Pemberton, and Karen Brickman Emmons—for their assistance in helping me discover the nature and history of the Charleston single house.

Several people were kind enough to contribute photographs. Benjamin Hall, an architect and my Airbnb host in Phoenix, I want to thank not only for the photo that he contributed of his beautifully designed project, which made the perfect example of how concrete block can be used in an attractive and appealing way, but for also reading the chapter of the West and giving me his great advice regarding the western vernacular. Katheryn Ritter, at the Taos Historic Museums, for her photo of the Martinez Hacienda in Taos, NM, and Allegra Sleep of the same organization for her follow up information. Dr. Deanna Schmidt for the contribution of her photograph of the Polish flats in Milwaukee, WI.

It is with a great deal of gratitude that I thank photographer Carol Highsmith for her extremely generous gift of over 30,000 images to the Library of Congress for public use. These beautiful photographs were taken across the country on a seemingly limitless number of subjects.

I wish to thank the many students who I had the privilege of teaching over my years at Wentworth Institute of Technology in Boston. They challenged my assumptions, taught me more than I could have ever predicted, and brightened my days.

Finally, my editors, Nicole Solano, Judith Newlin, and Krystal LaDuc, who brought it all together and made it into this book.

Chapter 1

Addressing the Future of the Evolving American City

Since the end of the Second World War, American cities have undergone numerous, significant changes that have dramatically impacted their physical development, our way of life, and ultimately, the environment. These changes have come so quickly and dramatically that they may more aptly be described as a revolution or an upheaval. By the 1970s, this transformation was well established. As a result, the current generation of homeowners does not perceive a significant change and accepts the present circumstances as given, but they are far from what their parents knew.

Until the 1940s or 1950s, our cities were places where different functions were blended together, overlapping one another. Housing, commerce, government, education, industry, and entertainment frequently were intermingled or located nearby. But after the Second World War, this model started to unravel. Those previously blended functions became more segregated and distant from one another, connected only by a vast system of roads. Cities expanded ever outward and suburbs became a much more important element in the scheme of urban development. Americans began to live at a distance from their jobs, in these "bedroom communities" far from city centers. As a consequence of this shift, our very way of life took a major turn and cities adapted to the change.

This postwar revolution in the cities was enabled as a result of the fact that automobiles became affordable and readily available to most American families. An infatuation with the car ensued that has not yet ended. Like many love affairs, this one promised much in the beginning, yet over time has begun to show signs of stress, become tired, and may be starting to fray.

While this new model has given most Americans a taste of independence from the problems of cities, it has created other issues that may be even more dire. These new problems have numerous, serious negative ramifications relating to our social fabric and to the environment. Pollution from the daily commute, the consumption of land and natural resources, and the long hours spent away from family and friends in cars are a few such issues that we now must confront. As a consequence, the rapid and overwhelming growth of suburbs could prove to be the cause for its undoing. Its very success may ultimately be responsible for its failure.

If we are to look to the future and suggest new and better ways to build and inhabit our cities, we must first have a clear understanding of our current circumstances. It is important to examine the causes and subsequent ramifications, as well as potential future problems that our current course may present. A better direction for cities in the twenty-first century is predicated on a thoughtful and objective analysis of the situation.

The Development and Transformation of the American City

Early Colonization

European countries seeking to secure a foothold in the New World laid out many of the United States' most important cities. The Spanish were the first to establish a permanent settlement in 1565 at Saint Augustine on the Atlantic coast in northeast Florida. Much farther to the west Santa Fe, New Mexico (1598) followed, then San Antonio, Texas (1691), as well as hundreds of other smaller towns and villages.

Other European nations followed the Spanish initiative and were also successful in staking their claims to different parts of the future nation. In 1625, 60 years after the establishment of Saint Augustine, the Dutch established New Amsterdam (New York City) at the tip of Manhattan Island. The English followed suit with the development of their own major population centers along the Atlantic seaboard in cities like Boston (1630), Philadelphia (1682), Charleston (1670), and Savannah (1733). Not to be left out of this scramble for colonies, the French established their capital in New Orleans in 1718 at the base of the Mississippi River.

For the most part, these new towns were ports built around commerce and trade with their focus on their waterfronts. Despite the country of origin, all of them contained within their boundaries every aspect of daily life. Government, commerce, and industry functioned side by side and the people lived among them. As a consequence, they were busy places, frequently crowded and full of social interaction.

After the American Revolution, existing cities continued to grow, while the country expanded westward to the Pacific. All along this expansion route, hundreds of small cities

Figure 1.1
In The Late Nineteenth Century, The Lower-East Side Of New York City Was Teeming With Street Life, And Many People Often Lived In Overcrowded And Squalid Conditions

and towns were established. American town planning followed rather straightforward and time-proven guidelines. They were almost always laid out on a grid. More often than not, the focus of the town was an important government building, church, or the major commercial activity of the community, such as the railroad station or sea or river port.

Until the mid-twentieth century, city centers, often referred to as the downtown, typically contained a blend of all of the various uses required by a modern society to function. Among other things, the downtown was where one could find employment, entertainment, education, and housing. Families lived in these centers or within a short commute to nearby suburbs and towns.

During the second half of the nineteenth century and into the twentieth, the population of many of the well-established coastal cities grew much larger. Many served as entry points for a constant flood of immigrants, such as the Italians, Irish, Scots, Slavs, Jews, Chinese, and Latinos, who arrived by ship from across the Atlantic and Pacific. Many of these newcomers chose to stay and take advantage of the opportunities that these crowded cities offered.

In addition to the foreign immigrants, many young adults from farms of the surrounding countryside sought employment in cities, further expanding their populations. Both of these groups were usually composed of the poor, who frequently arrived without any resources and in need of jobs that cities had to offer.

As a result of this overwhelming flood of newcomers, numerous problems developed. Overcrowding, racial and ethnic inequality, filth, disease, crime, and pollution made some parts of these cities undesirable places to live. They were the slums, the ghettos of the new world. Regardless of the poor living conditions, these people had few choices, as cities were where employment could be found and represented the steppingstone to a better future. As a result of the problems that plagued such cities, they developed a reputation that did not represent the American ideals of freedom, individualism, and resourcefulness, but became something more akin to an American nightmare.

The American Dream

Thomas Jefferson, who articulated the American dream, "envisioned a country ruled by yeoman farmers. Jefferson felt that urbanization, industrial factories, and financial speculation would serve to rob the common man of his independence and economic freedom."[1] The realization of such an agrarian democracy required space and land.

Typically, cities have never represented the dream of an improved lifestyle. It was the countryside that Americans felt most suited that image. The reality was that the preponderance of Americans did not live in cities or towns. We have been essentially an agrarian society for most of our existence. Immigrants arrived in cities, but many, if not most, quickly moved to the frontier where opportunity beckoned. In 1800, only 3 percent of the Americans lived in cities. Until recently, the country homestead, farm, or ranch represented our nation better than cities did. Currier and Ives best captured this wholesome ideal in their popular engravings of nineteenth century rural life. The charming home, cows in the pasture, clean air, and tranquility made the image compelling. Needless to say, this prospect was attractive to many city dwellers as an alternative to the old, crowded urban centers, but the possibility of escaping cities was not in place until the turn of the twentieth century.

Figure 1.2
A Currier And Ives Vision Of An
Idyllic Homestead In Spring,
Representative Of The American
Dream (C. 1869)

The Move Away from Cities to Suburbs

Prior to the advent of the electric streetcar, which only arrived toward the end of the nineteenth century, cities were very compact because the distances that people could travel quickly and easily were limited. The transition from the slow pace of horse-drawn conveyances to the more rapid and efficient electrical ones happened quickly. "Streetcar lines grew from 3000 miles, all horse-drawn, in 1882 to 22,500 miles of mostly electric lines"[2] 20 years later. As a result of this innovation, city neighborhoods located functional uses according to the natural economic guidelines relating to the streetcar routes, not zoning. "Apartment houses were almost always built near them to take greatest advantage of the convenience they offered tenants. Streetcars did not carry large amounts of freight, so only less noxious commercial development, such as retail stores, was pulled out of the central city, while heavy industry remained concentrated around wharves and railheads."[3] The concept of mixed-use cities was still very much alive.

Many affluent families, who were now better able to move away from city centers to more spacious, greener environments at their periphery, did so. One of the first planners to begin to satisfy this demand was the landscape designer, Frederick Law Olmsted. He conceived of numerous, innovative developments located just beyond the limits of cities' urban cores. His creations were naturalistic places such as Riverside, IL, outside of Chicago, which had winding roads and large homes with spacious, shaded yards. They were free from the dirt, noise, and poorer classes of the city. These communities were tranquil, safe, and distant enough to be clearly separated from nearby cities. These early idyllic communities along with others were our first suburbs.

By the late 1920s, the automobile was beginning to affect city life in a major way. The number of cars in the U.S. "soared from 8,000 in 1900 to 500,000 in 1910, 8 million in 1920,

Figure 1.3
The Suburb Of Riverside, IL,
Designed By Frederick Law
Olmsted And Calvert Vaux
(1868–1869) Sought To Wed
Nature With The Emerging
Suburbs

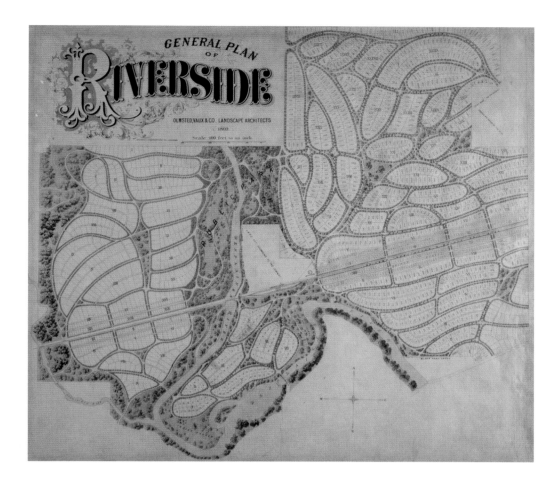

and 23 million in 1930."[4] By the beginning of the 1930s, New York City had "more cars than the whole of Germany, but it also had fifty thousand horses."[5] This multitude of cars began to crowd city streets, competing for space with horses, carts, trolleys, and pedestrians.

Distant travel and transportation of goods was still mostly done by rail, as roads outside of cities were not well-developed and were rarely paved. "The great, newly built Lincoln Highway—which proudly called itself the first transcontinental highway in the world —was continuously paved only from New York City to western Iowa. From there to San Francisco, only about half of it was."[6] During the 1930s and 1940s, this road network would grow exponentially due to the proliferation of cars and the subsequent need to serve their owners' ever expanding desire to have easy access to any destination. The development of a national system of highways was accelerated with the implementation of public policy that funded the construction of a massive new network, which was to blanket the nation from coast to coast. In 1956, President Eisenhower, reacting to the threats of the Cold War and corporate pressures, signed the Federal Aid Highway Act, thereby beginning the development of the Interstate Highway System. Today, there are nearly 50,000 miles of interstate highways in place, which represent the backbone of our transportation system.

The unprecedented surge of industrial activity initiated during the Second World War brought about a much higher concentration and a wide assortment of affordable goods; not the least of which was the automobile. Car styles changed yearly and millions upon millions were sold. The automobile represented the future with a new and unprecedented freedom for its owners. Coupled with an extensive highway system, most Americans could now begin to capture the dream of living a wholesome, tranquil country life away from the strife of the city.

The popularity of automobiles could not have happened without the aid of inexpensive gasoline. It was available in abundance and was left for the most part untaxed, therefore cheap. By not taxing gasoline, government was, in essence, subsidizing the flight from cities to suburbs.

This exodus was also bolstered by a measure to alleviate some of the economic hardship of the depression and foster home ownership. In 1934, the federal government began offering guarantees for mortgages through the Federal Housing Administration to homebuyers. These guarantees gave banks greater incentive to loan money for the purchase of first homes by many young families who would not have had adequate credit otherwise. Along with the income tax deduction for mortgage interest, the government made the ownership of a single-family home very affordable.

Developers, seizing the opportunity to capitalize on these new markets, began to offer small starter homes at very low prices outside city centers. Suburbs burgeoned and Levittowns began to spring up across the nation, as great numbers of middle class families chose the single-family house with its yard over the dense urban townhouse or apartment. The national ideal of home ownership now became a real possibility and we evolved into a suburban nation. The realization of the American dream into the now ubiquitous suburban lifestyle was codified in the fifties and sixties and was subsequently played out on television in programs such as *Ozzie and Harriett, The Brady Bunch*, and *Leave It To Beaver*.

As a result, enormous numbers of subdivisions supported by their requisite shopping malls, recreation centers, and schools have spread across the country. They have grown and prospered by providing wholesome environments for families to raise their children and, no doubt will continue to do so well into the future. However, as a consequence of their success, city centers have been greatly changed.

The Transformation of the Downtown into the Central Business District (CBD)

American city centers continued to grow and prosper through the early days of the twentieth century. In many cases, cities engulfed smaller, surrounding towns and communities, as their populations expanded outwardly. As the need for office space increased, they also expanded upwardly and saw a surge in the construction of high-rise buildings. Bill Bryson captured the mood of the day in his book *One Summer: America, 1927*, when he wrote,

> In the 1920s America became a high-rise nation. By 1927, the country boasted some five thousand tall buildings—most of the world's stock. Even Beaumont, Texas, had six buildings of ten stories or higher, which was more than Paris, London, Berlin, or any other European city.

> As buildings grew taller, the number of workers pouring into city centers from their outskirts grew and grew. Boston by 1927 had 825,000 people a day coming into its downtown or more than the entire population of the city. Pittsburg absorbed

355,000 workers every day; Los Angeles and San Francisco 500,000 each; Chicago and Philadelphia over 750,000 apiece; and New York, superlative in everything, took a whopping daily load of 3 million.[7]

It was not until the Great Depression in 1929 that all of this development stopped rather abruptly. There was nearly a 20-year hiatus in major construction across the country while we grappled with the staggering economic crisis and fought a major war in Europe.

After the end of the Second World War, middle class families began the mentioned exodus to the suburbs and downtowns went through a period of decline, losing a significant portion of their populations. Many buildings were abandoned and left to deteriorate. In some cities, these buildings were eventually torn down and vacant lots took their places. The poor—frequently minorities, the elderly, and foreign immigrants—were left behind often in old, poorly maintained buildings or in equally decrepit public housing projects. As racial tensions rose, in many cases, the urban fabric began to break down and once-safe family neighborhoods degenerated into dangerous slums.

To make matters worse, zoning codes implemented during the twenties and thirties began to define separate areas for different functions. The main rationale for redefining the city structure was to protect the property values of homeowners from the negative effects of heavy industry. The result, however, was that cities and towns began to develop distinct and separate zones with housing in one area, shopping in another, and offices in their own. This modernist concept of the ideal city did a great deal to destroy the once-

Figure 1.4
The Towers Of Downtown Los Angeles Shrouded In Smog Produced By Automobile Emissions

vital centers by alienating residential areas from them. Gone were the days of mixed use. "The worst offender in this urban destruction is the monofunctional mega tower, which paradoxically has become an icon of modernity and progress,"[8] claims Sue Roaf in *Adapting Buildings and Cities for Climate Change*.

By its very existence, the city's skyline is a reflection of not only current technology, but also societal values representing its citizens' collective goals and aspirations. Up to and through most of the nineteenth century, government and religious buildings were the most prominent elements that projected above the city. The dome over the state capital or county courthouse or the church steeple marked the important buildings of any city or town until well after the Civil War. For the most part, the modern skyline that we see today gives witness to the fact that our downtowns are now primarily places of business and commerce.

Throughout this transition, the city cores, which have always been important financial and governmental centers, remained unchanged. Even though many corporations moved out of cities, many stayed. In the 1960s, cities began to regain some of their importance, as larger, local, and international corporations saw an opportunity to consolidate their operations in even taller buildings than those of previous generations. They built skyscrapers not only to house their operations, but also to create an image, an iconic building befitting their corporate status.

In addition to corporate offices, other functions stayed downtown or were added to the mix. Local and state government offices located there from earlier times remained and were augmented, as the need for bureaucracies grew. Civic functions, such as museums and art galleries that represented the culture of the region, found a place in the centers. Sometimes, entertainment zones sprang up from past hot spots in older sections of the town. In some cases, even sport venues found their home downtown as in Baltimore and Houston, while others like Boston's Fenway Park remained. However, shopping came back only sparsely as families preferred the ease of parking at malls, in front of a strip mall, and little housing found its way back.

The Suburbs Have Maxed Out

The commute is now an instilled ritual of everyday life for most working Americans. The vast majority (128.3 million) of American workers must commute to jobs each workday. Of that number, 18 million (14.2 percent) commute from suburbs to cities. Nearly 27.5 million (21.4 percent) commute within cities. Another 8 million (6.2 percent) commute from cities to suburbs. Nearly a third (40.75 million) commute from suburb to suburb.[9] Freeway life in Los Angeles, considered by many to be the epicenter for commuting, was put in perspective by Reyner Banham when he wrote, "that coming off the freeway is coming in from outdoors. A domestic or sociable journey in Los Angeles does not end so much at the door of one's destination as at the off-ramp of the freeway, the mile or two of ground-level streets counts as no more than the front drive of the house."[10]

Consequently, highways in, out, and around cities are faced with gridlock during peak commuting hours, making life a great deal less pleasant for anyone caught up in it. The inevitable solution that traffic engineers propose is to add more lanes making highways wider and taking even more land. However, it has been shown in numerous studies that this is no solution, as more lanes only spawn more traffic. The only real, lasting cure for this problem is not wider roads, but to reduce the number of people on them.[11]

Figure 1.5
This Monday Morning Rush-Hour Traffic Coming And Going Into Chicago Is An All Too Common Scene In Any American City

It seems that in many places, we are beginning to reach the limit that commuters sitting in traffic are willing to endure. If we have not done so already, we certainly will soon. When that point is reached, there will be fewer people willing to drive such great distances and spend so much time and money doing so; the seemingly relentless development of housing farther and farther from downtowns will slow. Leigh Gallagher notes that fewer potential homebuyers are willing to commit to endless hours stuck in their cars in her book *The End of the Suburbs*. "The rate of suburban population growth has outpaced that of urban centers in every decade since the invention of the automobile, but in 2011, for the first time in a hundred years, that trend reversed. Construction permit data shows that in several cities, building activity that was once concentrated in the suburban fringe has now shifted primarily to cities, or what planners call the 'urban core'. Due in part to shifting demographics and aging baby boomers, demand for large, single-family homes that characterize the suburbs is dwindling, and big suburban home builders like Toll Brothers are saying their best markets are now cities."[12]

By the same token, the mall, which has for over the last half century been the main focus of suburban shopping, is showing signs of waning popularity. PBS's Paul Solman asks, "Why spend money on gas to schlep to the mall, when you can get the lowest prices possible online?" He follows up with the fact that "fifteen hundred [malls were] built from 1956 to 2005 . . . but barely a thousand are left today. Not a single new one built since 2006." It is expected that 15 percent of malls will "fail or be converted into nonretail space in the next decade," while "online shopping has doubled in the last 7 years . . . tastes and habits have changed." Linn Schlesinger of Harvard Business School goes on to state that, "malls have been declining for years and will continue to decline."[13]

It is clear that more people are now considering the balance between that American ideal of a home in the country and the convenience that city living offers. Many suburbanites are recognizing that their quality of life is suffering due to the long drive times they must endure. The advantages of city living, such as access to shopping and restaurants, as well as less time required on maintenance, now appear to offset some of the disadvantages they once were perceived to have had. More people are realizing that the American dream, as it was conceived, may no longer be as desirable as it once was given the high human, environmental, and monetary price one has to pay to enjoy it.

Future Challenges

It is clear that the transformation that cities have undergone during the latter half of the twentieth century has left us with some significant problems, but they are not the only ones that cities will face. In addition to the physical and social issues that have developed as a result of this evolution, a new set of issues has begun to surface over the last couple of decades, which has never been faced before. They are global in scope and will be faced to some extent by every living soul on this planet in the near future. There is no doubt that their effect on cities both here and abroad will be profound. Also, it is entirely possible that they will require us to make some significant lifestyle changes. They are many-fold, but the most important ones are as follows:

1. Global Warming

Everyone today is acutely aware of the problems that the world is facing regarding the effects of pollution on the environment. Some may choose to disagree, but the facts are clear enough for most of us—we created the problem and we continue to make it worse.

The burning of fossil fuels, such as oil, natural gas, and coal, has been proven to be the major factor contributing to the introduction of the greenhouse gas carbon dioxide (CO_2) into Earth's atmosphere. CO_2 along with several other gases has begun to create significant changes in the globe's climate. Scientists have determined that the decade from 2000 to 2010 "was the warmest on record and that the Earth has been growing warmer,"[14] since 1960. Additionally, the frequency and erratic nature of droughts, floods, blizzards, super-tornadoes, and hurricanes seems to have increased. Icecaps and glaciers are melting and sea levels are rising as a result. It appears that if nothing is done, this process will intensify, and at some point (if we have not already reached it) will be irreversible. Elizabeth Kolbert writes in *The Sixth Extinction* that many scientists now consider that we are in a new era, which they now refer to as the Anthropocene. It is considered to have begun with the Industrial Revolution less than two hundred years ago. As geological time goes this may well be the shortest era and the only one where the dominant species brought about their own demise.[15]

In order to slow or stop this trend, each of us needs to reduce our "footprint" on the planet. This implies doing less with less, which may be an untenable prospect to most people. We talk and write a great deal about sustainability, but it is difficult to give up any of our conveniences or comforts for the sake of the environment. There certainly are no shortages of SUVs on the road. Our energy consumption increases yearly. If the problem grows greater as it is projected to do, then we will have no choice but to live with our creation.

In order to reduce our collective footprint, people will be forced by simple economics to occupy smaller homes in more compact urban communities where they can live more efficiently and use a minimum of natural resources. Public transit or walking to work in lieu of driving an automobile is certainly a big, first step in that direction.

2. A Much Larger Population

While population growth in the U.S. will eventually slow, it is estimated that the country will grow from the current 300 million people to well over 400 million by 2051. This represents a staggering one-third increase, which will have enormous effects on all aspects of American life.[16]

Recent census records tell us that most Americans now live within urban areas or urban clusters. Urban in this context refers to metropolitan areas that encompass most suburbs in contrast with rural areas. As of the 2010 census, there were 80.7 percent of Americans living in urban areas and only 19.3 percent in rural settings.[17] Another way of looking at it is that "83.7 percent of Americans live in 336 metropolitan areas and 10.0 percent live in 576 'micropolitan' areas (towns with between 10,000 and 49,999 inhabitants). In other words, America is 93.7 percent city folk."[18] But either way, this does not mean that these metropolitan areas are necessarily dense. Many cities annexed the growing suburbs as they developed. Houston represents an extreme example as it now encompasses over 600 square miles with a population of 2.1 million people or only 3,500 people per square mile. By comparison, Boston has an area of 90 square miles and 636,000 people, resulting in a density that is more than twice that of Houston. Beyond those statistics, what was once considered the "downtown" in Houston now has very few residents living there.

Like cities everywhere around the world, American cities are going to be placed under a great deal of pressure in the forthcoming decades due to this exceptional growth. Most of them will experience a surge in population and with it will come many and varied complex issues. Most certainly, a great deal of more affordable urban housing will be required to satisfy these growing numbers.

3. The Lack of Affordable Oil

Oil is the major natural element that has fueled the flight to the suburbs from cities. While oil is a finite resource, for the moment at least, there seems to be an abundance of it.

There are some skeptics, however, who believe that it is now on the decline, but every new discovery seems to refute that view. The simple truth is that it is now more difficult to obtain than in the past. It is deeper and harder to extract, hence the need for fracking; it is found farther offshores than ever and much of it is located in countries that may be unstable and/or not have our welfare in mind. In his book *The Race for What's Left*, Michael Klare states, "In all likelihood, we are looking at the last oil fields, the last uranium deposits, the last copper mines, and the last reserves of many other vital resources. These materials will not all disappear at once, of course, and some as-yet-undeveloped reserves may prove more prolific than expected. Gradually, though, we will see the complete disappearance of many key resources upon which modern industrial civilization has long relied."[19]

It is possible or even likely that we will be running low in a generation or two at the rate at which we are currently consuming these resources. Like all other commodities, oil will increase in cost, as the supply dwindles. Over the last couple of decades, oil prices have roller-coasted up and down with seemingly little relationship to our long-term reserves. For much of the latter part of the twentieth century, oil prices hovered around $1.00 per gallon. In January of 2000, the average price of a gallon of regular gasoline in the U.S. was $1.35.[20] Oil then reached prices above $4.00 per gallon, which represented a three-fold increase from 14 years previous. In 2014, prices subsided by about half to around $2/gallon due to a renewed sense that there was plenty of it. Clearly, gasoline prices are coupled to the global perception of supply and vary accordingly. The long-term reality is that there will be less and less and prices will consequently rise.

We seem to have become reconciled to this new reality and are taking it in our stride. While the Prius is the most popular car sold today, there is no lack in sales of SUVs either. Furthermore, the EPA's statistics show that the average miles traveled by licensed drivers are increasing. In 1970, that figure was at 8.69 miles per driver; in 2010, it was 12.62; and in 2040, it is projected to be 13.28.[21] These figures show clearly that we are not only driving more than previously, but we will continue to increase our individual driving distances.

We are not alone in our lust for oil, as the world's growing population wants the advantages that we have had for so long. This additional pressure on supply is, quite naturally, compounding the problem. With a dramatic population increase anticipated and greater individual prosperity in what we now call developing nations, we can expect a much greater demand on oil in the future. With this greater demand prices will rise.

But can the price of gasoline increase even further? No doubt it can and very likely will. If so, will we be able to afford it? As gasoline prices rise, a larger and larger portion of one's paycheck will be dedicated to this daily commute and all of the other shorter, but still necessary trips. Suburbanites without the fiscal ability to fuel their cars will not be able to get to where they need to go, which will be compounded by the lack of public transportation. Ultimately, it will reach the point where the commute becomes infeasible to our poorest citizens. One wonders, where that point may be?

The overarching question here is: what will happen if there is a stoppage of the flow of oil as occurred briefly in 1973–1974 and again in 1978 or if the price of it climbs to untenable levels? If either or both of these two possibilities occur, then the daily commute will become much more expensive and many suburbanites will no longer be able to afford it. Europeans commonly pay three times as much for gasoline as Americans and the results are clear. They have a great deal less sprawl than we do, better public transportation options, and their cities have remained vibrant.

4. Scarcity of Modern Construction Materials

Steel, concrete, aluminum, copper, and glass represent the majority of the materials that we have come to rely upon to build our modern cities, but they too may be more difficult and expensive to acquire in the future.

Each of these basic construction materials requires a specific, natural resource for their creation. Steel comes from iron, concrete from limestone, aluminum from bauxite, and glass from silicate. These basic minerals have all become more scarce, therefore more difficult to mine, and consequently more expensive. Copper, for example, which is used as wiring, piping, roofing, and elsewhere has already become so valuable that thieves not only rip it from deserted buildings, but occupied ones as well.

All of the finished building materials come from these natural elements that need to be extracted from the ground, which require fossil fuels to accomplish. Once extracted, they must be transported to a plant where they undergo a manufacturing process using more fuel to transform them into the final, usable commodity. They are then shipped to the building site, which may be a great distance away. This lengthy and expensive process requires extensive amounts of fossil fuels, which are not only running low, but are polluting. The manufacture of concrete alone accounts for approximately 3.8 percent of all CO_2 gases emitted around the world.[22] Some scientists believe that the figure is closer to 5 percent.

Equally concerning as Michael T. Klare points out in *The Race for What's Left* is that bauxite and iron, both used commonly in construction, are not only becoming more scarce, but are now found only in areas of the world that are either unstable or potentially unfriendly. Like oil, our supply of construction materials that we have come to rely upon will not only become more expensive, but could be cut off entirely. As a result, we may find ourselves held hostage to tyrants and hostile governments.[23]

Our reliance on these finite natural resources will certainly become a problem in the future as they become more scarce and much more expensive. As a result, more traditional, and sustainable materials will need to fill this void. Materials, such as earth, stone, and timber, that were popularly used up to the mid-twentieth century, but were abandoned in favor of modern ones, will be available well into the future.

Can Technology Save Our Lifestyle and Our Cities?

When we hear dire predictions such as global warming and lack of oil, we often tend to rest easy, as we have an abiding belief that technology can solve all of our problems and life will continue uninterrupted or possibly get even better. We aspire to keep what we have, maybe get more, and eliminate any negative side effects through innovation. *Progress* is a keyword in our vocabulary, and in this context at least, it means that we can achieve greater and greater levels of longevity, comfort, and convenience through scientific advancement. Medicine, space exploration, and skyscrapers to name only a few, have all made our technical boundaries seem limitless. When it comes to solving life's problems, technology will find a way. We hope to find a way to run our vehicles without petroleum, but with a clean, renewable substitute. We are trying to get new sources of energy to propel our power plants that do not scar the Earth or pollute the atmosphere. We trust that someone will come up with solutions before time runs out. They always have so far, haven't they?

At this juncture, a qualified *maybe* is most appropriate, as no one has those answers yet. If we happen to find innovative, technical solutions to our issues, will they come with a new set of negative effects? We have experienced the negative results of our inventiveness with nuclear plant meltdowns, DDT, and the internal combustion engine among others. They all seem to have their price and the unanswered question is: Can we afford it, if it comes? This time there may be no easy fix, as even technology does have its limits.

New Directions

As shown, cities and their contiguous areas are evolving. The next generation will be different from previous ones in numerous and significant ways due to the unique problems that it will be facing. In order to make cities livable with the more limited resources that we will have available to us and still accommodate the expected large influx of humanity, it is clear that we are going to need to give much greater thought to the manner with which we rebuild them.

It is encouraging to see that in some cities across the country, a great deal of housing is once again being developed near their centers. But, it is being built mostly to accommodate young, prospering professionals, whether singles or couples, or the very wealthy, who are looking for an urban pied-a-terre in addition to their other home(s). Unfortunately, most of this new housing is contained in tall, elevator buildings with no

Figure 1.6
This Map Prepared By Regional Plan Associates Denotes *Emerging Megaregions* Across The United States

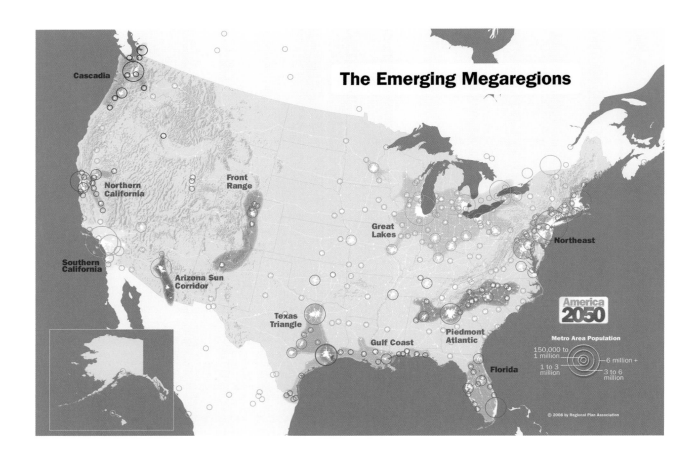

operable windows for fresh air and no outdoor space. Few families want or can afford to raise their children in such buildings, and as a result, they will continue to live away from cities in suburban single-family detached houses with yards until such time as adequate provision is made for them.

Obviously, tall buildings are the most efficient way to house large numbers of people, since they require very little land per individual, and similar units can be stacked to great heights. Therefore, they might seem to be the most economical, but that is not necessarily the case. They are very expensive to rent or buy unless subsidized by government as is the case with public housing.

In many instances, they have the advantage of a long-range view that can be initially appealing. They offer on one hand a high degree of security, as there is usually an attendant screening anyone entering the building, but on the other hand, in the case of fire or any other life-threatening issue, it can be problematic getting down and out to the ground level. However, the major concern when we are trying to build community is that the occupants are remote from the street level where community takes place. While they concentrate a lot of people in one place, people living in them are quite isolated from the street, since their view is of the horizon, not allowing for a focus on the more important factor—what is taking place near at hand in one's neighborhood. Also, they are built with the very materials that will be becoming scarce and inevitably much more expensive— steel, aluminum, and concrete. Ultimately, stuffing people into tall buildings is not the answer to creating new, vital, and sustainable communities.

It would seem from where we stand today, the next iteration of our urban habitat will need to be designed to accommodate a much larger population, including families. This will be done in the face of dwindling resources, which will present the future generations with some difficult challenges and the need for innovative solutions. Every generation before has had their own challenges, so this is nothing terribly new, but after decades of what we consider "progress," these new ones may require a certain amount of sacrifice. At the least, they will necessitate an adjustment in one's perception of wellbeing, accompanied by a redefinition of the American dream. In some people's minds, this may seem to be a rather hard pill to swallow, as change frequently is, however, in the long-run society and the planet may be much better off for it.

Our tendency is to pin all of our hope on technical solutions, but this may not be the way this time. There are more benign and traditional ones available to us currently, whereas future unknown technical ones are not and may never be available. It is not unrealistic to look to the past for advice, as many of the answers we seek may still be found in the adaptation of previous solutions. Our forefathers built buildings, societies, and cultures that were not only viable, but enviable ones. We must ask ourselves, what can we learn from them that may help us sort out and perhaps even solve many of our future problems? We clearly need to seek out a new urban vernacular.

Notes

1 Synonym. Summary of the Ideas and Values of Jeffersonian Democracy. Website: http://classroom. synonym.com/summary-ideas-values-jeffersonian-democracy-14320.html.
2 Cudahy, Brian J. Cash, *Tokens and Transfers: A History of Urban Mass Transit in North America*. New York: Fordham University Press (1990) p. 49.
3 Fischel, William A. An Economic History of Zoning and a Cure for Its Exclusionary Effects. Draft paper dated: December 18, 2001.

4   Fogelson, Robert M. *Downtown: Its Rise and Fall, 1880 to 1950.* Yale University Press (2001) New Haven p. 251.

5   Bryson, Bill. *One Summer: America, 1927.* Random House (2013) London p. 119.

6   Bryson, Bill. *One Summer: America, 1927.* Random House (2013) London p. 97.

7   Bryson, Bill. *One Summer: America, 1927.* Random House (2013) London pp. 219–220.

8   Roaf, Sue, Crichton, David and Fergus Nicol. *Adapting Buildings and Cities for Climate Change: A Twenty-First Century Survival Guide.* Architectural Press (2005) Oxford p. 249.

9   Bowman, Marcus. *About Your Commute.* July 2008. Website: www.slideshare.net/marcus.bowman. slides/us-commuting-statistical-analysis.

10 Banham, Reyner. *Los Angeles: The Architecture of Four Ecologies.* University of California (2009) Berkeley. p. 195.

11 Speck, Jeff. *Walkable City: How Downtown Can Save America, One Step at a Time.* North Point Press (2012) New York.

12 Gallagher, Leigh. *The End of the Suburbs: Where the American Dream Is Moving.* Portfolio/Penguin (2013) London p. 6.

13 Public Broadcasting. *The Rise and Fall of the American Shopping Mall.* Video Aired 11/28/2014.

14 National Oceanic and Atmospheric Administration. *NOAA: Past Decade Warmest on Record According to Scientists in 48 Countries.* Website: www.noaanews.noaa.gov/stories2010/20100728_stateoftheclimate.html.

15 Kolbert, Elizabeth. *The Sixth Extinction: An Unnatural History.* Picador (2015) NewYork.

16 U.S. Census Bureau. *U.S. Census Bureau Projections Show a Slower Growing, Older, More Diverse Nation a Half Century from Now.* December 12, 2012. Website: www.census.gov/newsroom/releases/archives/population/cb12-243.html.

17 *US Census 2010.* Website: https://ask.census.gov/faq.php?id=5000&faqId=5971.

18 *Madville Times. South Dakota Population Growth Fastest in Midwest.* Website: http://madvilletimes.com/2011/03/south-dakota-population-growth-fastest-in-midwest/.

19 Klare, Michael. *The Race for What's Left: The Global Scramble for the World's Last Resources.* Picador (2013) New York p. 16.

20 EPA. *Petroleum and Other Liquids* Website: www.eia.gov/dnav/pet/hist/LeafHandler.ashx?n=PET&s=EMM_EPM0_PTE_NUS_DPG&f=W.

21 EPA. Vehicle miles traveled per licensed driver, 1970–2040 (thousand miles). History Reference case 1970.00.

22 Marland, Gregg, Boden, Tom A., and Robert J. Andres. Global, Regional, and National CO2 Emissions. In *Trends: A Compendium of Data on Global Change*, Oak Ridge, TN: Carbon Dioxide Information Analysis Center, Oak Ridge National Laboratory, U.S. Department of Energy (2008).

23 Klare, Michael. *The Race for What's Left: The Global Scramble for the World's Last Resources.* Picador (2013) New York.

Chapter 2

Employing Vernacular Solutions to Future Urban Housing

We are going through a phase in the history of this country that represents extraordinary growth and change, but as it always happens at some point, we will enter yet another phase that takes us in a very different direction with new challenges. It is likely that this next one will reshape our cities and redefine our culture in many new, exciting, and innovative ways. These innovations may, in fact, rely more heavily on past solutions, as our future may not offer us as many options as prior ones did. As a result, prior traditional methods may be useful, as they could be able to satisfy our future needs in a more sustainable way. The time-proven vernacular approach still has lessons to teach, many of which we have discarded as passé and unsuitable to modern problems. It could offer us a way to improve our quality of life while shaping a new urbanity that can respond to a current national and global agenda. A new urban vernacular can go a long way toward establishing a basis for these objectives through a more sensitive and thoughtful approach that considers everything from the overall global environment down to the local neighborhood.

Figure 2.1
Century-Old Mixed–Use Brick Buildings Line Charles Street At The Foot Of Boston's Beacon Hill Creating A Vigorous Urban Village

Defining Vernacular Building

In general, the vernacular is considered anything that uses commonplace or traditional methods—techniques and/or technologies—as they relate to a specific place and time. We can speak in the vernacular when our language is local in its construct, vocabulary, or accent. One can refer to a regional way of dress, cuisine, or mode of transport as vernacular. It relies heavily on local traditions and customs for meaning and for its form, and therefore, in many respects, the vernacular can help to define a culture. As it relates to buildings, it is at times called a style, but it in fact, represents a pragmatic method for solving common needs and problems with locally available resources. It embraces simple, straightforward solutions that endure and surpass trendiness that style implies. Robert Flanders says it well when he writes "different house patterns of different cultures may usefully be termed 'types' as differentiated from 'styles,' because they derive from tradition rather than innovation, the intention to build the familiar rather than the novel, and indifference to any artistic tradition other than their own."[1]

Vernacular structures are the result of builders (1) accommodating climatic conditions, (2) carefully using locally obtained materials, and (3) satisfying basic functional needs efficiently and economically. To fit this definition, a structure must meet all three of these criteria as well as fit into a building tradition specific to the region where it is found.

There are many building types that fall into the category of the vernacular. Most older, agricultural structures such as barns, windmills, and silos do so. There are public, governmental, and civic edifices such as some small town courthouses and train stations, defensive ones such as castles as well as many others. However, more often than not, when one mentions the vernacular, they are relating it to housing—usually single-family dwellings—that is frequently found in rural locations.

This book seeks to adapt these defining characteristics of a vernacular building to multifamily housing because it is only by building more densely that we can hope to reinvigorate cities and their surrounding communities. The vernacular is not new to this approach. In many places around the world, we can find outstanding ancient examples of multistoried buildings that house many families under one roof. The mud skyscrapers of Shibam, Yemen, the Hakka round houses of Fujian province of China, and the German heavy timber houses of the Black Forest represent only a few examples. But there is no need to look so far afield or back to such a distant time. There exists a vast array of multifamily, vernacular buildings that still maintain their original function in American cities. The most commonplace would be the multistory apartment house with brick bearing walls and a wooden floor/roof structure that one finds throughout the Northeast in cities such as Chicago, Boston, Philadelphia, and New York City. Another is the three-decker found in Boston and many other New England cities and towns. These are relatively recent examples of regional, vernacular prototypes of multifamily buildings that continue to effectively serve the current occupants as they did previous generations.

Several of the precedents described in the following chapters were built toward the end of the nineteenth and into the first part of the twentieth century to satisfy the great demand for housing that arose due to a surge in the poor, immigrant population and an emerging wealthier middle class demanding better urban alternatives. Some critics may feel that these examples do not satisfy the strict definition of the "vernacular," as in many cases, professional builders and developers built them in large tracts for speculation. Nor were they crude, but refined with amenities, such as stoves in lieu of fireplaces, hot and cold running water, and bathrooms. They were in many cases not for poor indigenous peoples, but for clients of the rising and prosperous middle class. They used factory-built, standardized parts, such as windows, doors, hardware, and fixtures for bathrooms, appliances for kitchens, and gas or oil-fired heating systems. To construct them, they used new tools such as the lathe and scroll saw driven by electricity. But for the purposes of this book, these examples will be considered to fall under the broad category of vernacular, as they retain the general requirements for that designation. They were built primarily using evolving traditional methods and techniques, mostly of locally found materials and responded to the climatic needs of the region in one or more ways. While it may be tempting to exclude twentieth-century buildings from the list of vernacular examples, as some have done, it would result in a great loss. We may find that examples from the recent past have as much or more to teach us, as do more ancient ones.

Why Resort to the Vernacular in a Modern World?

Many believe that vernacular techniques relate solely to days gone by and are now dated, with no future. One could argue that times have changed, and we have advanced well beyond those "primitive" days of cute, stone cottages with thatched roofs—beautiful and charming, but irrelevant. They might say that we are at a point in our technical development that requires new and highly advanced solutions. However, we are entering a period where we could benefit even more from the vernacular approach, since it is one that is for the most part very practical, built at a human scale and normally sustainable, which many of our modern methods clearly are not.

Today, we have a wide array of materials to choose from, but focus mainly on steel, concrete, aluminum, and glass. Many, if not most, of them come from a great distance, and some may even be imported. All are manufactured at great expense to the environment. If transportation costs rise along with the price of fuel to a prohibitive level, this will have to change. In the past, people had fewer options of material choices than they have today and as a result used what was available. Usually, these resources were found close at hand and they were found in abundance or were renewable. Timber, earth, stone, and numerous other organic materials make up a short list of traditional building materials that are still available to us.

Now we acclimatize buildings through the use of mechanical equipment with the goals of stabilizing interior temperature and humidity in a very narrow band—our comfort zone. In order to do this, these systems are powered by fossil fuels. As previously mentioned, these fuels are finite and will ultimately run low and become much more expensive in time. They cause pollution and are the very cause of global warming that is threatening our existence. Sue Roaf writes, "the growth of the modern building paradigm was made possible only because of the advent of air conditioning, fuelled by cheap fossil fuel energy, and based, until perhaps now, on the belief in the availability of limitless energy to power the machines that provided buildings, wherever in the world.[2]

A vernacular approach to climate would involve living more attuned with nature and solving the challenges it presents through passive construction and energy strategies. Orientation to the sun and control of it lead the package of passive techniques. Wall and roof constructions that retain heat in cold climates or let breezes through them in hot ones are important methods that could be revived.

The vernacular builders seek efficiencies of space, as that is the best technique for saving time, money, and resources. However, over the past century, small, efficient buildings have not been an important priority; large, spacious ones are more often the goal. Currently, we are not concerned about saving space, rather we want to enjoy a luxury of it. Houses in the Northeast now average over 3,000 square feet in floor area. We are entering a time when savings of energy and construction resources will once again be a major priority and efficiency of space will play a major role in getting there.

Today one hears the word *sustainable* bandied about, but in fact, we are doing little to change our accustomed way of living. More insulation in our buildings, more energy-efficient lights, appliances, cars, some solar panels here and there, recycling trash, and water bans are some of the methods we are trying to cure major environmental problems. These are mild efforts, but palatable ones, as they represent no loss of comfort or convenience. We are reluctant to make any lifestyle changes and sacrifice any part of what we perceive as the good life we currently enjoy. Perhaps because we do not have a great enough impetus to make significant change, nor do we know what to do even if we wished change. This malaise will come to an end if and/or when gas, electricity, and building material prices increase greatly. While we feel that we are getting along just fine right now, that may reverse quickly and dramatically in the future.

Reviving and Reapplying Vernacular Principles to Modern Cities

If we are to revive our cities and make them into places where people will wish to return to live, their surroundings must be pleasant and offer as much or more than they can find in the suburbs. In order to do this, cities will need to be carefully restructured into places where one can live safe, comfortable, convenient, and stimulating existences.

Our goals in so doing must be to first satisfy the basic social and individual human needs by making them desirable places to live. This implies that we will need to build or rebuild neighborhoods where people will inhabit communities within the much larger whole. They will need to feel safe. They will need to have shopping, places of worship, schools, entertainment, restaurants, and all of the other functions that one requires for a complete life and these should be within a short walking distance. They will need a direct visual relationship with the street to maintain a sense of community that a high-rise building cannot offer. They will need private outdoor space in the form of a yard, balcony, or courtyard. They will need good public schools, playgrounds, and parks. They will need good, reasonably priced public transportation that will get them across town and beyond. Our future cities must be walkable with interesting streets that are filled with people engaging in numerous and varied activities.

Most importantly, we must create housing in a regional context that is functional and efficient, but has soul; that is climatically comfortable, but does not rely heavily on mechanical solutions; and is built with renewable and/or abundant materials. Putting people in more tall buildings will be counterproductive, as our cities will need people down at street level to give these places greater vitality. Our most wonderful cities rely on the connectivity and interaction between its citizens to make them vital.

Developing Regional Prototypes

The vernacular is the closest approach that we have to a truly sustainable construction method and with it comes a much more environmentally responsible and healthy lifestyle than our current one. Can these lessons that the vernacular has to teach be relevant today in a very complex and sophisticated world? Can they be made useful in the urban context where multifamily housing is going to be a requirement? Will a change of this nature increase or decrease the quality of our lives? All are worrisome questions that require good answers.

This book seeks to answer these questions and others by studying different regions across the United States, examining their particular traditions, environmental circumstances, and historically vernacular responses to these forces and to learn from them. It will also identify locally available construction resources currently overshadowed by modern ones that might be reemployed to help us build more responsibly. From this information are derived elements, components, and strategies that are still relevant for designing future urban structures with contemporary lifestyles in mind. The purpose of this exercise is to demonstrate the power, usefulness, and applicability of these principles to our modern society. The Appendix will contain examples of how these pieces can be combined into a single building for each of the six regions studied. These are only meant to be examples of the possible, not definitive designs. From them, it is hoped that other architects and students will take some inspiration and begin to develop their own solutions.

In designing future urban housing, the following general criteria must be kept in mind:

- Each building design is to relate to the specific, local region.
- Individual apartment units are to be comfortable living spaces that can accommodate a modern lifestyle.
- Buildings and apartments are to be as small and efficient as practical.
- Sustainable, locally found (traditional) materials are to make up the majority of construction resources.
- Private and public outdoor living spaces are to be provided for fresh air and sun.
- Buildings should be no higher than people are willing to climb—three to five stories—usually four.
- Buildings and their living units ought to engage the street wherever possible.
- Passive methods (orientation, shading from excess sun, etc.) are to be used to mediate negative environmental effects in order to maintain bodily comfort.
- The emphasis on the automobile and parking are to be minimized in favor of walking, biking, and mass transit.
- Retail, services, and other non-residential uses may be located on ground floors to create a mixed-use building.
- Public spaces need to be considered as a part of the buildings and neighborhoods.
- Proven technologies (solar, wind, and others) must be incorporated into the overall design.
- Water conservation strategies should be included in regions where scarcity is a concern.

After satisfying these broad goals, more specific criteria are suggested to help standardize the design of a new vernacular building. The next section is a summary of those criteria.

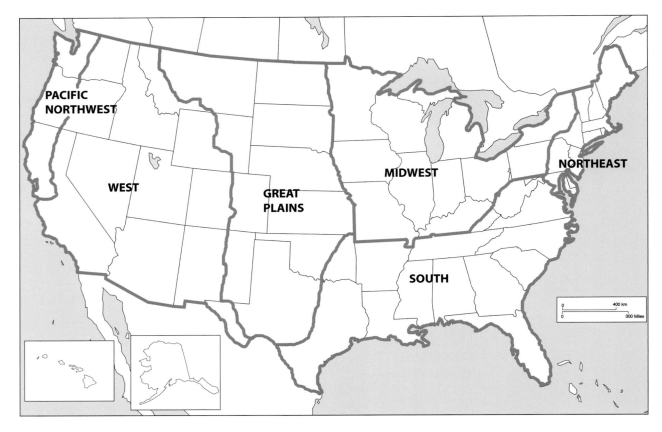

Figure 2.2
The Six Regions Of The Contiguous United States, Which Are Covered In This Study

Prototype Building Requirements

The structure should be substantially of sustainable materials. Acceptable materials include:

- Heavy timber or light wood frame for walls, floors, and roof structure
- Reinforced masonry bearing walls and columns
- Steel in a supplemental capacity
- Concrete for foundations
- Minimal aluminum
- Careful use of glass

Stairs will be the preferred method of vertical circulation; therefore, buildings should not exceed five floors (not including the basement level). Provide no more than one elevator for every twelve units when required. Avoid double-loaded corridors to connect units.

Natural daylight and ventilation will be used whenever and wherever possible, but will be required in all bedrooms and living areas. There will be no air-conditioning.

There will be suitable outdoor space (open air) provided to every unit on balconies, in courts, or yards. Every possible opportunity for plant growth will be used. Roofs will be green and accessible to all residents, whenever possible.

Building orientation to the sun and will typically follow these guidelines:

- Major glass on south side with protective overhangs
- Little glass on north side, if any
- Protected glass on east and west sides

Units will be modest in size with no more than three bedrooms. Maximum sizes shall not exceed:

- Master bedroom*   12' by 16'   192 s.f.
- Secondary bedroom(s)*   10' by 12'   120 s.f.
- Living area   12' by 16'   192 s.f.
- Dining area   10' by 10'   100 s.f.
- Kitchen   8' by 10'   80 s.f.
- Entry*   6' by 6'   36 s.f.

* Includes closets

Maximum sizes for units will be (measured to outside of wall):

- Studio   450 s.f.
- One-bedroom   600 s.f.
- Two-bedroom   850 s.f.
- Three-bedroom   1,000 s.f.

Basements will be functional beyond simple storage and mechanical areas, if possible.

Buildings will strive to include space for retail, cultural activities, community services, or common areas in addition to residential units.

Every building will include indoor storage for bicycles in an amount and location appropriate to the building program.

Water conservation in drier climates needs to be factored into the building design.

Energy efficiency is a major concern. Opportunities to incorporate passive strategies for heating, cooling, and electrical generation need consideration.

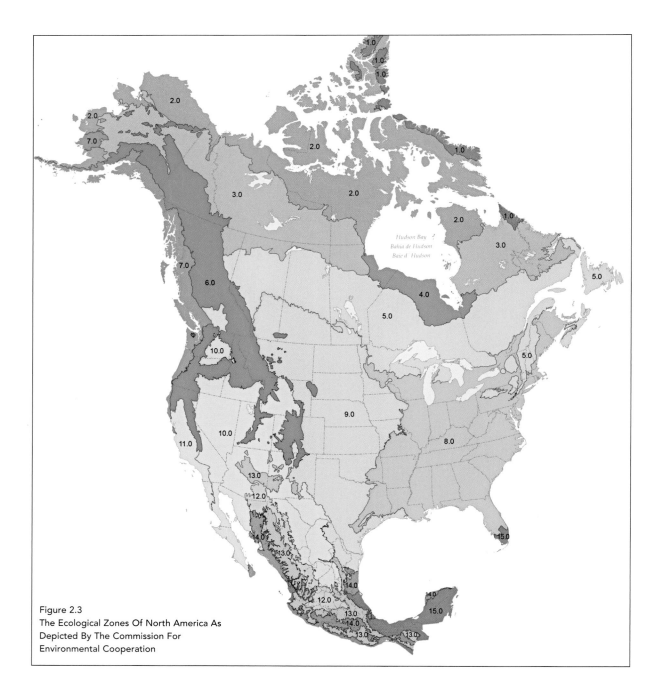

Figure 2.3
The Ecological Zones Of North America As
Depicted By The Commission For
Environmental Cooperation

Notes

1   Flanders, Robert. Ozarks Dwellings as Seen from the Road. *OzarksWatch*. Vol. IX, No. 2, 1996.
2   Roaf, Sue, Crichton, David and Fergus Nicol. *Adapting Buildings and Cities for Climate Change: A Twenty-First Century Survival Guide*. Architectural Press (2005) Oxford p. 219.

REINVENTING AN URBAN VERNACULAR

Chapter 3

The Northeast: New England and Mid-Atlantic Coasts

The Place

Located along the Atlantic coast in a rather narrow, but densely developed and populated band, is what we now know as the northeastern megaregion. It runs from Maine to the border of northern Virginia, stretching from one urban center to the next for nearly 600 miles, a distance that can be driven in fewer than nine hours. At times, it is also referred to as "Megalopolis," due to the fact that so many large cities are so near one another that they could be considered one super city. From Portland, Maine to Alexandria, Virginia, it includes some of the oldest and densest cities of the nation, which are connected to one another by a tightly knit transportation network. Interstate 95 and Highway 1, along with many other major roadways, in combination with some of the most heavily traveled railways in the country serve to form its spine or the northeast corridor.

Geographically, it is neatly defined or perhaps more appropriately stated—confined by the Appalachian Mountains on the west and north and the Atlantic Ocean on the east. Much of it occupies a gently undulating coastal plain that gradually rises in elevation to hillier terrain. It extends inland from the coast only a small distance, usually fewer than 80 miles, and includes all or most of nine of the original thirteen colonies.

It was settled first by Dutch traders and farmers in the New York area and by English Puritans seeking religious freedom around Boston in the early seventeenth century. In time, other western Europeans followed, clearing the land and eliminating the native population. Most of these new arrivals aspired to be farmers, but small cities began to develop along the coast based on trade and commerce. Portland, ME, Portsmouth, NH, Boston, MA, Providence, RI, New London, CT, New York City, NY, Baltimore, MD, Wilmington, DE, Philadelphia, PA, and Washington, D.C. now represent those tenuous embryonic footholds on the continent. By the late seventeenth century, they, as a group, became commonly known as "Yankees." No one knows exactly from where that nickname derived, but it is thought that it had Dutch roots. Whatever its origins might be, the connotation depends on the perspective of the speaker.

Most of these coastal cities were first settled because of their proximity to Europe and their advantageous locations on good, deep-water harbors. Their initial economic growth was based on trade and to an extent, still is. During the nineteenth century, manufacturing became an important element of the region's economy. That episode lasted barely over 100 years before manufacturers moved their operations to the South in the mid-twentieth century, where labor was cheaper and local governments more

Figure 3.1
Traffic And Office Skyscrapers
Lining Bustling Park Avenue In
New York City Exhibit The
Intensity Of Modern Urban Life

financially accommodating. Today, however, the fortunes of the region are supported by some of the world's largest service companies and institutions: financial, insurance, medical, high-tech, and education. In 2005, the region had a $2.4-trillion economy equivalent to one-fifth of the nation's gross national product, making it truly an international economic powerhouse.[1]

The people are generally regarded as industrious, politically liberal, and well-educated. Initially, the English settlers had the greatest impact on the culture of the northeast. Under British rule until 1778, it maintained a racial homogeneity well into the nineteenth century when it gave meaning to the words "melting pot" by absorbing millions of refugees from Europe. Scots, Irish, Germans, Italians, Scandinavians, and Chinese came in waves to escape the tyranny of their respective governments. This trend may have slowed, but has never ceased as immigrants continue to seek a new start here. Over the course of time, urban neighborhoods change in their ethnicity as one wave moved on and another took its place. As a result, the northeastern coastal cities are cosmopolitan in character, with any number of foreign nations represented.

The region's population, which totaled over 50 million people in 2015, continues to grow and is expected to pass 58 million by 2025. The current number represents "about 17 percent of the U.S. population on less than 2 percent of the nation's land area, with a population density of 931.3 people per square mile, compared to the U.S. average of 80.5 per square mile."[2] Even though growth may be slower here than in some other parts of the country, particularly the southeast and southwest, it will be significant.

Tempered by the sea, the region has a milder climate overall than its adjoining interior, even still its winters are cold and its summers are warm. Coastal Connecticut is the broad transition zone from the colder climates of the north to the milder temperate/subtropical climates to the south. Fierce coastal storms come with some frequency. While hurricanes, such as Sandy, can be disastrous, the most commonplace are the *nor'easters*, which blow in from the north Atlantic at gale force and can cause blizzard conditions as well as flooding of low-lying areas. In addition to strong coastal winds, there is a great deal of precipitation year round. It comes not only as rain, but a significant amount of it falls as snow and ice, which can be much more problematic. However, for most of the year, the weather is temperate and spring, summer, and fall along the coast can be very pleasant with sun and warm breezes.

The northeastern coast is a place with a long history of change and growth; therefore, with the expected increase in population, this trend will not be ending soon. Because so much of the region's land is already built upon long ago, new buildings will be needed to replace much of the crumbling development in cities and their adjoining suburbs. Likewise, it will require a careful restructuring and rehabilitating of antiquated infrastructure if these major cities are to continue to prosper. Many of these cities' future plans should look to previous examples for inspiration, as they have provided sound solutions in the past and offer many answers for the future by building upon its regional identity.

Early Development Patterns

Figure 3.2
A Reconstruction Of A Primitive Medieval House At Plimoth Plantation, MA, Similar To Those That The First English Settlers Built Using Traditional Methods

The cities that now line the northeast coast had their genesis under widely varying circumstances, which created innumerable, unique layouts. In the early seventeenth century, the first northeastern cities and towns were established as ports to secure a

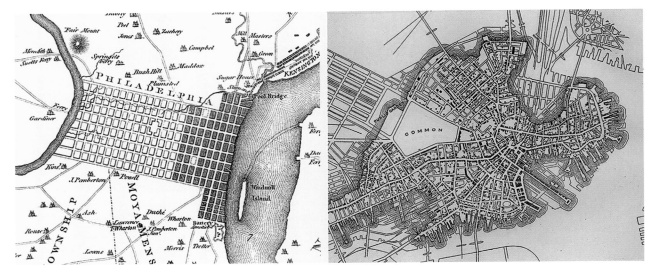

Figure 3.3
Early Plans Of Boston (1814) And Philadelphia (1777)

foothold on the continent. The cores of these earliest settlements were unplanned and displayed their medieval roots in a confusing tangle of streets that we have inherited. They followed Indian trails, skirted steep hills, passed by fortifications, and serviced bustling waterfronts from which they derived names such as Wall Street, Canal Street, and Broadway in New York City and Milk Street, Water Street, Tremont (three mountains) Street in Boston. William Penn, Philadelphia founder, planned the city as a straightforward yet sensitive checkerboard of blocks and squares. Washington, D.C., and to a lesser extent Annapolis, MD, which came much later, based their plans on the Grand Manner principles of boulevard, axis, and focal point, which were in vogue at the end of the eighteenth century.

From these beginnings, each grew into the modern cities that we know today and more often than not that growth was accommodated by means of a gridded street pattern. Cities expanded in stages, as was the case in Boston where smaller areas, such as Back Bay and the South End, developed independently from one another with unrelated grids. On the other hand, Manhattan imposed the most all encompassing one that now covers nearly the entire island within an unrelenting rectangular matrix of streets and alleyways oriented in a north-south direction.

As a result, the Northeast now has distinctive cities with great variety not only of layout, but also character. Blocks vary considerably in size and shape from one to the next, making it difficult for strangers to find their way. Public spaces such as parks and the placement of governmental and religious buildings over time found special niches within their local framework in often-unpredictable places. Mass transit evolved into individual systems, with little resemblance to one another. All in all, finding one's way around and through many of these streets is not an easy feat, and congestion can be a nightmare. However, they have developed into some of our most interesting, exciting and, in some cases, beautiful urban environments. They are walkable and populated by residents who by their presence give the urban context a special vitality.

Precedents

Mankind has been putting its mark on the Northeast for millennia, creating a rich and diverse vernacular heritage. Native Americans developed a wide variety of habitats to protect themselves from the cold winters in structures generated by necessity and evolved through long periods of trial and error. The white man had much the same need, but initially imported their methods and quickly adapted them to the new land.

The Wigwam

The term wigwam has been considered by some to represent any or all Native American house types, but this generalization is incorrect. It is, in fact, a specific type of dwelling that is found in a wide array of forms over most of the Northeast and well into the Mid-West. Across northern New England and southern Canada, "wigwam" has come to mean a conical, bark-covered structure framed with straight poles, much like the tipi, but not mobile. However, to those Algonquian-speaking Native Americans living along the Atlantic coast of New England the traditional wigwam was dome-shaped. Giovanni da Verrazano first reported these structures to Europeans when he visited Rhode Island's Narragansett Bay in 1524 as houses that were "of circular form, about 10 or 12 paces in circumference . . . covered with mats of straw ingeniously worked, which protect them from rain and wind." Within one of the larger structures, he counted twenty-five to thirty people living there.[3]

To the indigenous people, "the basic social unit was the village: a few hundred people related by clan or kinship structure. Villages were temporary and mobile. The people moved to locations of greatest natural food supply, often breaking into smaller units or recombining as the circumstances required."[4] This type of village structure dates back thousands of years. In the 1950s, archeologists uncovered a small encampment at Assawompset Pond in southern Massachusetts, where they found evidence of six circular structures averaging 36 feet in diameter that dated back to 2500 to 1800 BC. These structures were clustered around a ceremonial building that measured 60 feet in diameter.

The wigwam was this culture's most common housing type. It was generally used as a semi-permanent, summer dwelling for one or two families, but could be made more tightly for winter habitation as well.

It was a straightforward, yet sturdy structure that could be built in a short period of time by a single individual. The wigwam's basic framework was constructed out of green saplings of any readily available hardwood. These thin (about 2 inches at the base), supple poles were cut to lengths of 10 to 15 feet long. To increase their longevity, their bark was stripped, and it is believed the ends that were to be placed in the ground were hardened by fire. Construction usually took place in the spring or early summer when saplings are most malleable. The thick ends of the poles were set in the ground in a circular or oval pattern. The tallest saplings were placed opposite one another, as were the shorter ones. The saplings were then bent into arches to meet and lashed together, thereby creating its traditional dome shape. Another layer of poles was then wrapped horizontally around the first to form a sturdy structural grid.

Slabs of bark for winter dwellings or cattail mats for summer ones were placed shingle style over the frame. The covering was secured with leather straps or cordage obtained from the stripped bark to form a weather tight covering. In some cases, an additional frame, similar to the first, was constructed over the exterior covering to ensure

that it was held securely in place during stormy weather.[5] In 1634, William Wood described the wigwam's ability to protect one from the elements as, "covered with close-wrought mats of their owne weaving, which deny entrance to any drop of raine, though it come both fierce and long, neither can the piercing North winde find a crannie, through which he can conveigh his cooling breath, they be warmer than our English houses."[6]

The compact dome or hemisphere shape of the wigwam (similar to that of the igloo) has the least surface area of any possible volume, which makes it thermally the easiest to keep warm, therefore, an ideal form for a living space in cold climates such as that of the northeast coast. Similar to the earth lodge of the Great Plains, the rounded shape of the wigwam made it less vulnerable to winds. As it has no flat walls to push against, the wind would normally pass easily over and around the structure without causing great problems.

As with other circular indigenous dwellings, a fire for cooking and warmth was located in the center of the space. A smoke hole was provided above the fire that could be covered during rainy times. Unfortunately, due to the wigwam's low ceiling height, once the smoke hole was covered, there could be such a smoky build-up that it would be difficult to abide.

All in all, the wigwam was ingenious in its simplicity. Furthermore, it was an extremely weather-tight structure that was easily and quickly assembled, providing adequate protection from even the harshest weather. Developed over time through trial and error, it proved an invaluable shelter for the Native American for millennia before the white man came.

REINVENTING AN URBAN VERNACULAR

The Cape Cod House

The Cape Cod house of New England, often referred to as a "cape," was derived from the medieval prototype, the "hall and parlor," which was brought to the New World from England by the early colonists and adapted to their new homeland. Capes were "developed from the last quarter of the seventeenth century to about 1830."[7] Their popularity spread and "by 1740, such houses had been built throughout most of New England, and also on New York's Long Island. By 1790 it had made its way into southern New York State."[8] As circumstances and climate required, its shape was a simple one. It was rarely adorned with detail except around the entry door, as the Puritans would have had it. The typical cape is rectangular in plan, one story or one-and-one-half stories tall with a steeply pitched gabled roof with little or no overhang. It is symmetrical both inside and out. Normally, two windows flank a central entry door on the front façade, with one or two more on each end and another on either end of the attic/loft.

The interior layout is composed of a tiny central entry hall containing a steep stairway to an attic or loft. The first versions of the cape had only two rooms, one on either side of the entry. Later versions or the "full" cape had additional rooms to the rear. In these later versions, the "keeping room" was centered on the chimney and used as a kitchen/family room. A large portion of the space behind the entry hall was filled by a substantial brick mass, which held a fireplace for each of the rooms that surrounded it.

Figure 3.5
The Ubiquitous Cape Cod House
Of New England In Winter

The first carpenters and craftsmen that came to these shores built capes in a manner in which they were accustomed, using the prevailing technology of the day. These builders were fortunate to find locally an abundance of stone and wood with which to build. Softwoods, such as pine, spruce, and hemlock, provided excellent structural timbers; oak, maple, and cherry were used for floors and trim; and cedar made good siding and roof shingles. Usually, there was a hand-dug cellar with a fieldstone foundation. The main structure was composed of a traditional post and beam frame made up of large timbers, which were pegged together or joined with mortise and tenon connections, as manufactured nails were not then available. The space between the timbers was filled with the traditional wattle and daub. Wattle was a lattice of sticks, and daub was a mud plaster composed of water, soil, straw, and dung. Typically, the interior was then plastered or paneled in wood to give the home a finished appearance. Unlike their English counterparts where the wooden frame and wattle and daub infill was left exposed, the New England capes were covered with wooden clapboards to help fend against the harsher winter weather.[9] The entire structure was roofed over with cedar shingles. This assemblage, even though uninsulated, gave the house a weather-tight enclosure.

Glass was expensive at the time, as it was often imported from England and heavily taxed. Even though it was manufactured in America from early colonial times, most of it was shipped as small diamond- or rectangular-shaped pieces. Consequently, out of necessity, colonists made their windows small. The typical window was either a casement that was hinged to swing out or a double hung type that slid up and down. Double hung windows were composed of upper and lower sashes with multiple panes, usually four or six in each. Hinged exterior shutters were placed on both sides of the windows to protect from storms, as well as to retain heat in the house when closed.

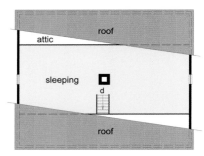

Second Floor Plan

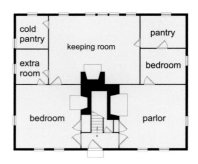

First Floor Plan

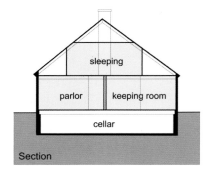

Figure 3.6
Cape Cod House

The cape was well-suited for the harsh northeastern coastal climate for a variety of reasons. Its compact shape reduced the exterior surface area exposed to the cold and at times buffeted by gale force winds. The ceilings were low, and therefore retained as much heat as possible near the occupants. Also, the central chimney, once heated by the wood fires in the fireplaces, would retain and radiate heat evenly to the surrounding rooms helping to make them comfortably warm. Usually, these houses were oriented with their fronts or long sides to the south with the strongest sunlight to help warm the interiors. At times, the houses would even be built over a small stream or spring to make fresh water accessible and convenient, without the need to go outside in the cold.

Saltbox

Figure 3.7
The Saltbox House Built By John Adams In Quincy, MA (C. 1681)

The saltbox house is a very close relative to the cape and springs from similar, post-medieval, English roots. Similar to the cape, it is symmetrical with a massive, central chimney and a room to either side; however, the saltbox is composed of two stories with a one-story, lean-to addition on the rear.

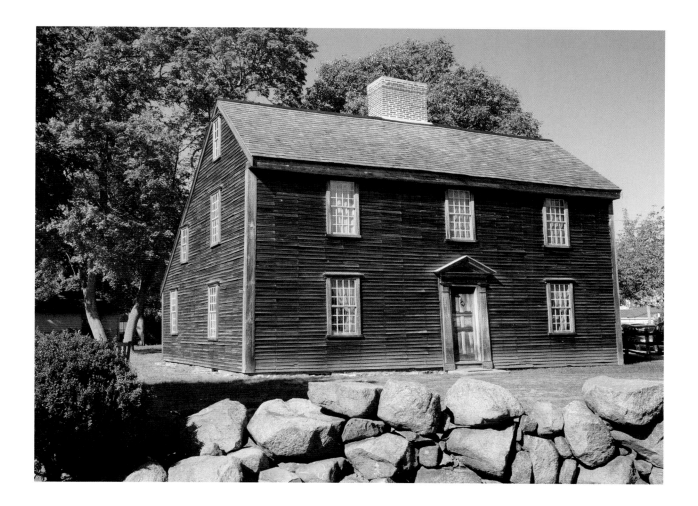

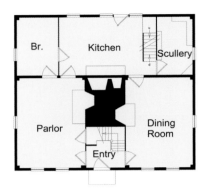

First Floor Plan

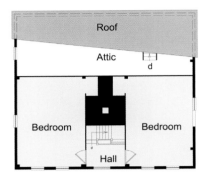

Second Floor Plan

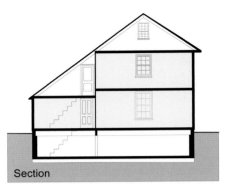

Figure 3.8
Saltbox House

The roof is the main discerning feature to the home and is the source of its name—it resembled a saltbox used at that time. Originally, the two-story section had a traditional steeply pitched roof with gabled ends with the shed roof attached at the rear over the addition. By 1700, these rear additions were usually included under a single main roof in new construction, or under reframed and lowered roofs remodels of earlier houses, hence the characteristic wedge shape.[10]

As the family grew, the kitchen was moved out of the main body of the house to an addition on the rear. In most saltboxes, the rear lean-to addition was divided into three rooms: a central kitchen with fireplace and oven, a room reserved for childbirth and nursing the ill, and a pantry or scullery.

Like the cape, it was framed with large timbers in the post and beam method. The spaces between the structural members were filled with either brick, or wattle and daub, then it would all be covered with wooden clapboards and plastered inside.

The saltbox was well-designed for the cold, damp, and windy New England coastal climate with its tight, compact form, and the central fireplaces to distribute heat efficiently to adjoining rooms. However, the saltbox had an additional virtue to that of other two-story houses; its roof had an aerodynamic shape, which directed strong winds over its mass. By so doing, strong winds would not directly confront vertical walls where it was most likely to infiltrate, but circulated past them.

Both the cape and the saltbox demonstrated how local resources were effectively used to create an innovative design that not only worked well with local climate, but also was economical to build. These virtues have served to make both of these designs favorites to this day.

The Row House or Townhouse

By the turn of the nineteenth century, many major northeastern cities had become quite crowded, the demand for housing within their restricted limits had grown beyond which the detached single family home could easily satisfy, and it became necessary to build homes more densely. As a result, the medium-density row house or townhouse became a favorite building type in urban areas. The American townhouse was based in part on

Figure 3.9
The Charming, Brick Row Houses In Boston's Back Bay Neighborhood Denote The Density Of The Typical East Coast City Of The Eighteenth Century

the Anglo settlers' tradition, the English terrace house, which was very popular in the seventeenth century and later. They were first introduced to this continent in Philadelphia and soon were adopted in neighborhoods such as Boston's Beacon Hill, Brooklyn's Heights, and much of Baltimore. As their popularity grew, they proliferated throughout major cities and their surrounding towns. Within a short period of time, it became the dominant urban dwelling prototype in most coastal cities and towns of the northeast.

By definition, the townhouse is a single-family, two- or three-story dwelling separated from its adjoining neighbor by a common, fire-resistant wall, known as a party wall. This arrangement saved precious city land that normally would have been the side yards in the typical standalone dwelling. They are also distinguished from other forms of attached dwellings by their uniformity. They are almost always set at a consistent distance from the sidewalk or front property line, are of the same height, and have a similar façade treatment with only minor details distinguishing one from the next. Their roofs are almost always flat.

Masonry was a favorite construction material, as fire was such a common hazard in these early cities. In colonial America and into the first half of the twentieth century, they were built with brick-bearing walls and wooden floor and roof structures. Stone rose in popularity as a facing material during the second half of the nineteenth century, the Victorian era, as Americans gained wealth and wished to express it. Brownstone, which is a sandstone commonly found in southern New England, became such a ubiquitous façade material that it is now in many places synonymous with the word townhouse.

Windows were double-hung and often trimmed with stone to add detail. The bay window was introduced by the Victorians to add interest to the otherwise flat façades, more space, and light to the interiors, as well as giving one the ability to look up and down the street, which a flat window could not do.

Usually, the row houses were somewhat raised above the street level over a functional basement, perhaps the kitchen. There was rarely a front yard, as the buildings were set near the sidewalk, but there could be a modest rear yard, which was not for personal enjoyment or play, but served utilitarian functions and as the location for the home's privy. The first floor was used as living space for the family and their guests with an entry, one or two parlors, and a dining room. Upper floors were reserved for bedrooms. Even though the roof was flat, it was rarely used.

Figure 3.10
Row House

First Floor Plan   Second Floor Plan

They were significantly more energy-efficient than a freestanding building, as they had a great deal less-exposed surface area. The shared party walls with the adjoining homes served to reduce the amount of energy required to heat them, and as a result, fuel cost was a great deal lower than in a standard detached dwelling.

As developers seeking profit built them on a rather large, block-by-block scale rather than individuals building homes for themselves, family, or neighbors, the townhouse might not be considered vernacular by some. But in most other ways, it fits that category quite well. The typical townhouse was a practical solution to an urban problem, built by local artisans from materials that were obtained locally. Even though it was a type built around the world for millennia, it was particularly well-suited to the climate of the northeast.

New York City Tenements

Today, the very word "tenement" has a negative connotation that was well-earned due to the often overcrowded and squalid conditions. They were built to house the enormous wave of poor emigrants surging into Ellis Island and settling in New York City after the Civil War, by landlords, with the intention of making as much money as possible. They were then and still are equated with slums due to their previous unsanitary living conditions, but they were the first home in America for many millions of people, and as cheap shelter, managed to give them a foothold in this new land.

Figure 3.11
Tenement Buildings In New York City Provided Shelter For Many New Arrivals To This Country Albeit In Frequently Overcrowded And Unsanitary Conditions

In those early days, New York's streets were vibrant and teeming with life. Immigrants settled into enclaves of their countrymen and neighborhoods developed individual ethnic character—Chinatown, Little Italy, Hell's Kitchen (Irish), and Yorkville (commonly known as Germantown), to mention a few. All such streets were lined with tenements and over-filled with these new American families.

Legislation that regulated the tenement design evolved from the first Tenements Act of 1879 through others up until the last in 1901—each designed to make the tenement a healthier place in which to live. The first tenements are now referred to as *pre-law* (before 1879) buildings,[11] as they were designed with practically no health or safety regulations other than a requirement for fire escapes.

They were designed to fit the standard New York City lot that typically meas-ured 25 feet wide by 100 feet deep. These five- or six-story walk-up buildings could accommodate twenty-six families in tiny, 325 square-foot apartments. They were often

Figure 3.12
New York Tenement

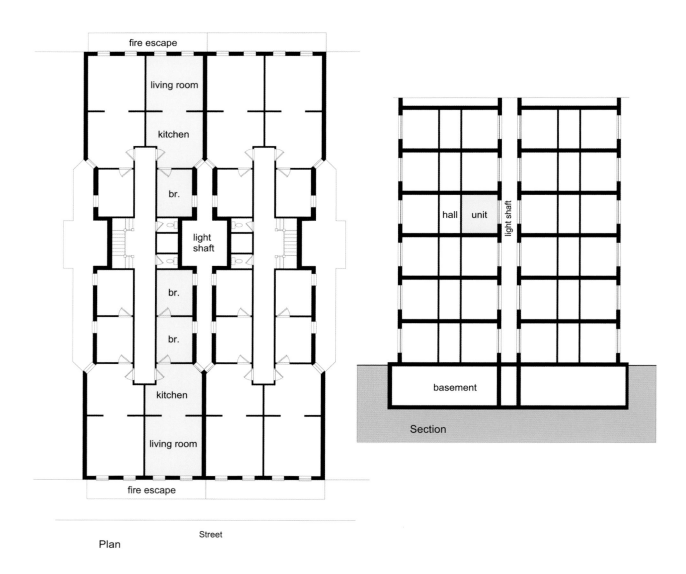

Plan

Street

Section

REINVENTING AN URBAN VERNACULAR

overcrowded with a family living in one room. They had no running water. Often these apartments had no windows, apart from those in the living room. Privacy was nonexistent as rooms were often accessed through one another without the use of corridors. Living rooms were also used as kitchens where cooking was done in a fireplace or coal stove. Water for cooking and washing would have been brought up in buckets from a tap in the backyard, which served dozens of families. Sometimes residents had to use a public water pump down the street. There were rarely bathrooms on the same floor as these apartments. "Privies or latrines (for the entire building) would have been in the basement or backyard, and be basically outhouses without running water, just a pit."[12] Not only were the apartments minimal in size, there were few outdoor spaces where children could play, adults could socialize or simply get fresh air and escape the apartments' stuffy confines other than the street, the adjoining fire escape, or the rooftop.

In order to resolve some of these problems, the legislature passed the 1879 Tenements Act, which mandated that each habitable room have a window opening to the outside, so that every room would be naturally lit and the whole apartment would have cross-ventilation. The plan that evolved from these requirements pulled the apartments away from each other in the mid-section of the building by 3 feet each, thereby creating a 6 foot wide airshaft that ran up through the building. The resulting layouts were called dumbbell apartments because of their shape, narrow in the middle and wide at both ends. This act ended in failure as the tenants threw their garbage down the shafts, making for an even more unsanitary situation. To make matters worse, "the airshaft acted as a flue spreading fire from apartment to apartment. The 1901 law did away with the airshaft, replacing it with the large courtyard for garbage storage and removal."[13]

These structures were constructed by many of the same immigrant laborers, carpenters, and masons who might be occupying similar ones. They built them well and most are as sturdy today as they were then. They were built upon a stone foundation with thick, brick-bearing walls, wood floor, and roof joists. They have now been converted into updated apartments in recently gentrified neighborhoods for a new generation of city dwellers.

Boston Three-Decker

The typical three-decker, also known as a triple-decker, is a free-standing, three-story apartment building built on narrow urban lots. There are identical units on each floor, except in some cases, the first floor could have had space taken out of it for the building's entry. Normally, there are only three units in a building, but some were built as doubles with six units.

They originated during the later part of the nineteenth century in eastern Massachusetts cities such as Boston, Cambridge, Somerville, Worcester, and Fall River where large working class immigrant populations needed affordable housing. They developed along the expanding electric trolley lines that fed newly developing neighborhoods, where land was relatively cheap, yet near city centers and employment. The building type proved so successful that subsequently it was constructed in most of the larger, industrialized New England cities and towns. They now represent a ubiquitous building type in eastern cities such as Boston, where over 15,000 were built and most still stand today.

They were frequently the first home for many families just starting out. Often, the building owners would live in one unit with their family, while the other two were rented

Figure 3.13
The Typical Three-Decker, Such
As This One In Cambridge, MA,
Could Provide Several Families A
First Home With Adequate
Sunlight, Ventilation, And Space

out to help pay expenses. It was smaller than a house, but larger than many apartments with each unit having two or three bedrooms, adequate for most urban families.

Following the development of the basic prototype, Arthur J. Krim notes that the three-decker took on different stylistic designs that included an Early Classic Period, a Late Classic Period, and finally, a less-imaginative Functional Period. Not everyone admired the proliferation of this building type. In *Streetcar Suburbs*, Sam Bass Warner, Jr. described, "cramped streets" of three-deckers that turned the notion of the city beautiful into an "ugly joke."[14]

Because the buildings were free-standing, unlike the New York tenement, the three-decker had windows on all four sides offering a great deal of light and natural ventilation. The front often had a porch, but the rear always provided an outdoor family living space as well as a useful outdoor space for such necessary activities as hanging clothes to dry. It also could be a place for a back staircase, which served as a second means of egress, to save space inside.

Addressing the nature of the builders of triple-deckers in a report to the Boston Landmark Commission historian, Arthur Krim wrote: "Since the building of three-deckers was a competitive business, which did not require large amounts of capital, the builders themselves tended to be drawn from the ranks of local tradesmen. Evidence suggests the existence of a community of builders—an informal alliance of tradesmen and speculators who worked for and with each other, borrowing and inventing designs. It is they who were most responsible for the lively vernacular quality of the streetscapes of porches and cornices . . . While some of these builders were Yankee carpenters, most of the three-deckers were constructed by newly emergent immigrant groups—Irish, Canadians, Jews and Italians, the very people the triple-deckers were meant to attract."[15]

They were framed of light wood members, which is still a standard method of home and commercial building construction used today. The exterior was usually covered with wooden clapboards, but some of the finer examples were built with brick-bearing exterior walls. The first floor was usually elevated above the street level over a basement with walls of stone. The roof was most often flat, but could also be pitched depending on the preference of the builder or current style at the time or place. Double-hung windows were the norm, but colored glass was frequently introduced in some windows to add a touch of interest.

Construction of three-deckers ceased toward the end of the 1920s with the onset of the economic depression, a lack of new building sites, and more stringent zoning requirements. However, these iconic buildings have proven to be extremely adaptable to modern lifestyles and will no doubt be of service well into the future.

Figure 3.14
Boston Three-Decker

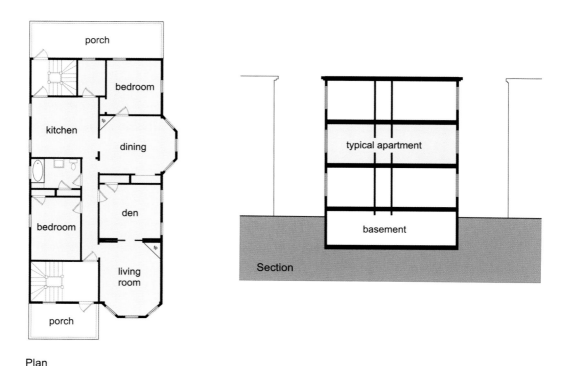

Plan

Common Themes Found in Traditional Buildings Along the Northeast Coast

Shape and Placement

Along the northeast seaboard, the main climatic concerns have been overwhelmingly those of its cold winters and storms, which can bring harsh, often gale force winds. Under these circumstances, the vernacular buildings all share the trait of being compact with a minimum of surface area exposed to the elements. The wigwam with its hemispheric form, the compact cape, saltbox houses, urban townhouses, and tenements sharing walls with adjoining buildings all sought to reduce the impact of wind and cold weather through their differing configurations.

Roof shapes, whether they be domed or pitched, were designed to shed the copious amounts of rain and snow, which the region regularly receives. Flat roofs, while not shedding snow, have the advantage of retaining it, thereby creating a blanket to protect the interior from even more intense exterior temperatures and wind.

In this region, the most desired placement has always been to orient buildings with their broadest side facing south or southeast where the largest number of windows will catch the maximum amount of sunlight. Likewise, under the most advantageous circumstances, the worst winds will have come from the north, so that the buildings would have their backs to it. In most cases, windows have been small to minimize the amount of heat loss through the glass and infiltration through cracks around them.

Shelter, Construction, and Materials

In many cases, structures and building materials varied from the country to town as circumstances dictated. From the wigwam onward, construction in rural locales was almost invariably of either a light wood or heavy timber frame covered with wood bark, clapboards, or shingles. Brick became the material of choice in towns and cities along the coast due to its durability and incombustible nature. Brick was used for bearing walls as well as façades, so all exterior surfaces were protected from weather and fire. Brick and wood alike provide weather-tight enclosures that could maintain a reasonable level of heat, and therefore comfort. Insulation was a rarity, but some resourceful Americans used whatever materials they could find close at hand, such as seaweed, corncobs, horsehair, or wool.

Basements were typical, as any foundation needed to extend below the frost line (usually about 4 feet down) to avoid heaving when the ground went through its normal freezing and thawing cycles. The need to go down 4 feet meant that with little extra effort one could dig a bit farther and obtain additional, full height storage space, while at the same time, keeping the house with its wood siding and structure well above the damp ground outside.

In addition to climate, tradition played a large role in determining the form these vernacular buildings took. The English of Pennsylvania and New England and Dutch of New York, all came from reasonably common European traditions that were translated into similar, yet somewhat different forms in their new homeland. Basically, a medieval technology was employed to craft capes, saltboxes, and other similar structures with their heavy timber frames and wattle and daub infill.

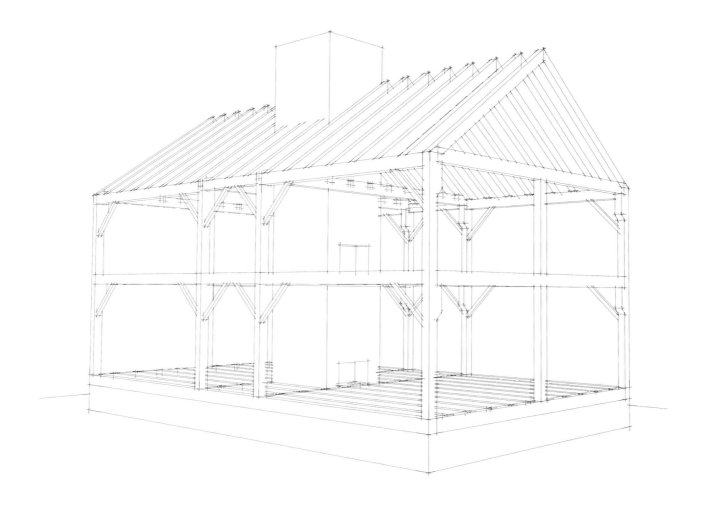

Figure 3.15
This Diagram Illustrates The
Traditional Post And Beam
Method Of House Framing

The first masons to build in America were part of a long European tradition of fine stonework. They were the descendants of masons who built such great exemplars as the large tithe barns, magnificent manor houses, or even humble country cottages. The earliest American masons built their structures in much the same manner as was typically done in England or Holland from where they came. While it was necessary to make some adaptations to these traditional techniques to accommodate local conditions and resources, much remained the same, and brick became the prominent building material in northeastern cities.

By the nineteenth century, the basic urban building types, townhouses, tenements, and apartment buildings had been developed, defined, and employed throughout the region. The townhouse form was an imported building type; whereas the tenement and apartment buildings of these major American cities were developed locally from the need to house large numbers of city dwellers. All three relied upon common walls for economy of construction as well as energy efficiency. As a result, they became the urban vernacular of northeastern coastal cities.

Heating, Cooling, and Ventilation

Providing not only a tight home, but one where heat could be maintained and efficiently distributed has always been a paramount concern in these early homes. In the Native American longhouses, the fire was the central element around which family life took place during the long, very cold winter months. Likewise, the cape and the saltbox of English settlers were built around several fireplaces composed of a mass of bricks that absorbed then gradually let off the heat from the fires. When the cast iron stove supplanted the fireplace in the nineteenth century, it became the focus of most, if not all, family gathering spaces. In winter at least, the kitchen was the place where families spent the most time due in part to the warmth of its cook stove. Some rooms, usually bedrooms, may have lacked any heat and occupants huddled together in bed under whatever type of cover that they had at their disposal.

Even in these northern latitudes, cross-ventilation has been a valuable asset historically. However, it must be achieved without compromising the ability of the structure to retain heat, which is the overriding environmental factor. Even though ventilation is not the prime concern, summers do get uncomfortably hot and muggy for weeks at a time requiring that a current of air be introduced to make life indoors bearable. Unlike the South, where every room requires good cross-ventilation, in this northern region, it is adequate to provide it to an apartment or unit as a whole. Consequently, many homes and apartments only had windows in the front and rear as they may have shared a common wall with neighbors as in a townhouse. Traditionally, double-hung windows were adequate to provide a sufficient current of air through the unit. Ceiling, window, and whole house fans can aid in producing an even greater flow during still periods, which will normally ensure a comfortable environment throughout hot times.

Natural Resources Available for Construction

Wood, stone, and clay for brick-making composed the short list of the most common, natural building materials used in the construction of vernacular buildings found in the region. These resources are still abundantly available and might well-constitute a significant percentage of future ones.

Wood

When the first colonists arrived on the northeastern shores of America, they found the land mostly covered with forests, impenetrable in places. This abundant growth was found not only on the coastal plain, but also on the rolling, hilly, and semi-mountainous terrain of the interior and well into present-day Canada. Timber has ever since been the most widely available building material. While greatly reduced from those early days, the northeastern forest is still vigorous and vast and now well-managed to supply a continuous source of construction products. Today, nearly two-thirds of the total land area in the Northeast is covered in forest. For statistical purposes, the Northeast region, considered to be New England, the Mid-Atlantic States as well as Ohio, contain approximately eighty million acres of privately owned timberland suitable for lumber production.[16] In 2014, this region shipped just over 853 million board feet of white pine and dimensional lumber products. White pine, which is typically produced in 1" thickness, is used for finish applications in building. "The dominant species used for dimensional lumber in this region are typically Eastern Spruces and Balsam Fir, as well as some Red Pine and Jack Pine."[17] Beyond these local forests, neighboring Canada has the third largest timber reserves in the world (only Russia and Brazil have more).

Future construction will rely heavily on these natural and renewable resources, which the region is very fortunate to have close at hand. Unlike the founding fathers that settled here and used their traditional heavy timber frame method of building, builders now employ thinner members (dimensional lumber), as they are more economically practical. It is most likely that this practice will remain the standard for construction well into the future.

Stone

Many parts of the northeast coastal region are well-known for their often dramatic, rocky landscape. In many places along the Maine coast down to Massachusetts is a very thick layer of bedrock, which can be commonly found near the surface or displayed as outcroppings where wind and waves have worn away any covering. Long, white sandy beaches make up much of the remaining coast. "Loose sediments that have not solidified to become rock dominate the geology of the Coastal Plain" from Delaware to Long Island and up to Cape Cod. "Gravel, sand, silt and clay transported from inland form a wedge that thickens oceanward towards the continental slope at the edge of the continent."[18]

Farther inland, large and small fieldstones that the glaciers rolled around millions of years ago until smooth still litter much of the land. The region is well-known for its stony soil, which has plagued generations of farmers trying to make a living by growing crops in these difficult-to-plow fields. The result was that many of them gave up and left, but not before extracting millions of rocks, large and small, from the fields and piling them in long, loosely stacked walls to define their property

For construction purposes, granite, slate, marble, limestone, soapstone, and sandstone were and remain to this day the most popular types of locally found stone.

Traditionally, stone, such as brick, was used as bearing walls that served to support buildings, detail around windows and doors, to reinforce corners, or to provide a more elegant facing over brick structures. Unlike their European predecessors, who built monumental buildings of stone and took it to a high art, the colonists used it more frugally. The vaults and domes, which their forefathers perfected, for all intents and purposes were never employed in the colonists' constructions.

Brownstone, a variety of sandstone, was used so frequently to face townhouse exteriors all along the northeastern seaboard that it has become synonymous with that building type. Philadelphia, New York City, and Boston still have large neighborhoods composed of these structures. Quarried in Pennsylvania, New Jersey, and Connecticut, it reached its greatest popularity during the latter part of the nineteenth century and into the early part of the twentieth.

In Boston, the Roxbury Puddingstone, also known as Boston conglomerate, became a prominent building material during the latter half of the nineteenth century due to its proximity, durability, and beauty. It was used in the construction of many major public buildings, walls, and bridges around the area. It can be seen in its natural state in many

Figure 3.16
Locally Found Stone Has Been
Used For House Construction In
The Northeast From The Early
Eighteenth Century

Boston neighborhoods as outcroppings. Similar to brownstone, puddingstone is a sedimentary rock, but it is composed of "a fine-grained matrix, or silt (the pudding), within which are inclusions of rock, mostly rounded granite."[19] The result is a stone rich in texture and visual interest.

Granite and marble have long been favorite exterior surface materials due to their hardness and resistance to weather. Found in deposits around New England and New York, they come in a wide variety of colors, shades, and textures, which lend a sense of elegance to any structure.

When a long-lasting roofing material was required in the past, slate was the traditional solution. It was split into thin sheets or tile that could be fashioned to overlap one another shingle style. Weather and fireproof, it could last for hundreds of years with minimal maintenance. Still found in large quantities in the interior of New England and New York as well as eastern Pennsylvania, it was quarried throughout the nineteenth century and into the twentieth when petroleum-based roofing supplanted it and others.

While stone is still a favorite facing material, today it is generally only employed as a thin applique or veneer over wood or steel structures, intended to give the look of a more solid stone building.

Brick

Brick has been the building material of choice in cities along this section of the Atlantic coast since early colonial days and remained so through the first quarter of the twentieth century when materials such as steel, aluminum, and glass began to take its place. In the early colonial times, both the English and Dutch settlers imported brick from their homelands, which came over in the form of ballast used to stabilize ships. This practice of importing brick, however, proved to be impractical and unnecessary, as brick-making resources were plentiful and readily available nearby. Soon after their arrival, colonists established numerous brick kilns on the outskirts of port cities and towns to satisfy the growing demand for more permanent, fire-resistant buildings. By 1628, the Dutch West India Company had built a brick kiln in New Amsterdam that produced "small, yellow, and black brick called Holland brick to distinguish them from the larger British variety," which gave a distinctly Dutch character to the architecture of that city. New England's first brick kiln was established in Salem, Massachusetts, in 1629. Significant brick production facilities followed in Fort Orange (now Albany), New York City, Philadelphia, and Burlington and Trenton, New Jersey as well as many others. By 1810, the total "U.S. brick production stood at about ninety-five million; in the single year of 1883, 300 million bricks would be shipped from Haverstraw Bay" north of New York City.[20]

Clay and shale, the main components of brick, were found and easily dug locally from various sources. The banks of the Connecticut River, the Hudson, the Raritan River in New Jersey, and many others all had major deposits. In addition to riverbanks, clay was dug from large deposits found inland. Glaciers that had covered the region as far south as northern Pennsylvania, New Jersey, and Long Island had created numerous lakes as a result of their vigorous scouring activity. In the bottom of these long dried-up lakes, clay formed in abundance, which was easily extracted.[21]

Today, clay is still readily available in the northeast, easily removed and can be fired efficiently at low temperatures. With such little embodied energy required for the production of brick, it makes one of the more sustainable construction materials that we still have available to us. Its strength, long life, and ease of maintenance only add to its attractiveness.

The Current Approach to Design and Construction

Urban Development Today

Megalopolis is running out of land that has not already been built upon. Due to this fact, sprawl is somewhat better constrained than elsewhere. Consequently, those remaining sites are generally expensive or difficult or both, so suburban growth is slower here than most other parts of the country. In addition to the flat land found along the coast, the northeast has a great deal of rolling topography, as well as wetlands, ponds, and watercourses and much of that is designated as conservation land; all of which tend to further limit where one can build.

As a result, in both cities and their suburbs, much of the new development today is replacing older buildings that are being torn down. In cities, whole blocks have been acquired, razed, and rebuilt. In almost every case, the density is increased in order to make the new project viable due to the high cost of the property.

Architectural Character

More and more people are wishing to locate near these urban centers and that is fuelling most of this new growth. Much of the construction is related to commercial or business activities, but a good portion is being dedicated to housing. Many of the newer buildings in these cities are condominium or rental apartments, and many of these only the upper middle class or the very wealthy can afford. They are almost always taller than their predecessors on the site, more luxuriously outfitted, and filled with amenities and services that the previous occupants would not have conceived of or dreamed possible.

In some other cases, midrise buildings are being constructed closer to shopping and jobs, even adjacent to malls where land is made available in place of open-air parking lots. This trend of filling in underutilized land near community amenities is one that should grow relatively quickly, as the need is great for more affordable middle-class housing options. In some cases, they eliminate the need for a car, as public transportation is more likely available.

In the cities where the new housing is glassy and tall, housing takes on a much different character in the suburbs. After World War II, the suburbs in the northeast burgeoned as they did elsewhere in the country. Modest "cape" and "ranch" style homes offered the emerging middle class starter homes in large-scale developments, where Levittowns set the standard. During the sixties and seventies, the "colonial" or "garrison colonial" style house gained popularity, usually in smaller developments. It was a two-story box with a pitched roof shape that echoed the original colonists' homes. Now fitted with a kitchen/family room in lieu of the keeping room and an attached two-car garage helped to adapt them to a modern lifestyle. This trend continues to this day although greatly subdued in scale.

Figure 3.17
This Low-Rise Apartment Building In Boston, MA, Is Being Built With Light Wood Framing Methods Employed Across The Country

Toward the end of the twentieth century, more families amassed greater means than in any previous generation, and these families began to build very large houses often referred to as McMansions. These large homes sought to emulate the stately houses that the European aristocracy built for themselves in previous eras. This was frequently accomplished by replacing an original, smaller house with a larger one.

Popular Design and Construction Methods

Single-family and low-rise apartments are typically built of light wood framing as one finds elsewhere across the nation. In some cases, the ground floor is used for parking, requiring that level to be made with a concrete structure that is fireproof. A stair or elevator shaft may provide stability to the overall structure by building it with concrete masonry units.

Larger projects being built in city centers are taller, often extremely tall, and constructed with steel or concrete frames. As mentioned, they are often covered entirely or mainly with a glass curtain wall. There is only a small proportion of that skin that has operable windows.

Future Environmental Concerns

According to the EPA, the northeast has already begun to experience noticeable temperature increases. Since 1970, "the average annual temperature rose by 2°F and the average winter temperature increased by 4°F." For example, it is expected that New Hampshire's summers will be more like those of North Carolina's today by century's end. Boston could have an increase in the number of days reaching 100°F from 1 currently to as many as 24 days per year by the end of this century. Likewise, Philadelphia and Hartford could go as high as 30 days per year."[22] This scenario portends at the least, worsening air quality, which can compromise the health of vulnerable people in urban areas and beyond.

In addition to rising temperatures, the region should expect more heavy precipitation events with more of it in the form of rain and less as snow. This trend will no doubt increase the number and impact of flooding events, which will increase the risk of waterborne illnesses caused by sewage overflows and pollutants.

Most important will be the future threat of rising sea levels to coastal cities and towns. As sea levels rise, there will be more storm surges, coastal erosion, and the destruction of many important coastal ecosystems.[23] We saw the consequences of Hurricane Sandy in 2012, which caused an estimated 65 billion dollars in damages, second only to Hurricane Katrina. It destroyed or damaged nearly 650,000 homes and 250,500 vehicles in New York and New Jersey and took the lives of 159 people, according to NOAA.[24]

Even with this knowledge, more and more people continue to populate the coast, as the allure of the ocean has a strong tug on the human spirit. In 1983, there were 218,000 people who lived in the low, at-risk areas of New York City, but that number had nearly doubled to over 398,000 at the time hurricane Sandy arrived.[25] This trend of populating the coast appears not to be abating. It is likely that we will witness even more devastating consequences, if more and more people continue to move into these vulnerable areas, as sea levels inevitably rise and storms increase in their ferocity.

Design Strategies and Building Components for the Future

Climatic Imperatives

In this sometimes-harsh climate, the major design concern is to stay warm during winter months, which can be bitterly cold for extended periods. Associated with the cold are ice, wind, and an abundance of snow. In locations near the ocean, high tides and storm force winds create powerful surges, which can result in beach erosion and flooding. Milder summers can bring heat waves with temperatures of over 100°F for a week or more, and with global warming already taking place, the summers may prove to be even warmer. Rain is usually plentiful during the milder times of the year.

Orientation

As elsewhere, the major orientation of any multifamily building should be toward the south, but greater latitude is acceptable in the Northeast because the sun is usually not too strong for comfort in summer and winter sun is always most welcome. On either side of true south, a 30° variation is permitted to the southeast or southwest. Living areas are most appropriately located on the sunny, southern side, with the bedrooms facing northward. The south side should have the preponderance of glass to let in warming sun, while the north wall only requires enough for light, ventilation, and view.

Buildings should be located on high ground away from the coast and river valleys where the exposure to flooding and storm damage is greatest.

Figure 3.18
Idea Drawing For The North East

common areas and usable roofs

rear decks

bay windows

the "stoop"

deciduous shade trees on south side

sunken lower floor entry and yard

Overall Suggested Configuration and Layout

The most typical precedent for a low-rise city dwelling found in the northeast is the row house, also referred to as the townhouse (see page 34), which is found in profusion in all its major cities. This general building type can certainly work well in the future, as each unit shares a common wall with its neighbor, thereby reducing heat loss and saving valuable construction material and urban space. In this scenario, each apartment unit would have a presence directly on the street as well as to a rear yard. The height of the older buildings of this type is usually only three stories, whereas future ones need to be taller to accommodate greater urban density with the four- or five-story buildings becoming the new normal. This overall arrangement produces an energy-efficient compact mass that is well-accepted in the cities of the region.

Normally, row housing of this sort has very little width, as it is designed for narrow city lots, which are often no more than 25 feet wide. With the short side facing the street, the townhouse arrangement gets most of its square footage in its depth, which results in an elongated, rectangular-shaped plan.

Three-bedroom units can occupy the ground floor, where they can open out onto yards. Smaller apartments can then be placed on the floors above them. Rooftop use can then be made available to all units for recreation and social gatherings.

The internal organization of most units ought to be with living areas in an open plan layout. Living and dining areas should be located on the street side, kitchen and bath in the middle, and bedrooms at the rear.

Ceiling heights should not be high, as the conservation of heat is a paramount design issue. It is recommended that no ceiling height be more than 8.5 feet with the optimum around 8 feet and the lowest at 7.5 feet.

Building Circulation—Halls and Staircases

The lowest floor can be depressed a few feet into the ground below the sidewalk level wherever feasible. This bottom or ground floor level can be accessed by way of a short flight of exterior stairs in both the front and rear. Small courtyards may provide a pleasant front entrance and yard space in the rear.

To access the upper units, it is suggested that buildings have a main front stair that opens directly on to the sidewalk and a rear one connecting all units to the roof. Semi-private porches can be used to access the rear stairs from each unit, as is seen in triple-deckers. By having only two units per floor, which utilize these stairs, the need for corridors can be avoided, which will save money and give greater exclusivity to the apartments. Both stairs should be enclosed and provided with operable windows to allow air to ventilate them in summer.

Roof Type

Even though it might be possible to cover this type of building with a pitched roof, the size and layout make the design of such a roof somewhat convoluted and consequently difficult to build, so a flat, green roof is recommended. The flat roof makes it easier for the installation of insulation and can further protect the unit below from the cold by allowing snow to accumulate and create a protective blanket. Also, the opportunity to create a green roof with its environmental and recreational advantages is not to be missed. With the exception of winter, roof access for residents will allow for a safe outdoor place for children to play and for adults to enjoy fresh air and sunshine.

Windows and Window Treatments

As noted previously, to gain the maximum advantage from the sun's heat, the largest glass areas should be placed on the south side. A modest amount of glass can be placed on the east and west sides as mid-summer sun is not so hot that it cannot be controlled. If the suggested row house configuration is followed, then there will be few, if any, windows on the east or west sides. There should be much less glass on the north side, which is subject to the cold, where little to no sun falls.

Skylights can add light and some ventilation to the uppermost apartments, but strong overhead sun in summer can serve to overheat these units. Too many of them in the wrong place can be problematic, so discretion in their number and placement is advised.

On the other hand, the very common, traditional bay window is a vernacular icon in Northeast cities. Projecting from the face of the building with windows typically on three sides, they add to a room's interior light, space, air, and view. This view of the street is of particular note, as they allow one to look not only out onto the street and sidewalk, but up and down them through side windows. This connectivity to the activities of the neighborhood make them a valuable addition, as they provide not only interesting views of local comings and goings, but useful surveillance that can help to keep street crime in check.

Even though much of the year windows will be closed, they should be operable as some fresh air is desirable year round. An adequate airflow, especially during summer, is very important to maintaining good health and a comfortable temperature balance without the need for air conditioning. In this region, double-hung windows are the traditional type and are still a valid one today, but sliding windows and door, casement, and awnings types are also appropriate choices.

Overhead shading devices, such as overhangs, arbors, and trellises, on south-facing windows help to block the sun's hottest rays in summer. Rarely is there a need to worry about too much sun coming in from the north, so shading is usually not necessary on that sides.

Window coverings play an important role in maintaining interior comfort during both the heat of summer days and cold winter nights. Venetian blinds can be a worthwhile addition, as they not only provide privacy and allow for a free flow of air, they can control the amount of sunlight coming into a room, but they provide little protection from the cold. Curtains are the standard solution and generally for not only room darkening and privacy, but they serve well to keep cold drafts to a minimum. An insulated window blanket is even more effective for keeping the cold from the glass contained. These can be located either over or on the side(s) of a window and operate by rolling up and down, sliding, or swinging.

Materials and Construction

Before World War II, traditional housing in east coast cities was built of wood, brick, and stone, with the masonry apparent on the exterior. They were cities that exuded a sense of permanence because of their solidity. The colonial brick-faced townhouses were understated and staid, while the Victorian façades were lively, varied, and greatly detailed. The masonry, while practical and fireproof, was enriched through various patterns and textures, carvings, cantilevers, and trimmed with multiple colors and shades of stone and brick. The common theme of solid, adjoining buildings running along the streets, block after block gave a pleasing sense of visual continuity to neighborhoods.

This vernacular construction approach is one that we can benefit from today as well. The sustainable nature of masonry coupled with its durability and beauty make it a material of choice for the future. However, unlike current practices where it is simply used as a thin covering on the exterior, it can serve a structural function as well. Solid masonry party walls between units are the obvious first choice for the future as they were in the past, as they make a good barrier to the spread of fire from one unit to the next and they can support floors and roofs. However, front and rear walls of masonry are more problematic, as they are difficult to insulate adequately and are not required to be structural when floors and roofs rest on the side walls. Even still, the exposed façades can benefit from the use of a masonry covering, even if it is backed up with an insulated, interior wooden partition, as it is durable, fireproof, and beautiful.

Of the masonry choices for the future, it would seem that stone would be less desirable due to the difficulty and expense of excavating, handling, and placing it, but brick and hollow concrete block will very likely find their niche here. Both are manufactured, but the process is much more benign than that of concrete or steel. However, foundations most likely will by necessity remain concrete or hollow concrete block. They are both fast and can provide a stable base for the masonry that will bear down upon it.

Wood is plentiful in the region and will without doubt be represented in future housing. Floor and roof structures will continue to rely on it for their basic support. These elements can be composed of heavy timber, engineered lumber, or dimensional lumber, any of which can be designed to span from one masonry-bearing wall to the next, if distances are not unusually great.

With regard to interior finish, masonry and heavy timber can be left exposed, as they have a desirable finish and have a pleasing aesthetic. Where engineer and dimensional lumber are used, one might choose to cover it with wood paneling, gypsum board, or plaster, as this type of construction requires covering.

Dark-colored floor and wall surfaces where the sun hits them are recommended to absorb its warmth and help reduce heating costs.

Outdoor Spaces

Balconies are always considered an amenity and that is true in the northeast as well, but they are not a necessity and are often unusable. Due to the fact that at least half of the year the weather is too cold or otherwise unpleasant for sitting outside, this space might be eliminated in favor of more shared open space on the roof or adjacent to the building. The rooftop can be shared or divided into separate spaces for private use. Regardless, some sort of roofed shelter where one can get out of the rain or a vine covered arbor to avoid the sun when it gets too hot make sense. These types of community gathering places will give the residents a place to come together in the fresh air.

Landscape

As is typical elsewhere, housing in the northeastern cities can take advantage of well-located trees and shrubs for shade in summer and to protect the buildings from wind in winter. Deciduous trees, which lose their leaves in winter, should be located on the south side to ensure that sunlight gets through their branches and into apartments.

Renewable Power and Mechanical Equipment

Solar power is, at this point, the best bet for producing energy for individual buildings, but wind power may come into its own at some point in the future. In a northern area, the sun moves from very high in the sky in summer to a much lower position in winter, which means that solar panels would benefit from being adjusted periodically to track the sun's inclination. These panels may be adequate to heat or power the building, but significant improvements need to be made before they will be able to do both.

If the units are well-insulated, little heat will be required due to their use of shared walls and the resulting compact mass with little exposure to the cold. More often than not, heat for the building would be by hot water or hot air. Ceiling fans are always recommended to keep the occupant comfortable during those hot, humid summer days and nights, which can last for several weeks.

The Prospect for Future Urban Development in the Northeast

It would appear that the region will continue to grow and prosper, but in order to do so, it will need to provide not only more and improved housing, but it will have to address major environmental, infrastructure, and energy issues that as time goes by will become ever more pressing.

As with other coastal regions, the northeast faces the ever-present threat of storms, even hurricanes, but it is sea level rise that will need to be addressed seriously and most urgently. All of the major cities and their adjacent low-lying suburbs situated along this coast will be in jeopardy unless meaningful steps toward preventing future, devastating inundations from another Sandy-like catastrophe are taken. This will require a great deal of planning, which has begun in several places, and then a huge amount of money to implement those plans. While most people would enjoy a home with a sea view, these plans must include the development of higher, inland locations.

Likewise, much of the existing infrastructure (roads, bridges, rails, and utilities) is old and much of it is in need of either repair or total replacement. Mass transportation systems that link city to city and city to suburb must be expanded, improved, and made less vulnerable to flooding, as the automobile becomes a less viable means of travel.

Sources of affordable, clean energy also are a prime, future concern. Even though coal, which is found in Pennsylvania, is a tempting fuel, it is not a clean one. The experiment with atomic energy during the last half of the twentieth century seems to be drawing to a close and may not return unless safer means of harnessing it are found. Currently, most of the energy generated in this area comes from oil and gas, which is imported from either other regions of this country or foreign ones. Even though it is possible to "clean up" coal, that process is expensive. Natural gas is much cleaner than oil and may offer an immediate solution, but not a long-term one, as it, like both coal and oil, is finite and at some point will become more scare and the price will rise to levels that many will not be able to afford.

Figure 3.19
The Homes At Old Colony In
Boston, MA, Designed By The
Architectural Team Use Solar
Energy And Other Sustainable
Strategies While Creating A
Sense Of Community

The future appears to be in alternative power sources such as solar, wind, and tidal. The amount of solar energy available to the area is much less than in other, more southerly parts of the country, so its potential may be somewhat limited. Tidal has promise in the Bay of Fundy and perhaps elsewhere, but it too has definite limits. Of the three, wind may prove to be the most useful, as the coast offers a good and steady source. Offshore wind farms along the Atlantic seem to offer a reliable opportunity, as the space is available in an otherwise crowded, built-up shoreline. The first of these in the nation, Cape Wind, is to be located in federal waters of Nantucket Sound off the coast of Massachusetts and Rhode Island. It will be composed of "130 Siemens 3.6-megawatt offshore wind turbines with a capacity of 468 megawatts." Its developers claim that will power 200 homes or it "will produce 75 percent of the electricity used on Cape Cod and the Islands of Martha's Vineyard and Nantucket with zero pollution emissions."[26]

Besides the need for power, more housing for people moving closer to urban centers with shopping and jobs will account for a great deal of the future development. Some of this effort will be to rebuild and replace the existing units. Wherever possible, adaptive reuse of older structures that were previously used for functions other than housing, such as mills and factories, will save valuable pieces of the region's historic fabric while accommodating a new need. Most importantly, however, will be new construction, particularly which will be built in areas that were once of a lower density. Where feasible, city zoning will need to change to provide land for multifamily housing and local retail. All of these changes will be driven by inescapable economic pressures as they have always been.

In some respects, the northeast has a head-start toward the goal of promoting a new urban vernacular, as their cities have a long tradition of building urban row housing and other similar forms of dense city dwellings. Most of the downtowns are once again vigorous and the longstanding housing stock has for the most part been restored. Public transportation, albeit old and in need of renovation, is well-established and heavily used. Construction resources are available near at hand and they are plentiful. For the foreseeable future, lumber and brick can be supplied in adequate amounts to add to the necessary housing stock. Alternative energy is ready to be tapped. The investment will be substantial, but the ultimate outcome should be a better living environment for a large portion of the American population.

Summary of Components for Reinventing An Urban Vernacular in the Northeast

Main environmental objectives: Defend against cold winters with frequent strong winds.

Orientation

- Living areas should be south to southeast facing
- Share as many walls as possible with neighbors
- East and west walls should have only few or no openings

Layout

- Compact volumes
- Enclosed stairs to service units on both sides to eliminate the need for double-load corridors
- Provide shaded areas for living and working outside, such as courtyards and porches
- Low to moderate height ceilings to keep heat near occupants

Construction

- Build into the ground over a basement
- All exterior surfaces need to be well-insulated
- Timber beams for floor and roof structure
- Leave wooden ceilings exposed
- Reflective roof colors (white, silver, or similar colors)

Recommended Construction/Structural Materials

- Brick or stone
- Timber and light wood framing
- Wood siding and roof shingles

Roofs

- Steeply pitched with wood shingles or light colored, reflective metal or
- Flat roofs with opportunities for resident use
- Wide overhangs to help protect exterior walls and windows (most valuable on south side)

Shading

- Moderate overhangs, particularly on south side
- Exterior solid or louvered shutters, particularly on the west side, less important on east side

Windows

- Moderate openings for summer air flow—double-hung are desirable
- Should be modest on west- and east-facing walls
- South side can afford a lot of glass (if shaded for summer sun) to warm interiors in winter
- North side can have very little glass

Ventilation

- Keep the heat in—modest openings to exterior except south side where more glass can be allowed
- Cross-ventilation is important in summer
- Windows should allow full or partial ventilation when desired
- Fans can be used to augment air circulation within dwelling and to exhaust hot air build-up

Cooling

- Encourage air movement with fans and good cross-ventilation in summer
- Shady walkway—portico and other covered outdoor living spaces
- Roof color is less important here with a slight preference to the darker shades
- Dark exterior wall colors

Heating

- Central heating or space heating in each room required
- Fireplaces or wood stoves can help to add warmth in winter

Water

- Channel rainwater away from the structure as quickly as possible
- Collect all gray water for flushing toilets and watering garden plants

Notes

1   The Business Alliance for Northeast Mobility. *The Future of the Northeast Corridor*. Website: www.cqgrd.gatech.edu/sites/files/cqgrd/files/northeast_corridor_2009.pdf.

2   Wikipedia. *Northeast Corridor*. Website: http://en.wikipedia.org/wiki/Northeast_megalopolis.

3   Nabokov, Peter and Robert Easton. *Native American Architecture*. Oxford University Press (1989) New York. p. 52.

4   Wikipedia. *Algonquian Peoples*. Website: http://en.wikipedia.org/wiki/Algonquian_peoples.

5   Woodland Indian Educational Program. Website: www.woodlandindianedu.com/wigwamframes.html.

6   NativeTech: Native American Technology and Art. *Early Historic Descriptions of Wigwams*. Website: www.nativetech.org/wigwam/wigwamdoc.html.

7   Cape Cod Houses Recorded by the Historic American Buildings Survey. *Introduction*. Website: www.loc.gov/rr/print/list/170_cape.html.

8   Old House Online. Website: www.oldhouseonline.com/original-cape-cod-cottage/.

9   Shelter. *The New World*. Shelter Publication, Inc. (1973) Bolinas, CA. p. 27.

10 McAlester, Virginia, and Lee. *A Field Guide to American Houses*. Alfred A. Knopf (1991) New York p. 105.

11 Wikipedia. *New Law Tenements*. Website: http://en.wikipedia.org/wiki/New_Law_Tenement.

12 Shags of New York City; 1800s and 1900s tenements. Feb. 6, 2013. Website: https://approachaarch.wordpress.com/2013/02/06/shags-of-new-york-city-1800s-and-1900s-tenements.

13 Wikipedia. *Old Law Tenements*. Website: http://en.wikipedia.org/wiki/Old_Law_Tenement.

14 Warner, Sam Bass *Streetcar Suburbs: The Process of Growth in Boston, 1870-1900*. Harvard University Press (1962) Cambridge, MA.

15 Krim, Arthur J. A Community of Builders. In *The Three-Deckers of Dorchester: An Architectural Historical Survey*. Boston Redevelopment Authority (1977) Boston, MA. p. 13.

16 USDA Forest Service, Forest Inventory Analysis Program. 2006.

17 Northeastern Lumber Manufacture's Association. *Total Lumber Shipments for 2014 Highest Since 2007*. Website: www.nelma.org/total-lumber-shipments-for-2014-highest-since-2007/.

18 The Teacher-Friendly Guide to the Earth Science of the Northeaster US. *Glacial Deposit Resources of the Northeast*. Website: http://geology.teacherfriendlyguide.org/index.php/non-mineral-resources/glacial-deposit-resources.

19 Hobin, James. *Dorchester Reporter*. *Ancient Souvenirs: Discovering Roxbury Puddingstone in Dorchester*. March 13, 2014. Website: www.dotnews.com/2014/roxbury-puddingstone-dorchester.

20 Vogel, Michael N. *History of Buffalo*. *Up Against the Wall: An Archaeological Field Guide to Brick in Western New York*. Website: www.buffaloah.com/a/DCTNRY/mat/brk/vogel/#Foundations.

21 The Teacher-Friendly Guide to the Earth Science of the Northeaster US. *Glacial Deposit Resources of the Northeast*. Website: http://geology.teacherfriendlyguide.org/index.php/non-mineral-resources/glacial-deposit-resources.

22 EPA. *Climate Change*. Website:www.epa.gov/climatechange/impacts-adaptation/northeast.html.

23 EPA. *Climate Change*. Website:www.epa.gov/climatechange/impacts-adaptation/northeast.html.

24 *USA Today. One Year after Sandy, 9 devastating facts*. Oct. 29, 2012. Website: www.usatoday.com/story/news/nation/2013/10/29/sandy-anniversary-facts-devastation/3305985/.

25 *The Huffington Post. Hurricane Sandy's Impact, By The Numbers*. Oct. 29, 2012. Website: www.huffingtonpost.com/2013/10/29/hurricane-sandy-impact-infographic_n_4171243.html.

26 Cape Wind, Energy for Life. Website: www.capewind.org/what.

Chapter 4

The Midwest: Eastern Prairies and Northern Woodlands

The Midwest, while seemingly homogeneous, is most importantly defined by its diversity. Midwestern climate goes from extremes with hot, humid summers to severely cold, snowy winters. The landscape is punctuated by the skyscrapers of some of America's largest urban centers, which are framed by vast stretches of open country. It is the heart of the country's manufacturing sector, but one of our greatest farming regions. Its people are considered typical Americans, but they actually come from widely disparate parts of the world and retain much of those ethnic characteristics. It is thriving in places, yet depressed in others.

The Place

Bounded by Canada and the Great Lakes on the north, constrained by the low Allegheny Mountains to its south and east, yet open to the Great Plains and the vast farmland to the west, the Midwest represents a part of the United States that is clearly defined by a similar geography, but made up of contrasting development patterns. With the exception of the western farmland and the northern forests, most of the region is included in what we now call the Great Lakes Megaregion, which corresponds roughly to the boundaries of the region's urban development—its most heavily populated and interconnected parts.[1] The exact definition of its boundaries varies depending on the source and can be contested. For the sake of this book, the region will be considered to be composed of the western part of both Pennsylvania and New York states, all of Ohio, Indiana, Illinois, Iowa, Wisconsin, Michigan, Missouri, and Minnesota, as well as a large portion of northern Kentucky.

Migrants from Asia, who crossed the then-existing land bridge to North America, settled the region over 10,000 years ago. They subsequently spawned a large and prosperous agricultural society along the fertile flood plains of the region's many river courses. To honor their gods, they built monumental mounds of earth that remain today as a reminder of their society's ingenuity and organization. Numerous Indian tribes evolved from these early people into the Iroquois and Algonquin speaking tribes.

Toward the middle of the eighteenth century, the growing pressure by the American colonists to expand beyond the Allegheny Mountains into this fertile, highly prized land was held in check by a confederation of French and Indian nations. Once the Americans fought and won their struggle for independence from England, there was little to stop the ensuing invasion that quickly swept across the Midwest. The native population was subdued in short order, and by 1800, much of the land was platted into neat 1-mile squares, which were then divided further into 160-acre blocks. Wave upon wave of families crossed the Allegheny Mountains and rushed in to claim their piece of farmland. They were Yankees from New England, whose land was difficult to farm,[2] Quakers and Mennonites from the Mid-Atlantic States, veterans of the war who were given land for their service, and hordes of Europeans emigrating to escape widespread famine and tyranny in Europe.

Unlike the milder maritime climate of the north Atlantic coast from which many of the early settlers came, the Midwest's inland position is in what is termed a continental or temperate zone. It is beleaguered by long, cold winters with copious amounts of snow and ice, which bring the region to a halt from time to time. Its summers are warm and humid, ranging to very hot for brief periods, yet long enough to provide an excellent growing season. Plentiful rainfall keeps the crops green and growing and the rivers and lakes full. Tornados visit southern Illinois and Iowa from time to time, wreaking havoc and destruction on whole neighborhoods.

The first settlers found a rather flat to gently rolling landscape of rich farmland drained by several of the mightiest rivers on the continent—the Ohio, Mississippi, and Missouri Rivers. They cleared the land and established the nation's most prosperous agricultural region of the time. It became known as the Corn Belt or the heartland due to its high level of production of corn, soybeans, and wheat, which still feeds much of the

Figure 4.1
Pristine Farms Such As This One Have Become An Integral Part Of The Wisconsin Landscape

nation. Its grasslands sustained large herds of cattle, which grazed on it. Later, great stockyards were developed to slaughter and process beef and pork coming from its farms and the ranches of the Great Plains.

With the advent of the Industrial Revolution in the early nineteenth century, the region developed into a powerhouse of manufacturing. Serviced by a ready-made, natural transportation system of lakes and rivers and later railways, an almost limitless source of natural resources such as timber, coal, and iron and copper ore, and with the addition of cheap immigrant labor, the region surged ahead at breakneck speed. Dubbed the America's Foundry, it was once unrivaled in the world for its manufacturing production. Steel foundries drove the industries that produced everything from automobiles and household appliances to construction materials. It provided the resources to win the Civil War as well as both World War I and II.

Unfortunately, its industrial base has been undercut in recent decades by foreign competition and has fallen on hard times, assuming the derisive title—the Rust Belt. Today, with about 18 percent of the total population of the U.S., its share of the nation's GDP is only 17 percent.[3] Enormous steel mills once fed by iron ore mined in Minnesota, Wisconsin, and Michigan that produced record amounts of steel are now closed. The region's automobile industry floundered for a time and is yet to fully recover. It has now assumed a much smaller share of the world market than previously. Those cities reliant on heavy industry suffered declines in population, which led to vacant, deteriorating housing and closed businesses, as workers left for other parts of the country in search of work. Detroit, the most noted city for the decline, now has about a third of its residential land vacant. Many workers and retirees have moved on and found employment and new homes in Sun Belt States and elsewhere.

The region has remained strong due to its agricultural base and now is in the process of reinventing itself by adding new sectors to its economy. While industry struggles to make a modest comeback, the service and intellectual areas—banking, insurance, finance, technology, education, bio, and medical research—are growing and seem to be taking up much of the slack.

Cities, such as Chicago, Pittsburg, Buffalo, Cleveland, Cincinnati, Detroit, Columbus, Indianapolis, Milwaukee, Minneapolis, and Saint Louis, that were built upon this foundation of agriculture and industry added trade and commerce to the mix. Chicago and its suburbs form the largest metropolitan statistical area in the region with 9.8 million people, the third-largest in the country. On the other hand, many of its main industrial dependent cities, such as Detroit, have had serious losses in population as jobs disappeared. The population for the Great Lakes Megaregion in 2010 stood at 55.5 million and is projected to grow by 28 percent by 2050 to 71 million people.[4] Overall, it appears that the future population growth will be slower here than in the southern tier of the country, but the projected growth will be significant. Meanwhile, its resources are still abundant, its people resilient, and its cities are primed for renewal.

Early Development Patterns

After the end of the Revolutionary War, the U.S. congress set down for the Midwest a pattern of development that would dictate the future of not only that region, but the rest of the country. The Northwest Ordinance of 1778, which responded to certain political imperatives of the time relating to the settlement of the region, also mandated the method by which the new territory would be subdivided. It relied on an almost limitless grid of squares to give a uniform structure to this future development, now known as the Public Land Survey System. Working on primary north-south and east-west coordinates, square blocks called *townships*, of 6 mile to a side were made the standard. Townships were divided into thirty-six 1-mile squares (640 acres) called *sections*. Within each township, one section was required to be devoted to public buildings and education. The section could be further subdivided into smaller lots.[5] The quarter of a section block became the basic Midwestern farm unit in the Mid-West. Starting in what is now eastern Ohio, quarter sections were disbursed at first to veterans of the Revolution in lieu of pay for service. Subsequently, most of the remainder was sold to new arrivals.

From this gridded format, the layout of roads, innumerable farms, villages, towns, and cities were shaped, not only in the Midwest, but also across the country—a pattern that is clearly visible from the air today.

As a result, long, straight streets became the norm in the Midwest and well beyond. They were frequently spacious and accompanied by sidewalks. Trees formed allées along them setting off the middle-class housing that lined them. Many of the resulting rectangular blocks were bisected by alleyways running through their centers, which became a popular method for separating service vehicles and functions from the more formal street side of the home. The alleys were where garages were located, deliveries made, and trash was removed.

Figure 4.2
This Diagram Illustrates The Divisions In A Typical "Township" By Which Most Of The Continental U.S. Was Subdivided

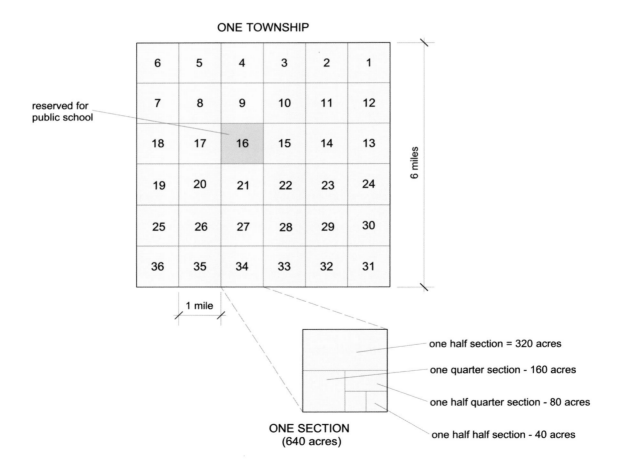

ONE TOWNSHIP

reserved for public school

6	5	4	3	2	1
7	8	9	10	11	12
18	17	16	15	14	13
19	20	21	22	23	24
25	26	27	28	29	30
36	35	34	33	32	31

6 miles

1 mile

one half section = 320 acres

one quarter section - 160 acres

one half quarter section - 80 acres

one half half section - 40 acres

ONE SECTION
(640 acres)

REINVENTING AN URBAN VERNACULAR

Precedents

Midwestern precedents were mainly developed after 1800, as so little of the region was settled before that time. Aside from the Native American structures, most subsequent buildings were based on prototypes developed previously either in England or by the east coast colonists. Once established, there were several innovative approaches that arose during the early twentieth century; some of which were ultimately adopted throughout the nation.

The Iroquoian Longhouse

Figure 4.3
Two Examples Of Palisaded Iroquois Villages As Portrayed In 1651 By Nicolas (Claes) Jansz Visscher

The Iroquoian-speaking peoples, who included the Iroquois tribe, as well as the Heron, Cayuga, Cherokee, Huron, Mohawk, Oneida, Onondaga, Seneca, and Tuscarora,[6] once constructed one of the most notable housing structures built by Native Americans, commonly known as the longhouse. These tribes were centered in upstate New York, but controlled a much larger territory that spanned both the Canadian and U.S., sides of Lake Ontario and the St. Lawrence River, most of New York state, and down into northern Pennsylvania.

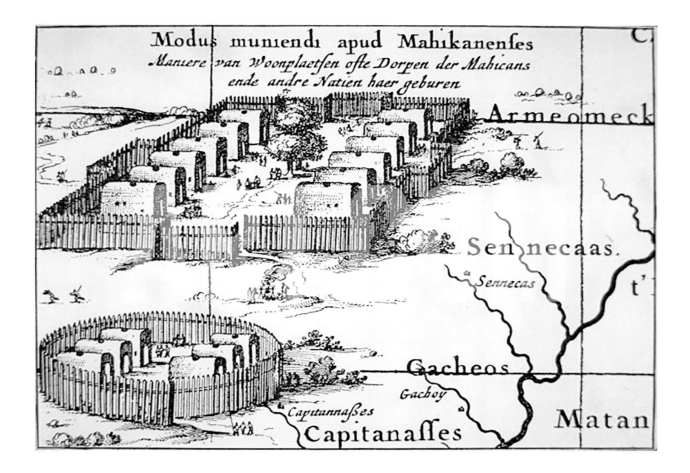

They were hunters, fishers, and farmers who built fortified villages surrounded with palisades constructed out of tree trunks spaced close together and sharpened on the tops. These villages were typically composed of four or five longhouses, but some of the larger ones could have hundreds of people living in them, with the largest containing as many as 3,000 people.[7] The typical village was located on a height overlooking a nearby river or stream with one or more steep sides to help make it more defendable. Their fields would be close by and surrounding the village. They needed to relocate their villages at least every 20 years.[8] This relocation was due to several causes: soil would become depleted, making it difficult to grow their crops; the depletion of easily accessible firewood; the fact that their longhouses would suffer deterioration and need rebuilding and for various sanitation reasons.

In their villages, each clan would build and occupy its own longhouses, marked with the clan's symbol, such as a turtle, a bear, a wolf, etc. These clans were composed of families related through the female line.[9] Once married, the husband would move into the longhouse with his wife's family. The females of the clan owned the dwelling and governed it.

The typical longhouse was 16 to 20 feet in width and quite long as the name implies. The shortest ones were no more than 30 feet in length with the average between 60 to 200 feet long, but many over 300 feet. The longest one that archeologists have discovered stretched out over a staggering 400 feet.[10] The heights averaged 15 to 20 feet.[11] An entrance, covered with hides or hinged bark would be located at both ends of the structure. In the very long structures, additional openings were placed at intermediate points along the length.

Longhouses were built in sections of about 20 feet in length with two families occupying each section. As the clan grew, sections were added to accommodate the new families. A corridor or passageway ran the full length of the dwelling, which connected the entire community within the space. This corridor divided each section in two, with a family occupying each side of it. Fire pits were built along the corridor between the two families, who shared it. A hole was left in the roof above the fire to let the smoke escape. The smoke hole was sometimes covered with a piece of bark that could be opened or shut from below by a pole.

The family living space was composed of a platform built a foot or more off the ground and filled most of the family's allocated area or compartment. Another platform was built about 5 feet above the first one and was used mainly for storage, but could also be used as a sleeping loft. Firewood was stored below the lower shelf.

It was constructed in a somewhat similar fashion as the wigwam, but among other things, it had a linear plan rather than a round one. Similar to the wigwam, it began with opposing rows of saplings, placed at 4 or 5 foot intervals, with their thick ends in the ground. Rather than being bent over to form an arch, the longhouse side structure was vertical. Another set of saplings was used as roof rafters, which were then added to the tops of the posts. These rafters were then bent to form an arch.

A horizontal layer of saplings was then added over the side posts and rafters, strengthening the whole structure. Another double row of vertical saplings was placed along the central corridor to help support the roof as well as define the corridor and each family's compartment. The structural frame was covered with bark sheeting—usually from elm trees—to form a weather-tight exterior skin. The entire structure was then covered by another grid of poles, which held the roofing in place.

The region around the Great Lakes where the longhouses were built suffers long, cold winters with chilling winds, which required the Native Americans to develop housing

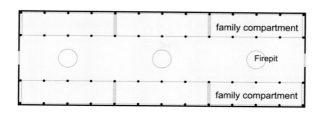

Plan

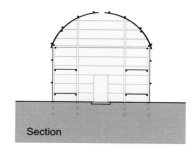

Section

Figure 4.4
Iroquoian Longhouse

that could offer adequate protection from this harsh climate. Tight and compact with a central fire heating each section, the longhouse provided a warm home out of the elements, as well as a place for social and family gatherings. They were not comfortable by today's standards as they were noisy, crowded, dark, and at times, smoky. Even though individual space was small (around 200 square feet per family), the focus was more on the clan or the community as a whole, which the longhouse could provide.

The I-House

The unassuming I-house type is spread widely throughout the eastern half of the U.S. and well into the Great Plains (also see Chapter 6, page 137 American Farm House), but it achieved it greatest level of popularity in the Midwest during the early and mid-nineteenth century. It was based on the medieval English hall and parlor house form. The early colonists built this type of house in large numbers during the seventeenth century in the mid-Atlantic and the south. The hall and parlor were composed of a simple rectangular plan, divided with a wall into two separate spaces—the hall and the parlor. It was usually a story and a half with a steeply pitched, end-gabled roof, and fireplaces located at either end. One entered the hall where much of the household work and cooking took place. The parlor was somewhat smaller and more private, often used as a living space and bedroom. If there was an upper half floor or loft, it was accessed by a ladder/stair and used frequently as additional sleeping space. Due to its uneven plan, windows were often placed asymmetrically in the façade.

Unlike the hall and parlor design, the I-house had two stories and was a bit more formal in its layout. Usually of modest size, it was one room deep and two rooms wide with the upper rooms directly above lower ones. It was common that the entire house was between 16 to 20 feet deep and up to 40 feet wide. In some cases, there was a central stair hall placed between the two sets of rooms, which gave the home a greater sense of spaciousness and the rooms more privacy. The roof ridge ran the length of the house and was gabled on the short ends. Fireplaces were located on both ends of the house so as to accommodate each room.

Easily recognized by its tall, rather narrow silhouette, it did not, however, derive its name from its shape or layout. The name I-house comes from the fact that many of its builders, who spread the type south into Louisiana, originated from Iowa, Indiana, and Illinois.

The I-house was especially popular through central Pennsylvania, Ohio, Indiana, and Illinois. Its design was "particularly favored as modest folk dwellings in the mid-western states where the relatively long and confining winters made large houses more of a necessity than farther south."[12]

Its plain, symmetrical façade lent itself to any number of decorative treatments. Most often, porches were added and embellished according to current styles. Federal, Greek revival, Gothic revival, and Italianate styles followed one another as the vogue dictated through most of the nineteenth century.

In both this country and in England, the earliest examples of the hall and parlor as well as the I-house were constructed using a traditional heavy timber frame. Some on the frontiers were made of logs and others of brick or stone, but later versions, those built after 1830, were made with the then-modern balloon framing method. Developed in the Chicago area, the balloon frame used thinner, milled lumber, referred to as dimensional lumber, in lieu of the much thicker post and beam frame. This new method used two by four wall studs, which ran up the full two stories and were nailed together, making the whole construction process easier for local artisans to build, taking less time than the heavy timber method and subsequently cheaper. The exterior was most often clad with wooden clapboards.

In addition to these construction advantages, the I-house's simple floor plan with its central hallway lent itself to the addition of a rectangular rear wing or ell, which resulted in an overall L or T shape plan for the house as a whole. The ell was either one or two stories in height and provided space for a kitchen on the ground floor and a bedroom above. "Building an ell rather than extending the entire rear of the house was not only cheaper, it also preserved one of the most attractive I-house features: a light-filled parlor with windows on opposite sides of the room."

The rear wing also created a void to one side, which was usually filled with a porch. This back porch provided the perfect place "where messy chores could be done, and family members and hired hands could wash up before entering the house. After the Civil War, the front porch became practically universal in I houses—an excellent spot to sit a spell on a warm evening and chat, maybe while carrying out some less demanding household tasks, such as shelling peas or mending tools." "The front porch was also an aesthetic statement. One of the reasons the unassuming I-house was able to maintain its charm for so long and in so many places is that its simplicity invited decoration. As tastes in architectural styles changed, and as an ever-expanding rail system rushed lathe-turned and flat-sawn ornaments across the countryside, the I-house presented an ideal venue for architectural embellishment."[13]

Chicago Bungalow

Springing from its genesis in San Francisco (See Chapter 8), the affordable bungalow became a phenomenon that spread across the country. Between 1910 and 1940, over 80,000 bungalows were built in the city of Chicago, which accounted for about a third of its total housing stock. Large tracts of prairie land were developed into subdivisions of bungalows, resulting in what we now refer to as "bungalow belts." Today, these belts form a crescent around much of the city of Chicago. They were also built in great profusion in all of the other Midwestern cities, but it was Chicago that gave its name to the very specific style that grew out of the larger national movement.

The Chicago bungalow was similar to other bungalows found across the country, in that it was either a one- or one-and-a-half-story rectangle with a low-pitched roof that had broad overhangs. These modest homes were cottage-like, as the typical ones had

Figure 4.5
These Three Examples Are Typical Of The Chicago Bungalows That Were Built In Great Abundance And Still Serve As Urban Housing For Millions Of People

only two bedrooms and a single bath, but sunny with plenty of windows. They averaged 20 feet wide on the standard lot that measured 24 to 25 foot in width.[14] They were also some of the first American homes to be built with standardized, mass produced features, such as windows and doors, and to incorporate central heating, electricity, and modern plumbing.[15]

The Chicago version of the bungalow differs from those found in other parts of the country. They were clad with brick, often with stone decorative accents, not the more typical wood siding. They had a full basement, which was normal for most houses in the region, which raised the house up off the ground. The entry was reached by a set of exterior stairs referred to as a stoop. The stoop served as a place for families to relax on hotter summer days and socialize with neighbors as the children played. Also, the gabled end was oriented parallel to the street, rather than perpendicular, as was the norm elsewhere. The sheltered front entrance was offset on the façade or wholly to the side.[16] Often times, it was smaller than that of the typical bungalow, becoming more of an entry porch than one for outdoor living. This entry porch frequently opened into a small entry space, not directly into the living room, as did so many others across the country, and therefore provided a bit of a transition from the weather outside. In many of these homes, a sunroom or solarium was added to the front of the house to take the place of the open porch, thereby providing a much more practical sunny refuge for many a long, cold winter's day.

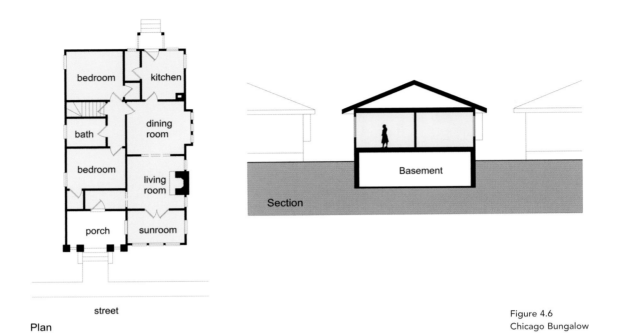

Plan   street

Figure 4.6
Chicago Bungalow

The Polish Flat

Around the world, there are many cultures where people build their houses in stages, as they do not have adequate financial resources to build everything that they want initially. In many developing nations, one can find housing with steel reinforcing rods projecting up from concrete columns, clearly denoting the family's expectation that additional floors will follow, topping the lower one(s). In other places, it has been normal to raise or remove the roof and interject a floor under it. The idea of adding a floor as finances allowed was popular throughout the Midwest as well, but in some cases, with a unique twist—the upper floor was built first and the addition built at a later date below it.

Starting in the 1890s, the Polish, Slovakian, and Russian immigrants came in large numbers to Milwaukee and the surrounding area where they found low-paying jobs. They rented until they had saved enough money to either buy or build a small, single-story house. In many cases, these houses only had three or four rooms and might have been shared by two families, resulting in extremely cramped living conditions. When the family's financial circumstances allowed, another floor would be added *below* the original one.[17] The new, lower floor may have been used as an extension of the home, doubling its size, but most often, it was used as another living unit for the extended family or as a rental unit to help generate extra income. "While highly unorthodox, it was an ingenious technique of building new accommodations without disrupting family life, in line with their growing wealth."[18] While this technique has little to do with the Polish vernacular architecture, it represents an innovative response to urban problems that immigrants encountered at the turn of the twentieth century. Aside from the economic issues that it addressed, it developed into a vernacular building type due to its efficient layout, spare use of local materials, and a satisfying response to the local climate.

The actual method for raising a house on a higher foundation varied. In some cases, an existing house would be pulled by horses on logs and rolled to another location where it was placed on a new, taller foundation. Others were simply jacked up off their foundation on beams and their foundations were then extended upward.[19] When an existing foundation was retained, earth might be excavated from the old cellar to provide more height. To this new, lower unit, plenty of windows were added, making it sunny, eliminating the below ground, basement feel.

These modifications gave the upper floor greater prominence than before as it was now set higher above the yard and connected to the sidewalk by a much longer staircase. However, the lower unit had a presence as well, as it had a direct, street entrance by way of only a few steps down.

This arrangement also had several advantages that helped the Minnesota home-owner cope with their long, cold winters. The resulting boxy, compact shape was ideal for heat conservation due to its modest exposed surface area. Also, by having it partially underground, the earth around it helped to keep it warmer in winter and cooler in summer. The windows not only allowed adequate amounts of warming winter sunlight in, but they provided good cross-ventilation during hot summers.

Figure 4.7
A Typical Street Of Polish Flats Elevated On High Basement Walls, Which Are Found In And Around Milwaukee, WI

The American Foursquare or Prairie Box

Much like the humble bungalow, the more expensive and spacious foursquare house served to house the burgeoning middle class that was composed of even more financially successful and affluent Midwestern families.

The exact origins of the American foursquare are not clear, but it may derive from a merging of the Queen Anne with Classic and Colonial Revival styles.[20] On the other hand, Virginia and Lee McAlester in their *A Field Guide to American Houses* give much of the credit to Frank Lloyd Wright and other Chicago architects of the time, who became known as the Prairie School. The McAlesters considered the resulting prairie-style house to be "one of the few indigenous American styles." Wright's first major work, the Winslow House, which he designed in 1893 for Forest Park, a suburb of Chicago, helped to popularize the foursquare house, but for him, it was to be only the springboard that subsequently led him in more creative directions.[21]

However, "it wasn't long before savvy builders simplified the shape and detail making it affordable to the middle-class"[22] and the foursquare house was born. It was

Figure 4.8
Foursquare Homes Such As This One In Chicago, IL, Make A Compact, Energy-Efficient Home That Can Be Added To And Changed With Seemingly Limitless Variations

built primarily during the first third of the twentieth century and while its popularity was great, it was brief—lasting no more than 25 to 30 years. During that short period, the style spread rapidly throughout the rest of the country, but the preponderance of them were built in and around Chicago and other large Midwestern cities. Examples were widely published in pattern books and by popular magazines of the day. Companies such as Sears Company, Aladdin Company, Harris Brothers Company, and others sold precut kits that offered several different plans and styles.

The basic plan layout was square or nearly so with the typical dimension of 28 or 29 feet to a side, but smaller homes could measure as small as 24 feet square. They were two- or two-and-one-half stories and rather cubic in appearance. This box was capped with a pyramidal roof with deep overhanging eaves. Normally, the roof had a hipped dormer, which was centered in the front. There was a deep, one-story front porch that often extended the length of the house from where one entered. Each floor was roughly divided into quarters from which the name foursquare derived. The entry, living room, dining room, and kitchen composed the first floor. A stairway led to the second floor where three or four bedrooms and a bathroom were located.

The foursquare was one of the most widely built house types of the time for several very good reasons. Having every important room on a corner, as this plan does, assured that each has plenty of sunlight and fresh air with good cross-ventilation. In a cold climate like that of the Midwest, its compact design with a reduced exterior surface area proved to be an energy saver. By the same token, its straightforward layout also meant that it could be easily standardized. Standardization saved on materials and resulted in more economical buildings. "All are key reasons for its popularity, but like a plain vanilla cake, it also took decorative details well,"[23] which allowed it to take on numerous and varied style adaptations that proved pleasing to its market.

The Chicago Graystone (Two-Flat and Three-Flat)

The urban housing that developed in the Midwestern cities during the late nineteenth and early twentieth centuries had much in common with those found along the northeast coast. Both regions developed their urban prototypes in response to burgeoning populations and all of the problems that came along with such rapid and relatively uncontrolled growth. Tenements, row houses, and triple-deckers were the east coast's solutions. Major Midwestern cities had their share of similar types, but in lieu of the New England triple-decker, Midwesterners, in particular Chicagoans, had a building type referred to as the two-flat and to a lesser extent the three-flat. Where Boston built theirs of wood frame, the Chicago counterparts were constructed of masonry-brick, often with limestone on the façades. Given the fact that the limestone had a grayish tint, these buildings as well as row houses and many single-family dwellings that used it became known as *graystones*. "Although many greystones have been demolished, about 30,000 still stand in Chicago. North Lawndale, a neighborhood just five miles west of Chicago's Loop, has the highest concentration of greystones in the city—over 1700. About 60 percent are two-unit buildings."[24] Because graystones were more expensive to build than frame buildings and had a more substantial look and feel, they were the choice of the middle and upper classes. With two or three bedroom units on each floor, they worked well to house this expanding group. The new homeowners could use them to either house an extended family or simply to gain extra income from the rental of the additional unit(s).

The graystone was efficiently organized and adequately impressive to satisfy the needs and aspirations of this rising class. From the sidewalk, a short set of steps led up to a sheltering and inviting porch and the front door. This opened into an entry and the main staircase to the unit above. In addition to the main stair, the required second means of egress was provided by an exterior, service stair at the rear. This rear stair allowed for ice and coal deliveries. Connected to the rear stair was a back porch. The layout of units was identical on each floor. The parlor faced the street and almost certainly had a bay window to enhance the view and add more sunlight to the apartment. Dining rooms were in the middle with kitchens to the rear, while bedrooms occupied the other side of this arrangement. Consequently, all habitable rooms had plenty of windows and cross-ventilation was not a problem with four sides exposed to sun and air.

Outdoor space was limited. Built typically on 25 feet wide city lots with a depth of 125 feet, little room was left around the home. There was a small, rather formal front yard, which provided a setback from the sidewalk and the street to give the home more importance. The backyard was equally small, but it was used only as a service yard to hang laundry and keep garbage cans. The distance between buildings on either side was only 2 or 3 feet wide, leaving only 20 feet or less for the building itself. As a result, these closely spaced, yet freestanding buildings, could appear to be attached row housing to the casual observer. Usually, there was a paved walk that ran in the space between them, which connected the public sidewalk at the street to the building's rear yard and stair.

Figure 4.9
The Chicago Graystones Are A Ubiquitous Building Type Found Throughout The City Of Chicago, With Their Limestone And Brick Façades

In some cases, the dining room would project out from the main body of the building over the walk, almost touching the neighboring building. In these cases, the walk stepped down and went under the projecting room at the level of the basement floor, which also allowed for a convenient entry to it. Roofs were flat, but inaccessible, so they were not used for any utilitarian or recreational function.

Graystones were set up on a basement that rose several feet out of the ground, giving the buildings an additional half story in height, which helped to convey a greater sense of importance and degree of elegance. By raising the building, it also meant that builders could create a full height basement by going into the ground by 4 feet required to get below the frost line, while not needing to dig too deeply so as to stay above the water table, which could be a problem in some locations.

These dwellings were built solidly with exterior walls made of masonry. They were either all brick, brick with limestone façades, or all brick with only limestone detailing on the façades. Limestone is a soft stone that is easily carved and builders made the most of this quality, adding simple or ornate flourishes to graystone façades, giving each one its own look. Architectural styles of the graystones ranged from Romanesque, Queen Anne, Chateauesque to Classical Revival (the Beaux Arts). Interior partitions as well as floor and roof structures were made of dimensional lumber that was plastered over creating a fire retardant barrier and a smooth interior finish.

Their flat roofs were made possible by waterproofing techniques that we now commonly refer to as built-up roofing. The process relies on covering the roof surface with multiple layers of wool felt on which molten asphalt or coal tar is mopped. The asphalt readily adheres to the felt and seals out moisture. In 1847, two brothers, Samuel and Cyrus Warren of Cincinnati, pioneered the development of this process by discovering that coal "tar—a waste product of the gas lighting industry—made an ideal adhesive."[25] Subsequently, asphalt was substituted for tar once oil was discovered in Pennsylvania in

Figure 4.10
Chicago Graystone

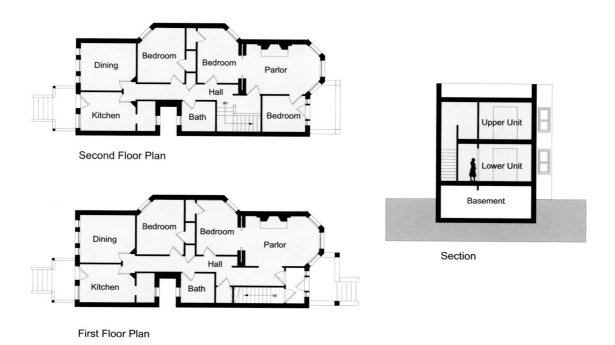

Second Floor Plan

First Floor Plan

Section

1859. This process allowed for the growth of cities where roof surfaces had become too large and difficult to cover with the more complex pitched roofs.

One might question the use of a flat roof in a snowy place like this, but it has certain advantages over a pitched roof. Because snow on a flat roof can create a blanket, wind will not be able to infiltrate that surface, and if the roof is well-insulated, it will serve to further protect the home from more extreme cold. Additionally, ice damming that plagues so many sloped roofs will not form at the edges of flat ones, avoiding a major roofing issue in this type of climate.

All in all, the Chicago two- and three-flat design worked well to satisfy the need for solid, healthy, and comfortable city housing economically and efficiently. It also satisfied, albeit with some degree of compromise, the climatic needs relating to the sometimes hot, sometimes cold Midwestern weather. As a freestanding building, it provided plenty of light even during dark winter days. It also allowed for adequate ventilation to all rooms when summer nights got oppressively hot and humid. The downside was that the large amount of surface area exposed during the cold winter months created more heat loss to the structure than is desirable. Whatever its disadvantages, it provided and continues to provide a good urban alternative to the single-family house.

Courtyard Apartments

In the larger Midwestern cities as in those of the northeast, apartment buildings began to be developed in great numbers around the mid-nineteenth century to accommodate the large influx of European immigrants. Like those of the northeast, the first tenements offered only small, overcrowded, poorly ventilated rooms with no running water or any other sanitary convenience. Many were often five- and six-story wooden buildings with only narrow exterior fire escapes as a second means of egress. There was no outdoor space for recreation other than on their flat roofs or in the streets. After the American Civil War, the Midwestern cities began to make efforts to improve these deplorable living conditions. In Chicago, the Great Fire of 1876 destroyed a large portion of what was the downtown area and with it many of these apartment buildings. As a consequence of this tragedy, a stricter building code was created here and elsewhere, in order not only to make future buildings safer from fire, but more sanitary and comfortable. Chicago's 1902 Tenement House Ordinance dictated a multitude of requirements from the quality of construction to living conditions in such buildings. Along with these mandated improvements, the nature of the tenant also changed. A growing, more affluent middle class, who could afford a better quality of housing, demanded a high standard for their families.

One of the most innovative and desirable building types to be generated by these factors was the courtyard apartment building. They came into being around 1890 and were built until the Great Depression put an end to their popularity. As the name implies, they were organized on or around a landscaped green space or courtyard. The functional intent of the open space was to provide increased exterior wall surface area for additional windows, which gave each unit more opportunities for fresh air, sun, and view. However, the courtyard did much more as it enhanced the overall living experience and created an elegant residential feel in an otherwise crowded city.

The typical building contained about twenty-four one- to three-bedroom apartments with a few containing as many as seventy-eight units.[26] They were developed around three-story modules with two apartments per set of staircases. An entry stair from the courtyard

Figure 4.11
Gracious Courtyard Apartments
Complexes Such As This One In
Chicago, IL, Provide Outdoor
Space To Each Complex In The
Heart Of The City

side and a rear, service stair with access from a public alley, accommodated each module. Unlike taller apartment buildings that had common public lobbies, this arrangement did away with the need for a double-loaded corridor to connect units and still satisfied the building code's requirement for two means of egress from every apartment. As a result, each unit could have windows on two or even three sides, as no corridor divided the building. This arrangement provided cross-ventilation and sunlight in every habitable room and gave the entry sequence a more domestic scale. Richard Gnat, an architect and educator, who has made a study of these buildings, says that he "has identified more than 25 variants of the courtyard building type, neatly integrated into a striking array of urban conditions." "More than 1,000 courtyard buildings dot the urban and suburban Chicago landscape, and that if you fly into the city you can spot them from the air—they resemble the letters 'C,' 'S,' or 'Z.' "[27]

These buildings were usually constructed no more than three-and-a-half-stories tall (three residential floors over a basement), since building codes were less stringent than for taller ones and no elevator was required. The code stipulated that for apartment buildings of this height, the exterior bearing walls and party walls between units must be constructed from solid masonry, but unlike taller buildings, the interior construction could be of more economical dimensional lumber.[28] In addition to helping fireproof the building, the masonry provided a sound deadening separation between the units. The façades on the public sides were often highlighted with carved limestone to give them a greater sense

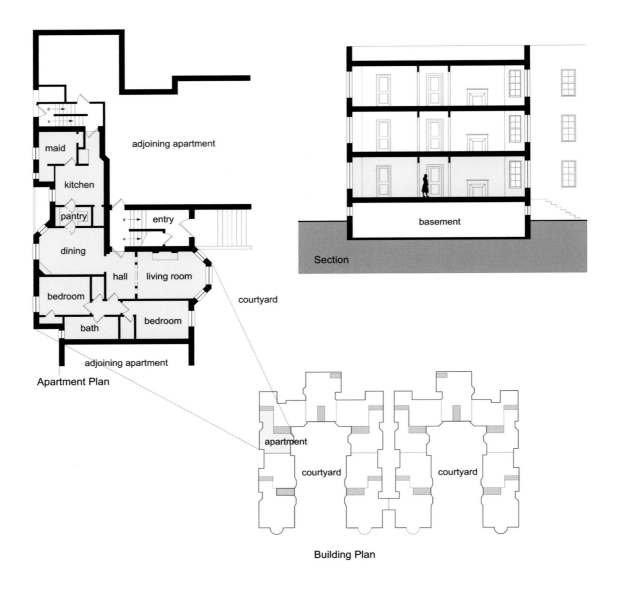

maid

kitchen

pantry

dining

adjoining apartment

entry

hall

living room

bedroom

bedroom

bath

adjoining apartment

Apartment Plan

courtyard

basement

Section

apartment

courtyard

courtyard

Building Plan

of elegance and style, while the rear walls were constructed with the much cheaper common brick. A covering of plaster protected the dimensional lumber that was used in the construction of interior partitions, floors, and roof structures.

In many ways, they represent the most successful sustainable, urban prototype to be built in the region. In addition to being well-made from local materials, they were efficiently laid out and provided a wholesome family living environment. Their compact, row-house-like design meant that they were more easily heated and kept cooler than freestanding buildings. Cross-ventilation and greater opportunities for sunlight added to their desirability. And finally, they introduced a modicum of vegetation into the city that high-rise buildings rarely match.

Figure 4.12
Courtyard Apartments

Common Themes Found in Traditional Buildings of the Midwest

Shape and Placement

In many ways, the earliest vernacular buildings in the Midwest resemble those of the northeast, the mid-Atlantic, and to a lesser extent the southeast due to similarities of climate, resources, and traditions—all the basic elements of the vernacular. As the pattern of settlement of the region was from east to west with people of English descent coming from New England, New York, Pennsylvania, and the mid-Atlantic coastal states, they brought with them their traditional building methods. Through Pennsylvania came a large number of northern European settlers—Germans (Pennsylvania Dutch), Swedes, and Scots (Scotch-Irish), who shared many of those same northern European construction methods with the English.

Climate played a role by reinforcing many of the lessons learned in Europe and along the Atlantic by the forefathers of the Midwestern settlers. The early buildings were compact and straightforward with their designs, driven by necessity and pragmatism, as the need to survive always dictates. At first, houses were rarely bigger than necessary and the reduced external surface helped to make them more easily heated over the long and very cold winters of the region. Roofs were pitched with small overhangs and windows were few. It was only at the end of the nineteenth century that this all began to change in the cities, where flat roofs and a greater number of windows became popular.

Of the prototypes discussed above, there was only a regard for solar orientation in the earlier ones—the longhouses and the earlier farmhouses. In cities, the orientation was to the street, which was not dictated by the sun. To make up for this, there was an effort made to have as many windows in a dwelling as possible. The sun was important, not only to gain heat, but for one's psychological wellbeing.

Shelter, Construction, and Materials

As a consequence of the large expanses of forest located in the region, timber became the most prominent building material. The early settlers built in the familiar medieval ways current at the time. Some made simple cabins of logs laid horizontally, one upon the other with overlapping corners. Many used the traditional post and beam framing method. Many of these initial shelters were crude, built only as a place in which to pass the first winter or two. As the family became more settled and their fortunes improved, these initial dwellings were replaced by those of a more permanent nature.

As in the rest of the country, in the early part of the nineteenth century, these methods gave way to framing with thinner wooden members and the use of mass-produced wire nails, which was faster and more economical. However, after the Great Chicago Fire in 1876, laws governing construction became more restrictive in the larger Midwestern cities, which demanded masonry exterior walls and two means of egress from upper floor units among other things. Fortunately, both brick and stone were readily available and quickly became fashionable.

In the country and in smaller towns where fire-resistant construction was not required by law, the two-by-four continued to make building easier and faster. This light framing method prevails to this day because it is still the cheapest method.

Midwestern roofs on single-family housing were almost always pitched, but not as steeply as might be expected, given the large amounts of snow that the region receives. This low-pitched solution was no doubt due to a combination of economy of resources and an ease of construction, but may have had an additional advantage that a steep roof did not. The lower pitches held the snow, which helped to form a protective blanket and also, it did not offer as much resistance to high winds as a steeply pitched one. As the region was susceptible to very high and continuous winter winds, as well as tornados, this lower angle could help keep the roof more stable and intact under the most turbulent of circumstances. The roofs of multi-unit city housing were for the most part flat, which gave them the same advantages as low-sloped ones. Wherever a house had wooden siding, a roof overhang was desirable to keep the moisture from rain and melting snow off, but they were not as important for shading from the sun as in the southern latitudes. A smaller overhang had the advantage of not catching as much wind, which could potentially tear a roof off.

Another common feature of the Midwestern home was the basement. In such a cold climate, builders must dig down far enough to get below the frost line—usually 4 feet or more—in order to have the foundation secure from disturbance by soil movement due to freezing and thawing. As foundations were required to go this deeply into the ground, there was no reason that a full basement could not be economically achieved. This added space was not only good for more storage, but it provided an excellent location for the heating system, without taking away from the living space above. The basement could be set deeply into the ground with only a small amount of foundation wall showing or it could extend higher with more of the basement wall exposed. This higher option was often chosen, as it required less digging to get the full-height basement, but more importantly, it set the building up on something of a podium, thereby giving it a greater presence or sense of importance, which the growing number of wealthy families found desirable.

Heating, Cooling, and Ventilation

As time went by, Midwesterners sought to have more and more windows to provide as much sunlight and cross-ventilation as could be afforded. Having housing with more than one side exposed to light and air was therefore a great advantage. Sunlight during the long winters not only warmed the dwelling, but also it gave some emotional relief to the dreary climate that tended to linger longer than one might wish. By contrast, once the hot, humid summers arrived, a good, steady airflow through the house was extremely desirable to keep it reasonably cool and comfortable. Windows were the traditional double-hung type from early on, but in the latter part of the nineteenth century, the out-swinging, casement variety became very popular as well. The casement window gave a greater open area, and therefore allowed more cooling summer air to enter the dwelling. Also, as a result of its design, they had fewer seams where infiltration can occur; therefore, they tend to be tighter and let in less cold air in winter.

As elsewhere, the wood-burning fireplace gave way to the cast iron stove as the main source of heat in most houses. Stoves were later replaced by central boilers and hot air systems, which were usually located in the basement, and relied on coal, oil, or gas to fuel them. Each of these innovations brought about added convenience and comfort, as well as small adaptations of layout and design to the building.

As mentioned, the Midwestern dwelling was an amalgam of European and American east coast traditions, with innovations evolving from the common factors of economy, climate, and necessity. Due to their attractive and practical designs, some of these Midwestern building types became very popular nationwide as in the case of the farmhouse, the foursquare house, and the courtyard apartment buildings.

Natural Resources Available for Construction

Stone

As mentioned previously, the ubiquitous graystones of Chicago got their name from the limestone used in their making. This limestone was quarried mainly in the vicinity of Bedford, Indiana. Unfortunately, we see very little stone used today in homes or even multifamily buildings due to the expense involved in quarrying, transporting, and placing the material.

Brick

Brick was the prevalent building material used as an exterior bearing and party walls until the mid-twentieth century in the Midwest. Some cities were even known by the color of their brick buildings. Milwaukee, for example, was referred to as the "cream city" due to the light color of the local brick used throughout the city. "Deep veins of red lacustrine clay run along the western shore of Lake Michigan, and one of the unique properties of this clay is that when formed into bricks, it turns a light golden yellow color after firing. Not only pleasant in color, these bricks generally possess superior strength and weather resistance characteristics, as well as excellent color-retention properties."[29] Other cities of the region were composed of the more common red brick, which often dominated neighborhoods.

Wood

When the first white men came to the region, it "was covered by virgin forests, of pine in the north and oak and hickory in the south."[30] Due to uncontrolled logging, fire, agricultural development, and urban sprawl in the nineteenth and twentieth centuries, these virgin forests were devastated. Through conservation efforts started in the 1940s (in particular, tree farming), they have rebounded dramatically. Currently "the Upper Midwest states of Minnesota, Wisconsin, and Michigan are among the most heavily forested in the nation, with 41 percent of their total area, or 20.4 million hectares (50 million acres), in forested lands. Forest diversity ranges from cool, near-boreal forests of Minnesota and northern Wisconsin to warm, oak-hickory forests of southern Wisconsin and Michigan, spanning 11 geomorphic sections in the Laurentian Mixed Forest and Eastern Broadleaf Forest provinces, populated by a dozen major conifer and 50 major hardwood species."[31]

Demand for lumber and other wood products both nationally and internationally has put increased pressure on these timberlands. Public policy has added to the problem by drastically reducing the amount of timber that can be harvested in National Forests in the Midwest as well as elsewhere across the country. Also, forestland is still being lost in large quantities due to "urban and commercial expansion, the 'rural sprawl' of second-home and recreational development, and other conflicting land uses."[32]

Also, the makeup of tree species in these forests has changed over time. By taking forest composition information as described in the Public Land Survey from the mid-1800s and comparing it with today's forests, researchers have concluded that the entire ecosystem has shifted. They "found that none of the areas surveyed—from Minnesota to Wisconsin to Michigan—have the same tree species makeup as they did 200 years ago." The original "system was made up of largely conifers with some deciduous trees, and now we have the opposite. Conifers—mostly pines and other evergreens—have gotten more scarce while deciduous trees such as aspen, birch and maple have taken their place. Trees in today's forests also tend to be smaller."[33]

Declining forestland and fewer conifers in the mix are not good developments for the building industry. Both tend to reduce the availability of lumber, so vital to the construction of small to mid-sized building projects. Whereas hardwoods, such as ash, alder, and poplar, are useful in the manufacture of trim, doors, and window sashes; conifers, such as pine, spruce, and fir, are used as basic elements in construction for structural purposes. With demand strong and these important species in short supply, the price will inevitably increase. Regardless, they represent our most sustainable major building product, and their availability must be encouraged over the long term to help satisfy the regions future needs.

Iron

Iron ore is a substance from which steel is made, and even though iron is one of the most plentiful elements on the earth, it is found in adequate concentrations for this purpose only in certain places. The area around Lake Superior in the northerly reaches of Michigan, Wisconsin, and Minnesota produces 99 percent of all of the U.S.'s iron ore due to significant veins found in the area.[34] Most of this production is from Minnesota, which produces about three quarters of that total amount from six iron ore operations. These mines produce about forty million tons of iron ore annually, with the richest being the Mesabi Iron Range, located in a narrow belt, approximately 3 miles wide and 120 miles long.

The region's mines were the source of iron from where steel came to fight two world wars and develop an industrial base that was not surpassed until the latter part of the twentieth century. From 1890 to about 1980, two-and-a-half-billion tons of high-grade ore was mined in this region, and this "natural ore" is all but exhausted. Mining of the low-grade ores began during the 1950s. About 20 to 30 percent iron, these low-grade ores are enhanced and upgraded to high-grade iron ore with an iron content of about 65 percent.[35] This refining process is expensive and fuel-intensive.

It is estimated that the reserve of iron ore remaining is about 2,100 million cubic tons,[36] which could last to the end of this century or possibly beyond. Even though this material is not sustainable over the long haul, it will be available, albeit more expensive. The result will be that its use will be restricted to projects that are large enough to afford the extra costs. The now-cheap all-metal building may soon be a thing of the past to be replaced with more affordable wooden structures.

The Current Approach to Design and Construction

Urban Development Today

The Midwest is still known for vast tracts of farmland and forests, but much of the natural wealth that the first white settlers found has been dissipated by urban development and its accompanying suburban sprawl. Even though this trend for development to expand outward will no doubt continue as land is cheaper the farther one travels from city centers, it has begun to wane. As with some other parts of the country, this slowdown can be contributed to a number of different factors already discussed in Chapter 1, but in the Midwest, the loss of population in the inner city is certainly the main reason. In once-vibrant urban neighborhoods, land now lies abandoned, even clear of the homes that once occupied them. Detroit is not the only city to experience a contraction. Akron, Buffalo, Cincinnati, Pittsburg, Rochester, Scranton, St. Louis, Wilkes-Barre, and Youngstown represent some of the more notable examples with decreases from 35 percent to over 60 percent declines since 1950. The question that politicians and city planners face is what to do with all of this now-vacant land, much of which has been claimed by the municipalities for tax defaults.

Architectural Character

Most Midwest cities have a plentiful supply of neglected housing that can be rehabilitated. Much of this is located near the inner city and is affordable. There are large sections of once-thriving neighborhoods that are still viable and worthy of reinvigoration. Chicago, for example, has established a "greystones initiative to help bring some of its housing stock back to life." Likewise, bungalows have become very popular for young families on small budgets, who have begun to repopulate the city. These once-neglected areas represent opportunities to house a new set of city dwellers.

Popular Design and Construction Methods

Today, the methods of low-rise, multifamily home construction are consistent with those across the country, with light wood frame structures predominating. However, new developments are still taking place on the urban fringes, far from city centers. Closer in, one finds a tendency to build tall, glassy buildings with few operable windows, relying on mechanical systems to modify interior climate. Conditions that will not be sustainable into the future.

Future Environmental Concerns

Global warming is expected to affect major changes in the region over the course of this century. Like most of the country, between 2000 and 2010, the Midwest experienced the warmest decade on record, a trend that is expected to continue. The EPA noted "the average summer temperatures are projected to increase by 3°F over the next few decades and could increase by over 10°F by the end of this century. This range would make summers in Illinois and Michigan feel like those in present-day Texas and Oklahoma, respectively."[37] In addition to this overall warming trend, severe weather-related events are expected to occur more often and with greater ferocity. Floods and droughts will become more frequent and prolonged with tornados more frequent and powerful.

Unlike coastal cities, evaporation could reduce the Great Lakes by 1 to 2 feet by century's end. A drop of this magnitude would very likely interrupt ocean-going shipping. On the positive side, warmer winters may mean that shipping could flow more freely throughout the year, as the lakes may not freeze over as completely as they currently do.

Also, agriculture and forest production may benefit from a prolonged growing season, but the composition of crops and trees in the northern forests is likely to change and new, potentially devastating pests and diseases will become an inevitable associated problem. With care and foresight, these may be manageable and not have a major detrimental long-term effect on the region.

On a more human level, the number of deaths related to heatwaves will become an even greater problem than currently, so future housing must begin to take improved ventilation into account. Reliance on air conditioning alone may not be useful to the poor, who will have difficulty paying the requisite higher utility bills.

Design Strategies and Building Components for the Future

Climatic Imperatives

When designing for the Midwest, it is necessary to take into account that the region has extremes at both ends of the temperature spectrum, with severe winters and summers that are often dangerously hot. Throughout the winter months, snow is plentiful and constant, while sleet, hail, and ice are additional, commonplace hazards. Sunlight is more than welcome most of the year for its psychological benefits, but especially throughout the winter for passive solar heating. Heat loss is the major factor in the layout and construction of this region's buildings, but good ventilation is also a necessity throughout most of the summer.

Orientation

In order to maximize passive solar gain to each unit, wherever possible, buildings should have their most prominent or longest side facing south, southeast, or southwest. While this is also generally true in the other regions, in the Midwest, the acceptable variation from west to east can be greater. The south side is also where the preponderance of glass should be placed with only a small amount on the northern exposure.

Overall Suggested Configuration and Layout

There is a great economic advantage to keeping the external surface area to a minimum in order to keep heat loss low, thereby conserving energy. This can be accomplished by keeping the volume of the typical, freestanding Midwestern building to a somewhat cubic shape, which, by its nature, reduces the overall mass, which in turn reduces the amount of surface area exposed to the elements. An apartment building, by its inherent layout, takes the advantage of the connectedness of units, with shared walls to reduce exposure.

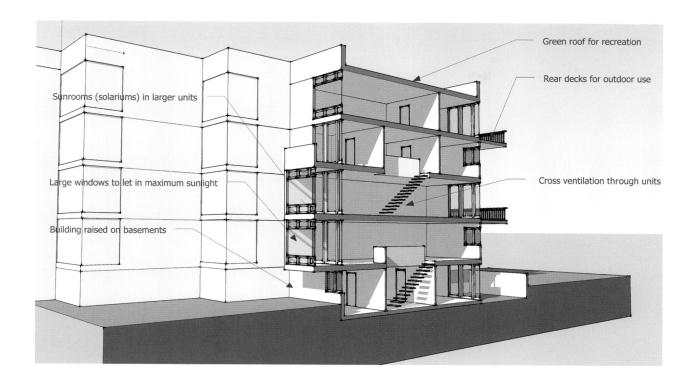

Green roof for recreation

Rear decks for outdoor use

Sunrooms (solariums) in larger units

Large windows to let in maximum sunlight

Cross ventilation through units

Building raised on basements

Figure 4.13
Idea Drawing For The Midwest

Even though it is important to keep surface areas to the minimum, every unit should have exposure on two façades (normally thought of as front and back).

One of the most interesting and practical overall building layouts is the traditional courtyard type, as discussed previously in the precedents section of this chapter. This approach maintains a presence on the street, with some units near the sidewalk and others set more deeply in from it. It also allows for enough surface area to accommodate an adequate number of windows for each apartment while keeping the units in a close proximity to one another. Even though some units are set in from the street with one in front of another, as shown in the example, the building can be configured to give each unit a sunny side.

Building Circulation—Halls and Staircases

In the region, more often than not, the first floor of housing is set up several feet above the sidewalk level and reached by a set of external steps. In the past, the space below the first floor level was used only as a basement, but future buildings could certainly take advantage of this near-ground floor space for more housing. These lowest units could also be the largest with three bedrooms for family occupancy. This arrangement would offer children direct access to yards, without needing to use the common stairway.

Following the example of many of the multifamily building precedents, it is recommended that the building be served by a public or front entry and stairs entered from the street or courtyard side, as well as a rear, more private stair for service and family use. Wherever possible, the rear stair should open out to backyard space and up to a usable flat roof. The rear stair could also provide more direct access to automobile parking, wherever available.

Staircases ought to be enclosed because in winter, it is necessary to keep snow from blocking them or ice and rain making them dangerously slippery. There is no need to heat them, but it is important that it is possible to open them up to a good airflow to keep them from becoming stifling hot and uncomfortably close in summer.

Unit Plan

If the larger family units are on the lower floors, studios and one-bedroom units for single people or couples without children could be appropriately located on the upper ones. Some of the smaller apartments might also be placed on the first floor for the elderly and those with physical challenges.

An open-plan layout for living areas not only makes the units more comfortable to a modern lifestyle, but also they are more easily ventilated, as no walls block the flow of air through the spaces.

In order to conserve heat, ceiling heights in units ought not be too high with 8 feet being the norm and 8.5 feet the maximum. Tall, cathedral ceilings may have a great visual appeal, but they should be avoided for this reason.

Roof Type

Even though the Midwest gets more than its fair share of snow, a pitched roof is not always the best solution, and a flat roof may have greater merit under the circumstances. Naturally, roofs must be extremely well-insulated to keep heat transfer through them to a minimum, but one of the less obvious virtues of the flat roof is that it holds the snow, which in turn further insulates the building while shielding it from the cold winter wind. Beyond the ability to keep buildings more weather-tight, the flat roof offers the opportunity for extra outdoor space.

In the cold Midwestern climate, a light-colored roof is of limited benefit for reflecting summer sun, as it is not as strong here as in other regions. It also has the drawback of reflecting the sun's heat in the winter. In this region, the color of the roof is not as important as in more southerly portions of the country and there is a slight preference toward the darker shades.

Windows and Window Treatments

Good windows and doors in this climate are extremely important to the maintenance of an effective thermal envelope. They should be of the best quality to provide the highest degree of insulation and air tightness to avoid air infiltration.

As previously noted, it is very desirable to locate the largest amount of glass on the south-facing wall. This is not only to provide solar heat, but also to capture as much sunlight as possible to give a psychological lift through the long, dark winter days.

It is very important that every unit has at least two exposures in order to provide cross-ventilation during the hottest times of the year. This may mean something of a compromise in summer as the living areas on one side and private, sleeping areas on the other will need to be somewhat open to one another to facilitate the movement of fresh air through the entire apartment.

The traditional double-hung or the more modern sliding window/door types are acceptable in this climate, as they provide an adequate amount of airflow. Windows with greater ventilating capability, such as awnings or casements, are not required now, but with warmer summers predicted, they may become the recommendation in the near future.

While external coverings help minimize heat loss and gain through glass windows and doors, they are not as feasible, since one must open the window or door to open or close the shade, letting cold air in. Internal coverings, such as thermal curtains and shades, seem most practical and effective. They do not keep the cold out, but can keep drafts to a minimum and help retain the warmth.

Materials and Construction

Brick, stone, hollow-core concrete block, and wood make up the shortlist of the most desirable building materials for the region. From the Chicago bungalow, the graystones and the courtyard buildings, brick and stone are the premier materials for covering the outside of Midwestern buildings due to their ability to withstand exposure to the harsh winter weather. Unfortunately, these masonry materials easily transmit cold. When used as an exterior covering, they will need to be backed up with a secondary, insulated wall, which makes the assemblage somewhat redundant and considered wasteful. On the other hand, this method of having a masonry veneer backed up with an insulated wood frame interior wall may still be appropriate whenever a very durable exterior is required.

The most logical location for an uninsulated, double-sided masonry wall would be between units where it can serve not only as a load bearing structural separation, but a divider that is fireproof and one with very good sound-deadening capabilities. If this sort of party wall is double-sided and left uncovered in its natural state, then there might be a saving, as no finish would be necessary. The added aesthetic benefit of natural stone or brick can serve to enhance the dwelling's interior.

Wood is indispensable and without doubt will compose a great deal of the structure. Dimensional lumber can be used for framing load-bearing walls and nonstructural interior partitions. Dimensional lumber, engineered lumber, and heavy timber are other possible choices for floors and roof structures. As with masonry walls, the heavy timber frame can be left uncovered to show its natural beauty, whereas the lighter frame construction will need something to sheath it. Typically, this covering is plaster, gypsum board, or wood paneling, which can be either painted or in the case of wood paneling, stained.

Outdoor Spaces

Courtyards, yards, and green roofs are all possible options for outdoor activities. These outdoor spaces can be either private for the individual unit occupants or semi-private for the use of all of the building's residents. By the same token, rooftop gardens can be used to create safe and sunny, open-air venues for residents to enjoy.

Balconies in this climate are not as useful as they tend to be in milder ones because the portion of the year that the weather is mild enough to make them pleasant places to relax is short. It is recommended that the space that would normally be used in this way be enclosed with operable windows to create a sunroom, traditionally known as a solarium or conservatory, which can be used year round. This space does not need to be heated, in which case, it might be considered a three-season room, which a resident might choose to not use during winter months. If unheated, it will become a buffer space from the cold outdoors, making the interior more comfortable and easier to heat.

Landscape

Trees that are placed around the building should be done so to shield it from summer sun and winter winds. This is done in the Midwest, as it is elsewhere with deciduous trees located on the south side of the building and evergreens thickly planted on the north or windward side. Certain site constraints may make this ideal arrangement impossible, but care should be taken not to block the sun from windows in the winter when the heat from it is most desired. Additionally, trees and vine-covered arbors located on rooftops and in yard areas can provide shady places to relax and protect from the summer sun.

Green roofs can accommodate any number of types of plants from grasses to small shrubs as long as their weight is not too great. This vegetation will not only serve to enhance the lives of the users, but will help to absorb some of the overabundance of unwanted CO_2 in the atmosphere, replacing it with oxygen. In addition to the plantings,

Figure 4.14
Built Above A Parking Garage, This Modern Apartment Complex Features An Entry Courtyard, So Prevalent In Chicago, As Well As Rooftop Outdoor Recreational Space

hardscape, such as wood decks and terraces, can provide useful places for gatherings and relaxing.

Renewable Power and Mechanical Equipment

For its part, solar is less dependable than the wind in the Midwest, as the sun does not shine reliably, nor is it intense in winter, so only a modest number of solar panels is recommended on this region's buildings. Because it appears that electricity will be coming from giant wind turbines located out on the plains, these solar panels can be used mainly to generate hot water for both domestic and heating purposes.

The Prospect for Future Urban Development in the Midwest

While the trend of urban flight and shrinking city populations has slowed or even begun to reverse itself in some places, many Midwestern cities are having trouble regaining their lost vigor. It is obvious that the reliance on an industrial economy is ending and that these cities must reinvent themselves in order to grow and begin to prosper again.

Like the major cities along the northeastern coastal corridor, the Midwest is also suffering from a problem of deteriorating infrastructure. Roads, rails, bridges, utility lines are old and deteriorating from a lack of maintenance resulting from a shortage of funds or political will. Buildings too have aged and many have been abandoned and left vacant or have been demolished. High crime and poverty have made some cities undesirable for redevelopment. Many of those families that chose to stay in the area moved farther away from the centers into suburbs to find stability and a good education for their families that the cities did not offer.

As a result, property values are now low, which could present the opportunity for investment to again flow back into these aging cities. Cities such as Chicago, Madison, Minneapolis, Buffalo, Pittsburg, and Milwaukee, have already regained a strong financial footing based on economies that do not rely on heavy industry and have begun their resurgence. The opportunity presented by abandonment can be a clean slate. The opportunity that deterioration presents is rehabilitation. Wherever neighborhoods have slipped into decrepitude, there are possibilities for regrowth to serve the needs of future generations in new ways.

As the Midwest begins to reinvent itself over the next decades, the process will gather momentum. Opportunities for revived urban growth are in some respects higher in the Midwest than elsewhere, as there is a great deal of urban land available and many more existing structures in need of rehabilitation.

Clean, cheap, and sustainable energy is being developed at a rapid pace in the region. Wind power seems to be the clear choice over solar. The open plains of these states make a natural place to harness the wind. As a result, the Midwest is represented by three states that rank in the top five for the generation of wind power—Iowa (2), Illinois (4), and Minnesota (5). Now one can drive for hundreds of miles passing by cornfields punctuated by mammoth towers capped with revolving blades of giant like proportions, which signal a new beginning of energy production and sustainability.

With the prospect for milder winters, adequate natural energy sources and more wholesome urban communities built of sustainable materials many may be encouraged to stay in the region and invest in its future.

Summary of Suggested Building Practices for the Midwest

Main environmental objectives: Provide heat in winter and good ventilation and shade in summer.

Orientation

- Living areas should be south, southeast, or southwest facing, wherever possible
- North-facing walls should have little glass
- East and west walls can have a modest amount of glass

Layout

- Generally, compact volumes are recommended to minimize the surface area and heat loss
- Separate units with masonry bearing walls
- Provide shaded areas for living and working outside, such as courtyards, and green rooftops
- Keep ceilings low (8' maximum) to ensure heat remains near occupants
- Use basement levels for storage, mechanical equipment, or living space

Construction

- Heavy timber or engineer lumber for floor and roof structure
- Brick, stone, or concrete block for bearing walls and separation between units
- Light wood framing for interior partitions
- Insulate exterior walls, roofs, and basements well

Roofs

- Flat or modestly pitched
- Green and/or usable flat roofs
- Color of roofing is not as important as in some other regions, but there is a slight preference for darker shades

Shading

- Use overhangs, particularly on the south side
- Interior, insulated curtains are helpful to keep units warm
- Cover usable portions of rooftop areas with either roofs or arbors

Windows

- Maximum opening for air flow—casement or awning most desirable
- Should be minimal on west- and east-facing walls, but some are acceptable
- South side can afford more glass (if shaded for summer sun) to warm interiors in winter
- Sunrooms provide useful interior spaces that also capture and hold solar warmth
- North side should only have a small amount of glass

Ventilation and cooling

- Design for good cross-ventilation
- Cross-ventilation must be controlled in winter, as it can introduce undesirable cold air into dwelling

- Windows should allow full ventilation when open
- Fans can be used to augment air circulation within dwelling and to exhaust hot air build-up
- Provide shady or covered outdoor living spaces on rooftops where airflow is the greatest in summer

Heating

- Design to keep the heat out in summer and contain it in the winter
- Central heating is required
- Fireplaces or wood stoves can help to add warmth in winter

Water

- Collect all gray water for flushing toilets and watering plants

Notes

1 America 2050. *Great Lakes*. Website: www.america2050.org/great_lakes.html.
2 Klingaman, William K., and Nicholas P. Klingaman. *The Year Without Summer: 1816 and the Volcano That Darkened the World and Changed History*. St. Martin's Griffin (2013) New York. p. 201.
3 America 2050. *Great Lakes*. Website: www.america2050.org/great_lakes.html.
4 America 2050. *Great Lakes*. Website: www.america2050.org/great_lakes.html.
5 Bryan, Dan. *The Northwest Ordinance of 1787 and its Effects*. American History USA. Website: www.americanhistoryusa.com/northwest-ordinance-1787-effects/.
6 *Encyclopedia Britannica*. Iroquois People. Website: www.britannica.com/EBchecked/topic/294628/Iroquois.
7 Native American Netroots. *The Iroquois Longhouse*. Website: http://nativeamericannetroots.net/diary/1081.
8 *Iroquois History*. Website: www.tolatsga.org/iro.html.
9 Nabokov, Peter, and Robert Easton. *Native American Architecture*. Oxford University Press (1989) New York. p. 52.
10 New York State Museum. *Longhouses*. Website: www.nysm.nysed.gov/IroquoisVillage/construction two.html.
11 Native American Netroots. *The Iroquois Longhouse*. Website: nativeamericannetroots.net/diary/1081.
12 McAlester, Virginia, and Lee. *A Field Guide to American Houses*. Alfred A. Knopf (1991) New York p. 96.
13 Old House Online. *The I House in Rural America*. Website: www.oldhouseonline.com/the-i-house-in-rural-america/.
14 Wikipedia. *Bungalow: Chicago Bungalow*. Website: https://en.wikipedia.org/wiki/Bungalow#Chicago_bungalow.
15 WTTW: Chicago Stories. *Bungalow: Sweet Home Chicago*. Website: www.wttw.com/main.taf?p=1,7,1,1,6.
16 Historic Chicago Bungalow Association. Website: www.chicagobungalow.org/about-us/what-is-a-chicago-bungalow.
17 Katie Steffan (Graduate Student). *Polish Flats*. Milwaukee Polonia, University of Wisconsin-Milwaukee Libraries. University of Wisconsin-Milwaukee. Website: http://uwm.edu/mkepolonia/polish-flats/.

18 Wikipedia. *Polish Flat*. Website: https://en.wikipedia.org/wiki/Polish_flat.

19 Turner, Nancy. *The Milwaukee Journal*. Polish Flats: Duplex Made Room for Newcomers. Website: https://news.google.com/newspapers?nid=1499&dat=19880312&id=nl0aAAAAIBAJ&sjid=AysEA AAAIBAJ&pg=7046,3566159&hl=en https://news.google.com/newspapers?nid=1499&dat=1988 0312&id=nl0aAAAAIBAJ&sjid=AysEAAAAIBAJ&pg=7046,3566159&hl=en Sunday, March 13, 1988. Section F.

20 Antique Home Style. *An Overview of 20th Century House Styles: A Little House Building History*. Website: www.antiquehomestyle.com/styles/stylehistory.htm.

21 McAlester, Virginia, and Lee. *A Field Guide to American Houses*. Alfred A. Knopf (1991) New York p. 440.

22 Antique Home Style. *An Overview of 20th Century House Styles: A Little House Building History*. Website: www.antiquehomestyle.com/styles/stylehistory.htm.

23 Antique Home Style. *Foursquare Style — 1895 to 1930*. Website: www.antiquehomestyle.com/styles/foursquare.htm.

24 Greystone Preservation LLC. *Greystone Features*. Website: http://greystonepreservationllc.com/What_Is_a_Greystone.html.

25 *Old House Online*. Amazing Asphalt: How 1920s Shingle Types and Designs Created the Golden Age of Composition Roofing. Website: www.oldhousejournal.com/magazine/2005/jul/amazing.shtml.

26 Kansas State University News Release, 9 April 2009. Website: www.k-state.edu/media/newsreleases/april09/gnat42309.html.

27 Kansas State University News Release, 9 April 2009. Website: www.k-state.edu/media/newsreleases/april09/gnat42309.html.

28 Gnat, Richard. The Chicago Courtyard Apartment Building: A Sustainable Model Type. p. 498. Paper delivered at the 98th ACSA Annual Meeting. Website: http://webcache.googleusercontent.com/search?q=cache:1XaZcpItHPQJ:apps.acsa-arch.org/resources/proceedings/uploads/streamfile.aspx%3Fpath%3DACSA.AM.98%26name%3DACSA.AM.98.60.pdf+&cd=1&hl=en&ct=clnk&gl=us&client=safari.

29 Seeing the Light. Cream City Brick. Website: www.terrypepper.com/lights/closeups/cream_city_brick/cream_city_brick.htm.

30 Clarence Mondale. *History of the Upper Midwest: An Overview*. The George Washington University, Summer, 1998. Website: http://memory.loc.gov/ammem/umhtml/umessay1.html.

31 Upper Midwest Research & Remote Sensing at Scales That Matter. *Forests*. Website: http://resac.gis.umn.edu/forestry/forestry_index.htm.

32 Agile Writer. *Michigan's Lumber Boom: Timmberrrrrr!!!!!!* Website: http://agilewriter.com/History/Mi_lumber.htm.

33 *Science Daily*. Upper Midwest Forests Are Losing Diversity, Complexity. October 17, 2007. Website: www.sciencedaily.com/releases/2007/10/071016181201.htm.

34 Tuck, Christopher A. Iron Ore. *U.S. Geological Survey, Mineral Commodity Summaries, February 2014*. p. 90. Website: https://minerals.usgs.gov/minerals/pubs/mcs/2016/mcs2016.pdf.

35 *Explore MInnesota: Iron Ore*. Sponsored by Minnesota Minerals Coordinating Committee. March 2013. Website: http://mn.gov/irrrb/images/IronOre.pdf.

36 Statista: Statistical Portal. *World reserves of iron ore as of 2015, by country (in million metric tons)*. Website: www.statista.com/statistics/267381/world-reserves-of-iron-ore-by-country/.

37 USGCRP. Karl, Thomas R., Melillo, Jerry M., and Thomas C. Peterson (Eds.). *Global Climate Change Impacts in the United States*. Cambridge University Press (2009) New York. Website: www.epa.gov/climatechange/impactsadaptation/midwest.html.

Chapter 5

The South: Coastal Plains and Interior Uplands

The southeastern part of the United States, which is sometimes referred to as the Deep South, Dixie, the Old South, or simply the South, is a unique part of the United States. History, tradition, geography, climate, and a wide range of ethnic groups mix together in a way that cannot be found elsewhere. A new and vibrant culture is evolving from this changing sociopolitical scene. Southern Whites and African Americans now share the region with an influx of Cubans, Asians, Latinos, and Northerners, both young and old. Cities are growing faster than anywhere in the country, as more and more people seek the warmth, jobs, and lower taxes that the South offers. It is a place where opportunity knocks and retirement beckons. More cosmopolitan now, it is the setting for exciting future growth and innovation. In *The Nine Nations of North America*, Joel Garreau contends, "change itself has become Dixie's most identifiable characteristic."[1]

The Place

The South covers a vast area that is bounded by the Gulf of Mexico to the south, the Atlantic Ocean to the east, into the Appalachian Mountains to the north, and to the hill country of central Texas on the west. The region includes the entirety of eleven states from Virginia to Louisiana, as well as the easterly parts of Kentucky, Oklahoma, and Texas. These states form a cohesive unit, as they share a common heritage, climate, and geography.

Geographically, the largest portion of this region is composed of flat or gently rolling coastal plains. The Gulf plain runs along the south coast of Texas to the southerly tip of Florida. It follows the Mississippi River up to southeastern Arkansas, western Tennessee, and Kentucky. This land area ranges "from sand hills and rolling longleaf pine dominated uplands to pine flat woods and savannas, seepage bogs, bottomland hardwood forests, barrier islands and dune systems, and estuaries."[2] The Atlantic plain parallels the Atlantic east coast from Florida to Virginia. Both of these costal plains begin to climb in altitude as one moves farther inland where they rise into hill country ultimately terminating in the Appalachian Mountains.

Generally speaking, the climate is mild with the yearly average temperature of "approximately 62°F, with the summer months (May through mid October) averaging almost 80°F; however, extremes range from 105°F to 110°F. Accumulated rainfall is 56 inches."[3] While these statistics can vary greatly depending on numerous factors, the general rule is that the South is hot and humid with copious amounts of rainfall, which can produce an extremely sultry environment at times.

Until the mid-nineteenth century, agriculture was the main economic driver for the region with cotton, sugar cane, rice, and tobacco as the primary crops. After World War II, this began to change as industry from northern states was enticed to move south by cheaper land and lower factory wages. Many people from the north were attracted by its low taxes and warm climate and took up residency either permanently or as a winter refuge. As a result, the population of the South has soared from what was once a sparsely populated region to the fastest-growing one in the nation. Commerce, industry, and trade have all flourished in this business-friendly atmosphere, producing cities such as Charlotte, Miami, Houston, and Atlanta, which are now major economic centers.

There is little doubt that the dramatic growth that the South has experienced the second half of the twentieth century, and to current times, is due to the advent and widespread use of air conditioning. This technological advance has made the region much more desirable, as those insufferably hot, humid summer days and nights can now be chilled to a much more pleasant level.

Figure 5.1
Houston's Central Business District With Its Concentration Of Tall Buildings Sprouts From The Coastal Plain And Is Ringed By Interstate Highways

REINVENTING AN URBAN VERNACULAR

Many of these southern cities are modern with tall, glassy office buildings and hotels, well-stocked shopping malls, and sprawling suburbs, which resemble other places around the country. Unfortunately, the erosion of a distinct regional character has compromised much of the charm that we associate with the South.[4]

Mimi Swartz, writing about Houston for the *New York Times* observed, "There are more newcomers than ever: about 1,550 new people a week by the latest reckoning, clogging the freeways and turning strip centers into international bazaars. These folks aren't just from Detroit: At the Ikea on any given Sunday, a Texas accent can't even begin to hold its own against Spanish, Chinese, Persian, Vietnamese, Arabic, French and the lilting intonations of several African nations."

Early Development Patterns

The Spanish, French, and English all played an important initial role in developing cities and towns in the South, but as might be expected, with distinctive differences. Many of the first of these towns were planned in Europe before any settlers arrived, and as might be expected, some worked better than others. Savannah (founded in 1733) is a wonderful example of an ideal plan created by James Edward Oglethorpe, which was drawn up thousands of miles from the intended site, which incorporated more open space into it than any other such layout in history. The result was the most beautiful (and perhaps, the most romantic) southern city. On the other hand, Charleston's founders made disastrous initial mistakes and had to move the town to its current placement on healthier, higher ground. The subsequent plan, developed with the benefit of first hand knowledge of the place, was also gridded, but somewhat less formal in its structure.

All of these early settlements were located on or at the mouths of rivers and near the ocean to facilitate trade between the hinterland and the motherland. Unlike their New England cousins, which developed from convoluted, medieval street patterns, all were designed from inception on a gridded street pattern. Lacking a common authority, there was no standard size or spacing to these blocks or street widths, but provision was always made for public places of differing sizes and purposes. Markets, churches, governmental buildings, and parks were placed strategically according to their importance within the checkerboard plan. Both the Spanish in San Augustine and Pensacola, Florida, and the French in New Orleans used similar gridded layouts as the English.

Rivers and harbors served as their economic and cultural lifelines, with the city growing out from the foci. New Orleans' main square that faced and opened out toward the Mississippi River is surrounded on three sides by major pubic buildings, which, to this day, form the heart of that great city.

In the nineteenth century, as the nation grew in population and expanded inland, small farms began to cover the countryside and country towns developed to service them. These agricultural-centered communities developed in much the same way as their earlier predecessors, but generally are of a more modest scale. A typical layout was one where the county courthouse occupied the central square and stores faced it and lined the main streets. The introduction of the railways brought to small southern towns a new element—the train station—where much commerce and social life was centered. These two elements became the main generators for future expansion in these towns and typified a southern lifestyle. In time, some of these inland towns developed into major cities, such as Atlanta, Charlotte, and Houston.

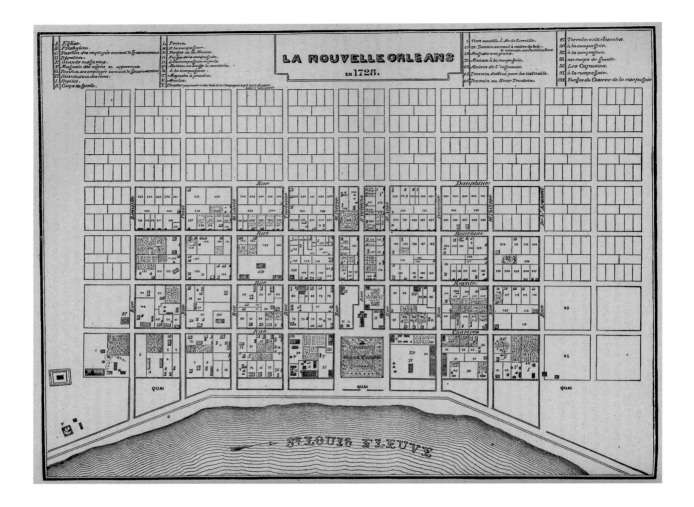

Figure 5.2
1728 Map Of New Orleans, LA,
Illustrating How Its Gridded
Street Plan Relates Directly
To The Riverfront

Even though the South was mainly an agrarian society, where the majority of the population lived in rural settings well into the twentieth century, cities grew and prospered. They developed in different ways due to local topography and specific need, which has given each its own individual character. Despite the regularity imposed by their rectangular formats, uniqueness has prevailed.

Precedents

During the eighteenth and early nineteenth centuries, the South developed a wide assortment of innovative vernacular building types. These ranged from large, formal, and imposing structures built by a new aristocracy to some rudimentary ones that housed the poor. They incorporated the traditions of several cultures—English, French, Spanish, African, and Native American. As with all such building, they were responsive to the southern environment and built with locally found materials, which gave them a distinctly southern look and feel.

REINVENTING AN URBAN VERNACULAR

The Antebellum Plantation House

When considering the vernacular tradition of the "Old South," colonnaded Greek revival plantation homes with wide verandas and spacious central hallways may come to mind. *Tara*, the plantation home of Scarlet O'Hara in *Gone with the Wind*, is representative of the most iconic building type of this pre-Civil War period. Primarily built during the first half of the nineteenth century, these homes took their imagery from classic Greek temples. This revival of an ancient Greek form represented the ideals of the time—purity, knowledge, and most importantly, democracy itself. In addition to imbuing homes with a level of beauty and sophistication, the Greek typology gave credibility to churches, banks, and government buildings, both large and small. These homes do not represent the vernacular tradition to many scholars, but they do have many similar characteristics and valuable lessons to teach. Even though some had the help of architects, the majority were designed from pattern books and the current local style of the day. Local carpenters using traditional methods built them from locally found materials. They always took climate into account.

Figure 5.3
Houmas House In Natchez, MS, Represents The Mid–Nineteenth-Century Southern Plantation Home That Expresses The Family's Wealth While Working With Climate To Make Life As Pleasant As Possible In An Age Before Air–Conditioning

Beyond the formal impression that these mansions were designed to create, they also reflected a practicability relating to the place and its climate. The Greek temple form, which made up many of the southern plantation homes' basic aesthetic format, was transformed through adaptations to local climate into a unique and appropriate southern building type. The basic building was usually two- or three-stories in height, somewhat square in plan and capped with a low-pitched roof. The result was a rather cubic mass, which does not allow for maximum cross-ventilation. To compensate for this less-than-desirable arrangement, a central hall punctured the middle of the house like the hole in a square doughnut. This void allowed most rooms that surrounded it to have open-ness on two sides—one to the exterior and the other to the hall itself. The central hall was frequently capped with a monitor or cupola, which could be opened on hot days, allowing the space to act as a chimney. This chimney effect induced air to flow freely from the exterior and through the rooms surrounding it. In addition, the wide verandas helped to capture any breeze and channel it into the spaces at the perimeter of the building. High ceilings kept the hottest air up and away from the occupants, and transoms over doors allowed air more freedom to pass. In some instances, the main living level was raised above an open-ground floor level on brick piers, facilitating air movement under these spaces as well.

Of equal elegance and grace, the typical French Creole house of Louisiana melded yet another European traditional style with southern climate in a creative manner. From 1765 to 1785, French immigrants, expelled by the British from Canada, settled in southern Louisiana and the lower Mississippi River region. They brought with them a traditional Norman building style that normally would not have been suitable for such an environment. With numerous adaptations, a northern French vernacular building type became a very southern one. "The most important features include: (1) generous galleries, (2) a broad spreading roofline, (3) gallery roofs supported by light wooden colonnettes, (4) placement of the principal rooms well above grade (sometimes a full story), (5) a form of construction utilizing a heavy timber frame combined with an infill made of brick (briquette entre poteaux) or a mixture of mud, moss and animal hair called bousillage, (6) multiple French doors, and (7) French wraparound mantels." The previously mentioned timber frame incorporated French joinery, that is, angle braces that are extremely steep, running all the way from sill to plate, in contrast to English joinery where the angle brace is usually at a 45° angle.[5] "Larger houses had from three to five rooms across the front. Sometimes, a second row of rooms were placed behind the first. In most Creole houses this second row incorporated a cabinet or loggia (a central open area flanked by a room at each corner). The houses usually lacked hallways; instead, the rooms opened directly into each other."[6] Rather than locating stairs inside the building, they were placed in the gallery, thereby eliminating the need to waste valuable interior space on vertical circulation.

The elegant Planters' homes are only a small part of the southern vernacular tradition, as there were many fewer in number than the humbler dwellings of the common people. However, the elegant planters' homes shared with other lesser-known building types of the South, many of the same attributes that were developed as a response to their locality.

The Dogtrot House

One of the most ubiquitous examples of the common man's home took its form as what has become known as the dogtrot house. It is typified by an open hall or dogtrot that connects a room on either side of it. The three spaces were covered with a roof that was pitched toward the front and back. A porch ran along the front or south side further connecting the spaces. Sometimes, a porch was added along the rear or north side as well.

Of the two rooms, one was used for cooking and eating and the other for sleeping. The dogtrot and the adjoining porches were cool places to socialize or work on long, hot days. Often, the porches sheltered the occupants from the frequent, and at times, torrential, blowing rains. As a consequence, a great deal of time was spent living outside of the two rooms in the home.

The dogtrot house developed from the basic one-room log cabin or "pen." As it is difficult to add on to a log building because of its overlapping log corners, any addition to an original structure was usually built apart from it. While this model was derived from farm buildings in the cold climes of Scandinavia and Northern Europe, the earliest pioneers to the South recognized its advantages with respect to the sultry climate they encountered. As construction methods became more refined, the log construction gave way to wood frame and clapboard siding.

The rooms on either side of the hall were usually square in plan and varied in size from 16 to 18 feet on each side. The width of the hall was frequently half that number.

Figure 5.4
A Humble, Southern Dogtrot
House In East Texas

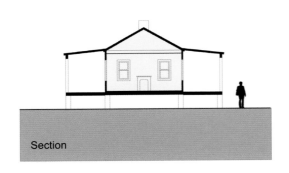

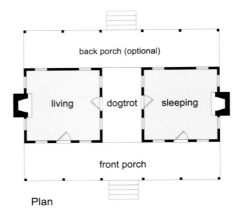

When the two rooms and hall were placed together, a long and narrow rectangular configuration was produced, which could vary from 16 by 40 feet up to 18 by 45 feet.

Figure 5.5
Dogtrot House

The great advantage of the dogtrot was the excellent ventilation that it provided, as both enclosed rooms had exposure on all four sides. Additionally, porches tended to capture breezes and channel them into the living areas. As the house was generally raised off the ground by 2 or 3 feet on brick or stone piers, air was allowed to circulate under the house as well.

Even though winters were mild, some heat was required during brief cold spells and chilly nights. For this reason, wood-burning fireplaces took on the function of heating both rooms. They were generally placed on the outside wall at either end of the building.

The Shotgun House

Another unique example of a truly southern building type is the shotgun house. "It was the most popular style of house in the Southern United States from the end of the American Civil War, through the 1920s."[7] Its introduction into this country is credited to black slaves who were themselves brought to the South from Haiti in the early nineteenth century. It is believed by some that the building type was derived from the slaves' native African house type, which they called "to-gun", which means "place of assembly."[8] In the book *Roots: Ethnic Groups That Built America*, John Michael Vlach addressing Afro-Americans' contribution to our vernacular heritage believes that it is "derived from the fusion of distinct ethnic architectural components: a Caribbean Indian building shape, European colonial framing techniques and African inspired proxemics codes."[9] Whatever the actual origin of the type is, we may never know definitively, but it is an extremely practical and logical design. While associated primarily with New Orleans, the shotgun house can be found throughout the South and well beyond. Even though many of them were constructed in the countryside, they are considered an urban type because they could be fitted neatly onto a narrow city lot—frequently only 30 feet wide or less. As a result, these neighborhoods could be quite densely populated. The buildings were not only closely spaced; they were frequently built on or very near the sidewalk with little or no front yard.

Figure 5.6
Single And Double Shotgun
Houses Such As These Abound In
New Orleans As Well As In Many
Other Cities And Towns Across
The South

They were composed of three to five rooms arranged all in a line, which formed a long, very narrow rectangle, usually no more than 12 feet wide. The first room was used as a living room, the middle room(s) served as sleeping areas, and the rear space was the kitchen. There were no hallways, which allowed every room to have either two or three sides exposed to the exterior. Needless to say, privacy was compromised, as family members would need to move through sleeping spaces to get from one end of the house to the other. Ventilation was apparently more important than privacy. In addition to exposure on all sides, the house was raised off the ground from 2 to 8 feet. Not only did this raise the house above floodwaters, the additional air movement below the floor added coolness to every room.

Space heating was provided by fireplaces, which were located between rooms. Each room would have its own fireplace while sharing a chimney with the one next door, creating a very economical arrangement.

Across the short end that fronts on the street and sidewalk, there was normally a shallow porch for sitting and socializing outside. John Michael Vlach states that the front porch "may be tallied as an African-derived trait. No antecedent for the front porch, as it is commonly found in the South, can be found in England or elsewhere in northern Europe."[10] Whether African in origin or not, it provided a wonderful sheltered space for family to gather on sultry evenings.

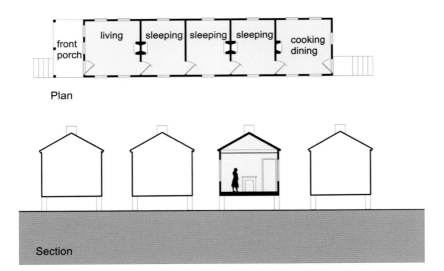

Figure 5.7
Shotgun House

front porch | living | sleeping | sleeping | sleeping | cooking dining

Plan

Section

Creole Townhouse of New Orleans

The French established a strong trading presence from the Gulf of Mexico and up the Mississippi River during the seventeenth century, with its cornerstone, New Orleans, being laid out in 1718. The Spanish took over control of the territory in 1766 and ruled it for 40 years. In 1788 and then again in 1794, the city was devastated by fire, which destroyed most of its earliest, wooden structures. The subsequent rebuilding in brick is what we now associate with the French Quarter of today. "While the architecture from this period is commonly attributed to French influence, characteristics of the French Quarter, such as multi-storied buildings centered around inner courtyards, large arched doorways, and the use of decorative wrought-iron, were most ubiquitous in parts of Spain and the Spanish colonies. This influence may be attributed to the fact that the period of Spanish rule saw a great deal of immigration from all over the Atlantic, including Spain and the Canary Islands, and the Spanish colonies. In addition, it should be noted that while the architectural style of New Orleans, with its wrought iron balconies and full-height windows may remind one of Paris, many of New Orleans' oldest buildings actually pre-date the Haussman projects that later renovated large areas of Paris in this same style."[11]

The typical townhouse of that day was constructed directly on the sidewalk with the building and its courtyard filling the entire plot of land on which it was built. The first floor had a carriageway entrance and was dedicated to service functions as well as commercial activities that took place along the street. A grand stairway led up to the second floor where the living areas were located. If there was a third floor, bedrooms were usually placed there.

Unlike many southern vernacular homes, which were designed to be very open, the New Orleans townhouse presented a solid and continuous face to the street. By contrast, the courtyard that occupied the heart of the house helped to provide more external surface area, but did so in the more private realm. A good circulation of

Figure 5.8
The Creole Courtyards, Often
Found In New Orleans, LA,
Provided A Quiet, Private Retreat
From The Busy City's Streets

air was thus achieved with the main living rooms having exposure on both the street and the courtyard.

This compact arrangement also facilitated keeping direct sun from hitting and heating up the majority of the structure. The shared party walls between buildings and many of the interior walls that fronted on the interior courts were never exposed to the heat of the sun. In this hot–humid environment, the courtyard provided, as in drier climates, privacy and good airflow in an urban context as well as welcome shade.

A bonus in New Orleans came from its high water table, which helped modify the interior temperature of buildings. The brick foundations that were sunken into the cool groundwater absorbed some of that coolness and gave it off to the interiors. This unique, but effective technique, helped make life much more tolerable on very hot days, of which there were many.

Figure 5.9
Creole Courtyard

bedroom | bedroom

parlor | parlor

Second Floor Plan

service | service

office | shop

courtyard

passage

street

UP

First Floor Plan

Section

The Charleston Single House

On a peninsula formed by the Ashley and Cooper Rivers sits Charleston, South Carolina, which was first settled in 1680 and quickly grew into a prosperous port town. Like many other east coast cities of the time, it was laid out with rather long and narrow building lots.[12] On these confining plots, the first structures were usually contiguous row houses. But in a short period of time, Charleston developed a unique standalone, single-family house type, which became known as the Charleston single house. As with other vernacular buildings, it was a practical solution to a variety of local demands.

These narrow, freestanding houses were normally placed in the corner of the property, with a short end quite near the sidewalk and one of the long sides at or near the property line with an adjoining lot. As with the southern plantation house, the more formal, main house was located nearest the street with the utilitarian structures behind it and out of the public view. As the required dependencies (kitchen, well, stable, slave quarters, etc.) were located at the rear of the lot, access from the street was achieved by way of a drive or carriageway that passed along the side of the home. Consequently, the drive separated one home from its neighbor. The separation between these houses allowed for a welcome airflow around and through them, which helped to keep the residents cool on the numerous muggy days and nights.

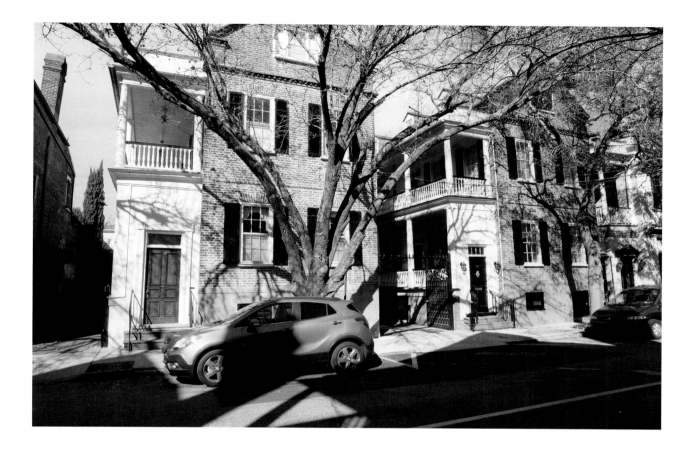

Figure 5.10
The Charleston Single Houses Of Charleston, SC, Responded To The Social And Environmental Needs Of The Region

Another distinction, multilevel porches, locally called piazzas, were added to one or more sides of the building. Piazzas were a practical response not only to the needs for additional space, but also to the demands of the southern climate. During the mid-part of summer days, they served to shade the house from the hottest rays of the sun. Additionally, they provided a comfortably cool alternative to the sometimes stuffy interior living spaces during times when pleasant breezes were available. This arrangement "so suited Charleston that even . . . shanty towns were built on similar lines."[13]

The residential buildings were further stratified vertically by function. In commercial areas of the town, the ground floor level was often used for business activities. In the larger, finer homes, this level was occupied by utilitarian functions associated with the running of the house. In each of these cases, the second floor was dedicated to family living and social functions. However, in the more modest houses, the ground floor was given over to these social activities. In all cases, the upper floor(s), where the bedrooms were found, were reserved for sleeping and private, family activities.

The houses were built of either wood or brick, but the lowest level was commonly brick due to its resistance to rot. If the ground floor was not being used for commercial or utilitarian functions, it was often raised above the ground a few feet over a crawl space on brick piers to add ventilation and keep the insects and damp away from the structure. The building was normally capped with a pitched roof with gabled ends. At first, they were covered with wood shingles, but due to the fire hazard that these posed in a city of closely placed houses, they were banned in favor of metal, clay tile, or slate.

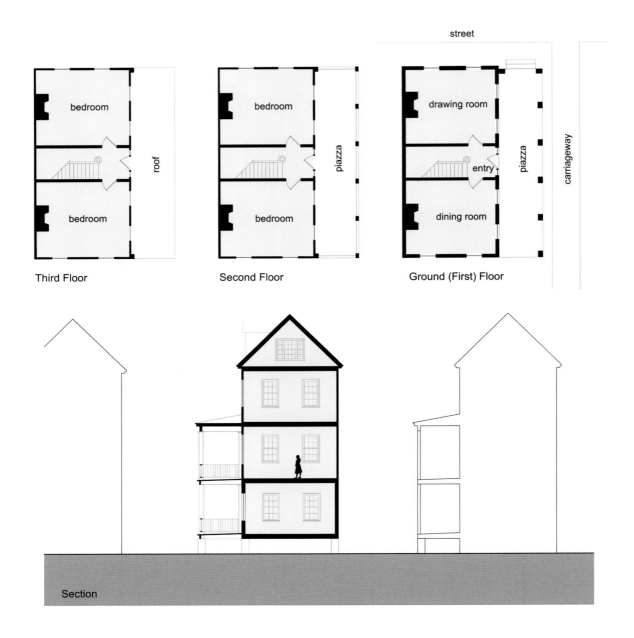

Third Floor

Second Floor

Ground (First) Floor

Section

The basic house was usually about 20 feet wide and 40 to 50 feet long. It was laid out with only two rooms on a floor, one to either side of a central stairway. This was an extremely efficient arrangement, as no space was wasted on hallways. Additionally, the vertical shaft formed by the stair created a chimney effect, which facilitated the airflow up and through the house.

In these homes, the elevation of rooms above the street mattered. Streets were usually unpaved, and therefore dusty and smelly from animal excrement, so getting up higher and farther away from the source of these problems made life more pleasant.

Figure 5.11
Charleston Single House

REINVENTING AN URBAN VERNACULAR

In addition, annoying or disease-carrying mosquitoes, which tend to stay low to the ground, were less of a problem in the upper story rooms.

As these houses were built close to one another and to the street/sidewalk, visual privacy was an important issue. To ensure both an unobstructed flow of air while keeping the interiors out of public view, exterior, louvered shutters were used as a standard solution to the problem. These could be fully opened, partially closed for airflow and privacy, or fully shut to keep out stormy weather.

In these various ways, the Charleston single house created a gracious and comfortable home in an environment that could be insufferably hot at times. Developed from an English tradition, it evolved through common sense and trial and error into a unique building type that reflects not only its local environmental needs, but also the social mores of a specific time and place.

Common Themes Found in the Traditional Buildings of the South

Southerners developed a distinctive approach to a unique place and time through their architecture. As with all vernacular buildings, the results of time-tested methods led to specific responses to the immediate environment. These responses are found from elegant plantation homes to the humblest abodes.

Shape and Placement

The best shape for a southern building is typically long and narrow with its long side running from east to west. It can be tilted somewhat to the southeast, without compromising the solar benefits. Unfortunately, in order to accommodate a typical city grid, many vernacular structures were oriented toward the street rather than to the sun. While obviously practical, this direct relationship to the street can diminish the environmental benefits one gets from a solar orientation.

In the South, pitched roofs have always been a requirement due to its copious amounts of rainfall. Until the introduction of petroleum-based tar and gravel roofing materials in the twentieth century, a flat roof was unfeasible. Traditionally, the roof pitch was not necessarily steep, as some examples were quite shallow, but adequate to ensure a speedy runoff during heavy downpours.

Shelter

When it comes to coping with the environment, keeping cool and dry is paramount in the South. It is the heat, humidity, and rain for which one needs to compensate the most. Of the common factors that run through all of the southern vernacular building types, the most common ones relate to satisfying these basic environmental issues. Above all, southerners have sought and continue to seek ways to escape direct sunlight, and at the same time, to catch a cooling breeze.

Deep overhangs shade buildings and protect their exterior surfaces from the elements. Shielded from direct sunlight, the interiors stay cooler. Overhangs also protect the wood cladding, which is a typical siding material, from the drying effects of this strong sunlight and the dampness that comes with frequent soakings. Wood that is protected in such a way will last much longer than the one that suffers from prolonged exposure to moisture.

Porches, which provide similar shelter from direct exposure to the sun and rain, also afford pleasant indoor/outdoor living spaces. In the past, much of the living was done in these covered exterior rooms, as the airflow was not constrained by walls. On a porch, not only can one find a cool, dry refuge, but a pleasant venue for socializing with family, friends, and neighbors. In some cases, like the shotgun house, it faced the sidewalk, allowing neighbors to exchange pleasantries as they pass by. The dogtrot house normally had one along the south side, which added outdoor living to its open, central hallway. The ubiquitous southern front porch, usually located adjacent to a sidewalk, provides an opportunity for maintaining closer relationships with passing neighbors. A back porch, which was frequently added to the rear of the house, opened to the backyard and was more service oriented. It provided a more private, family place. In many homes, porches were on the second level where they were used for afternoon naps and as the coolest place in the house to sleep through the night.

The greatest disadvantage was that mosquitoes could bedevil the occupants and force them inside after dark, but these open air spaces have been improved and made even more desirable by the addition of wire screening, which protects from mosquitoes and other annoying insect pests. This type of porch has been an important part of many southern homes since the advent of wire screening. Once porches were screened, southerners could live outside in coolness and peace.

Along with these building strategies for gaining a degree of comfort during long, hot summer days, some of these goals could be reached by manipulating the landscape. The South is well-known for its majestic alleys of spreading oaks draped in Spanish moss and glossy green magnolias whose shade provides pleasant outdoor settings for mid-day respites. However, shade trees planted on the east and/or west sides of a building do a great service by shielding the building from the rays of direct sun coming in at low angles. Additionally, vine covered arbors, pergolas, and trellises provided opportunities for shady walks and outdoor living during sultry afternoons and evenings.

Construction and Materials

Since the time when the first European settlers built here, brick and wood were the most common construction materials found throughout the South. Due to an abundance of natural resources, such as timber and clay, the new arrivals had few problems emulating the traditional structures that they left behind in their homelands of England, Spain, and France. At first, there was no great need to adapt their traditional techniques to the conditions that they found, as basic shelters were rudimentary and construction technology had changed only modestly. Medieval constructions with heavy timber frames and those with brick-bearing walls were commonplace here as they were in Europe. It was only over time that local conditions and climate helped shape more innovative approaches. Tabby concrete was developed and used along the Atlantic coast as long as oyster shells could be amassed. Stone was added to the list, as the settlers had more time and wealth to create finer structures.

Heating, Cooling, and Ventilation

Heating in the South is not a major design factor, as it may only be needed during some of the 3 months of winter. In the more southerly locations along the Gulf coast and Florida, it is rarely necessary. Naturally, inland locales of higher elevation do require a modest amount of supplemental heat, as temperatures can occasionally dip down below freezing from time to time. As in the rest of the country, most homes built before central heating relied on wood- or coal-burning fireplaces or gas space heaters.

Air movement is cooling because it dries perspiration as it passes over the skin. It is for this reason that a steady breeze through a building in a hot, humid climate is so desirable. In order to catch as much air movement as possible, most rooms of the southern home typically had windows on two or three walls as in the shotgun house. When multiple exposures were not possible, these spaces might open onto another internal space that would facilitate the flow, like the central hall of the southern mansion.

Similarly, the humble dogtrot house gave rooms an extra exposure by having them open to its hallway. In some cases, the breeze could actually be accelerated by its configuration. A volume of air that moves through a space and is subsequently forced through a more constricting one is accelerated, like in the dogtrot hall. Accelerating the air through a habitable room means that the cooling will be enhanced; as a result, occupants will be much more comfortable.

Figure 5.12
Adjustable Louvers Help Shade A Southern Porch To Provide A Pleasant Outdoor Living Space During Warm, Sunny Days

Windows in the early homes were usually the double-hung type or even triple-hung in the larger houses with higher ceilings. A double-hung window is divided into two panels with glass in each. They can both slide up or down, thereby allowing air to flow either through the bottom or top. However, they are limited in that they only permit half the space occupied by the window to open. A triple-hung window allows all three sashes to slide up or down to give a maximum of two-thirds of the window space as an opening. In some cases, louvers were used, which permit nearly 100 percent airflow while shading the opening.

Doors were sometimes louvered to allow air to pass through them while maintaining visual privacy. Also, transom windows were frequently located over doors and could be opened to help move air through closed rooms. Needless to say, acoustical privacy was sacrificed in order to achieve good airflow.

Typically, southern houses were raised off the ground to allow air to flow not only over and around the building, but under it as well. In most cases, these buildings were not insulated, so the air flowing below the floors could assist in keeping the building cool by moving any accumulated hot air away from its lowest surface. In some of the larger, more expensive homes, this raised ground floor level was enclosed and used for functional purposes, such as cooking and storage, that could be separated from the formal living above.

Another approach to keeping cool was to keep the hot air away from the occupants by raising the ceilings. As hot air rises, this simple tactic was used to keep the heat up above their heads. Ceilings in the more expensive homes were anywhere from 9 to 12 feet in height. Attics tended to overheat on hot summer days, so they too needed to be ventilated in order to keep the living spaces below them more comfortable. Eave vents, ridge vents, and cupolas all allowed cooler air to pass into attic space and exhaust the hot air without using any mechanical means.

After the advent of electricity and before air-conditioning became so prevalent, table fans, ceiling fans, and whole house fans were popular methods to keep the air moving. The table and ceiling fans have the advantage of cooling as they blow on anyone directly in their path. The whole house fan operates by sucking the hot air out the house through the attic and replacing it with cooler outside air, usually at night. This has the dual function of cooling the occupants as the breeze passes over them, while at the same time, lowering the overall air temperature within the house.

Other Considerations

As previously mentioned, buildings were frequently raised off the ground on piers to allow for better ventilation and to avoid flooding, but this technique had other advantages as well. By placing a metal shield over the piers, one could protect the wooden structure above from termites, which are an ongoing problem in the South. In addition to the native termite, the Formosan termite was introduced into New Orleans in 1965. Since that time, they have spread across all of the southeastern states and are beginning to slowly expand their range farther northward. "Among the 2,400 known termite species, the Formosan termite is considered one of the most destructive and aggressive species of termites in the world. They have been given the nickname 'Super Termite' and an active colony of Formosans has been known to eat 1,000 lbs. (454 kilograms) of wood per year compared to 7 lbs. (3 kilograms) per year by an active native colony."[14] Raising the house above the ground can also serve to keep at bay ants, cockroaches, and other crawling insects, vermin, and snakes, which are commonplace in the South.

The excessive amounts of dampness in the air when trapped and allowed to stagnate in the interior of southern homes can lead to the growth of mildew. Smaller confined spaces, such as closets, are particularly prone to this problem. Before air conditioning, people would resort to leaving a light on to help dry them out.

Natural Resources Available for Construction

Fortunately, the South is blessed with an abundance of building materials that are natural and sustainable. A combination of rich soil, abundant sun, and copious amounts of rainfall support innumerable timber plantations across the region. The soil itself contributes to brick-making upon which much of the Old South was built. These natural resources have helped define the nature and style of southern building throughout its history.

Wood

The South is typified by large, old live oaks with trailing Spanish moss, towering pine forests, and cypress-filled lowlands and swamps. Due to the preponderance of trees, the traditional building material from the earliest times has been wood. From the pioneers' log cabins to the grand plantation homes, wood played a leading role in home construction. The vast native forests that the early pioneers encountered have been greatly diminished by development. We now find large tracts of commercially grown trees that are planted and harvested on an industrial scale. As a result, wood remains the predominant material of choice in the construction of most residential and small commercial structures today.

Longleaf, loblolly, shortleaf, and slash compose the four main species of southern pine. It is "hard, dense, and possessing an excellent strength-to-weight ratio."[15] "It is fast growing, taking 30 to 50 years to grow a stand of pine saw-timber to economic maturity."[16] Southern pine "has the highest specific gravity of all common structural lumber species, providing superior fastener-holding power and load-bearing capacity."

"Pine forests are some of the most productive and sustainable timberlands in the world, capturing large amounts of carbon from the air and storing it in lumber used every day. Southern Pine is grown and manufactured in the U.S. South, further improving local economies, reducing transportation costs and minimizing impacts on the environment. Southern Pine is an abundant and renewable resource, growing in a vast band across the Southern United States from East Texas to Virginia."[17]

"*Taxodium distichum* is the scientific name for Bald cypress, the commercially harvested 'Cypress' that grows all along the Gulf Coast and prospers in damp, marshy, tidal areas. It grows as far north as the mid-continent states where it is found along streams and in lowland areas. Today, Cypress grows in abundance across the Gulf Coast and in hardwood bottomlands, and it is desired for its beauty and longevity. Though none of the second growth Cypress can be called the 'wood eternal' like its virgin predecessor, Cypress heartwood is still one of the most durable woods that can be purchased on the commercial market . . . the majority of our Cypress range in age from 100 to 150 years."[18] "Cypress grows in the Atlantic and Gulf coastal plains from Delaware to Texas and also in the Mississippi Valley north to southern Illinois. The species offers legendary durability and a naturally occurring preservative known as cypressene helps protect it from insects,

decay, and other damaging elements."[19] Unfortunately, it is not fast growing and can take 50 or more years to reach full maturity to be commercially useful. Consequently, this longer growth time is reflected in its comparatively high cost. Because of its ability to resist rot and insect damage, the best use is in areas where this is most likely—roofing, siding, and near the ground. It is also renowned for the beauty of its grain, color, and hue, making it desirable as interior paneling.

Figure 5.13
This Tree Farm In East Texas, So Typical Across The South, Grows Loblolly Pines

Brick

When traveling through the South, visitors are often struck by the seemingly ever-present red soil. This predominant feature of the countryside is reflective of the soil's iron-stain clay deposits. Throughout much of the region, soils are composed of "unconsolidated sands, silts, and clays transported to the eco-region by the weathering of the Appalachian Mountains."[20] They are classified as Ultisol, which "are reddish, clay-rich, acidic soils that support a mixed forest vegetation prior to cultivation. They are naturally suitable for forestry, can be made agriculturally productive with the application of lime and fertilizers, and are stable materials for construction projects. Occupying just over 8 percent of the nonpolar continental land area on Earth, they are found in humid temperate or tropical regions, including the southeastern United States. Ultisols are found in geologically old

REINVENTING AN URBAN VERNACULAR

landscape settings. They are enriched in kaolin-group clay minerals and in metal oxides and appear as red or bleached layers."[21]

Due to this plentiful supply of clay soil, brick and tile making began shortly after the earliest settlers arrived from England in the early 1600s. Evidence of an early kiln at the Jamestown colony has been dated back to 1630. During the eighteenth century, brick was usually made on the building site, so the brickmaker's life was an itinerate one. Today, there are numerous brick-production facilities all across the South, making brick an accessible commodity. Early production of brick depended on wood-fired kilns to harden the brick, and this traditional method continues to be used in some brick kilns today, there is a greater reliance upon natural gas to fuel them. Modern brick-making has become more efficient and environmentally friendly. Statesville Brick Company in North Carolina claims that it is "a company that makes masonry units out of Class C fly ash and cure the bricks at less than 200 degrees for only 12 hours so we use 81 percent less energy and generate 84 percent less CO_2 in their manufacturing."[22] As a result of improvements such as these, southern brick is now accessible, sustainable, and reasonably priced.

Stone

Unlike wood or brick, stone is a scarce commodity in the South. There is little or no stone along the Gulf coast, across and most of Florida, and very little along the Atlantic seaboard. It is not until one goes inland to the Appalachian Mountains that stone is encountered. In these inland regions, stone foundations, chimneys, and even complete stone buildings can be found. In Virginia, northern parts of Alabama, Mississippi, and Georgia, limited amounts of stone are used in building construction.

Along the Atlantic coast of Florida is found a sedimentary rock known as Coquina, which developed over time from the accumulation and adhesion of billions of tiny clam-like seashells, sand, and a wide variety of other desirous elements. The stone when quarried is too soft for construction and must be left exposed to the air for 2 or 3 years to harden before use. The earliest Spanish settlers of Florida built *Castillo de San Marcos* of this stone over 400 years ago. It served them particularly well, as the soft stone would not shatter from the impact of a cannon ball, but absorbed it. While quite beautiful, it is now protected and only a very limited amount is still used in the construction of floors and veneers on the exterior of buildings.

Tabby Concrete

Some of the earliest southern buildings found near the coast of the Carolinas, Georgia, and Florida were constructed of tabby concrete. Tabby is composed of readily available ingredients: equal parts sand, lime, oyster shells, and water. "The lime is obtained by cooking whole oyster shells in a kiln, then 'slaking' the shells by adding water to them—in this process the shells break down."[23] Once mixed together, the slurry is poured into forms. The wall goes up layer by layer; as the mix dries, the forms are stripped and fresh forms placed on the dried wall. Tabby produces strong walls that are impervious to insect damage, the damp, high winds, and fire. As a result, many old tabby structures are still standing today. This labor-intensive process was used through the nineteenth century, but only rarely today due to its expense. It can still be used in homes where a regional touch is desired.

The Current Approach to Design and Construction

Urban Pattern

Comparatively speaking, there is something of a housing boom in the South as people flee colder regions to find greater employment opportunities in the warmer ones. In 2010, "52 percent of single-family homes constructed were in the South."[24] In fact, the South has accounted for the largest share of home construction for the past 30 years. Naturally, with the addition of this greater number of single-family homes to the region comes the inevitable consequence of sprawl. Both large and small southern cities have grown in area and population since World War II. Houston, the most populous city in the South, had a pre-war population of 384,500, but is now inhabited by well over two million people covering 627 square miles of land. Even more spread out is the mid-sized city of Jacksonville, FL, which had about 173,065 people in 1940 and now has nearly 850,000. It now encompasses a vast 885 square mile area, which is approaching the size of the state of Rhode Island.[25] Most of the new land developed in these cities is in the form of subdivisions, shopping malls, and roads similar in nature to those found elsewhere around the country. The old downtowns have been converted to central business districts with many commuters but few residents.

With the exception of the beach-oriented cities of central and southern Florida, a few outside of Washington, D.C., and the old historic icons, such as New Orleans, Savannah, and Charleston, southern city centers are some of the least dense in the nation. Most southerners now prefer to live well beyond the centers in sprawling suburbs. For the most part, the old city centers now serve primarily as business districts and civic centers where one finds the major public buildings. Many of these cities' jobs are located in these concentrated areas, requiring large numbers of suburbanites to commute to work in their cars, as is typical elsewhere in the nation.

Figure 5.14
This Mid-Century Modern Home Is Similar To Many Others That Were Built In The South Over The Course Of The Last Half Of The Twentieth Century

Architectural Character

Today, people live enclosed inside their homes, with the once ubiquitous front porch virtually disappearing. More often than not, garages rather than porches are the dominant presence on the street. As one passes homes built since the advent of air conditioning, it is striking to notice that curtains designed to keep the sun out and ensure privacy are closed, covering most street-facing windows. The result is that there is little sign of life and less interaction among neighbors than in earlier times before the automobile gained such prominence.

From an energy point of view, however, it is fortunate that so many Americans have moved South, as research shows that it is cheaper to cool a house than to heat one. In addition, the typical southern home is somewhat smaller than those currently being built in the north. This trend is significant to the United States, because a typical house in the South will tend to consume less energy and fewer construction materials than its counterpart in the north.

The U.S. Department of Energy reports that in 2010, "the average household in the South required only 20.4 million BTUs for space heating, less than one-third the energy required for space heating in the average household in the Northeast."[26] With so little heating required, in most cases, space heaters can suffice. A common practice today, however, is to combine hot air heating with air conditioning. This arrangement is facilitated by use of an electric or gas fired heat pump, which uses a system of ductwork to circulate the conditioned air.

Because air conditioning and central heating are now standard features in most new homes, southern buildings are designed very differently from those our forefathers crafted; we have stopped treating climate as a design consideration. As a result, our needs and our priorities have changed. We no longer require a high level of ventilation, as it is more efficient to keep all windows closed and rely on an interior climate regulated by a thermostat. Under these circumstances, it is a great deal more efficient to have fewer and smaller windows. In this case, the window has ceased to relate to human comfort, as that function is now being handled mechanically; it serves only to let in light and allow one to enjoy any possible view. Today's house or apartment is designed to be a tight capsule, with windows that are only opened in the event that the air conditioning fails. If the air conditioning were to fail or if prices to run these systems were to become too high, then recently built housing, lacking adequate ventilation, will turn out to be insufferable during the hottest times of the year. Not designed to promote natural ventilation, they will be very difficult and expensive to retrofit to work with such a hot, humid climate.

With a mechanically controlled interior environment, the traditional, long, narrow building shape is no longer necessary. In air-conditioned houses, it is desirable to reduce the amount of a building's surface area; therefore, a cubic or square form is most appropriate. Equally unnecessary is concern for orientation to the sun, as the sun no longer has a major role to play in the overall design. As is also true in other regions across the country, most southern homes face the street instead of any particular compass point. Apartment units relate most closely to their respective parking areas.

Popular Design and Construction Methods

In many of these newer houses, roofs are low-pitched in order to save money on construction materials. A steeper pitch would be more beneficial, as it would get rainwater off more quickly, and thereby extend the life of the material. Almost all roof coverings are made of asphalt shingles made from petroleum. In some areas, they are light in color to better reflect the sun's rays, but this is not a consistent strategy.

Today, buildings are rarely elevated above the ground, except along the coast where it is mandated by code to be above flood levels; it is much cheaper to build a slab-on-grade. The slab-on-grade technique incorporates the foundation with the floor, thereby serving a dual purpose and saving money in the short term. With the first floor only inches above the ground level, the long-term may be the problem. As previously stated, much of the South is flat, and at low elevations, many of these newer structures could be in jeopardy of flooding. If flooding occurs these homes are much more at risk than those built before the 1950s when they were elevated. Global warming and the accompanying sea level rise will only exacerbate this problem in the future.

Slab-on-grade also exposes buildings to insects such as termites, which have only a few inches to travel up the foundation wall before encountering the wooden structure. Likewise, rot is a threat to the wood that is resting directly on the concrete slab. The concrete, which will tend to wick water up and into the structure will over time dampen the wood, thereby facilitating the rotting process. Under these circumstances, even treated wood, which has a guaranteed life of up to 30 years, can rot over time and will need replacing.

Future Environmental Concerns

The South will be greatly affected by global warming over the course of this century and many of those effects will be felt by mid-century. Sea level rise, rising temperatures, and greater precipitation are the main concerns.

The coastal areas lining the southeastern United States will face major environmental hazards this century due to an increased potential of flooding and storm surges brought on by sea level rise. This will cause a major reshaping of many major southern cities and towns such as New Orleans and much of south Florida. "I cannot envision southeastern Florida having many people at the end of this century," says Hal Wanless, chairman of the department of geological sciences at the University of Miami. Southern Florida has some 2.4 million people and 1.3 million homes, that sit within 4 feet of the local high-tide line. They represent nearly half of those at risk nationwide. Sea level rise will more than double the risk of storm surges in South Florida by 2030.[27] National Geographic predicts that as the oceans rise, the peninsula will shrink and freshwater wetlands and mangrove swamps will collapse in "a death spiral that has already started on the southern tip of the peninsula. With seas four feet higher than they are today—a distinct possibility by 2100—about two-thirds of southeastern Florida will be inundated. The Florida Keys will almost vanish and Miami will become an island."[28]

Rising sea levels will also add a threat to much of Florida's fresh water supplies, as about a quarter of the state's population depends on the Biscayne aquifer, where salt water is now seeping in from dozens of canals that were built to drain the Everglades.[29]

Additionally, temperatures across the region will continue to rise. The EPA reports that since 1970, average annual temperatures in the South have increased by about 2°F and that they should increase by 4° to 9°F by 2080. Rising temperatures will have an adverse effect on numerous aspects of life in the area from public health to agriculture.

Most areas of the southeast, with the exception of southern Florida, are getting wetter. "Autumn precipitation has increased by 30 percent since 1901. The number of

heavy downpours has increased in many parts of the region. Despite increases in fall precipitation, the area affected by moderate and severe drought, especially in the spring and summer, has increased since the mid-1970s."[30]

High temperatures and rainy weather are nothing new to the region, but the experts contend that they will be getting more intense. As a result, it will become more important to design buildings in a way that allows the occupant to stay cool, dry, and comfortable during the worst of these events.

Design Strategies and Building Components

Climatic Imperatives

In the future when one designs for southern living, the greatest challenge will be to develop strategies that will ensure that the occupants are comfortable on the hottest days, without the benefit of air conditioning. Heating can be done with a great deal less effort here than in many other parts of the country, as the climate never gets too cold nor does the cold last for an extended period. Rain, which is often frequent, intense, and accompanied by high wind, high humidity as well as hurricanes are all issues that need to be considered when designing for the South.

Orientation

According to the authors of *A Sustainable House for the Southeastern United States*, "the most significant energy savings derives from the strategy of correct building proportions and orientation. To abet cross ventilation, residences in hot-humid climates should have a minimum of a 1:2 proportion with the long axis oriented due east and west. The long sides receive the maximum amount of low angle of our winter sun during the 4 months of heating and, more significant, to reduce the solar heat gain on the east and west elevations during our 6 months of cooling. This proportioning will save 30 percent of the projected energy use."[31] More simply put, long, narrow buildings with a southerly orientation and adequate shading can minimize the heat gain and maximize cross-ventilation so necessary for comfort.

Overall Suggested Configuration and Layout

An attenuated design will assure that most of the entire unit is only one room wide much like in a shotgun house, where all living/sleeping spaces have at least two sides exposed to outside air. This type of elongated layout with windows on both sides will provide an opportunity for excellent cross-ventilation to an entire apartment, helping to ensure the occupant's comfort during hotter periods. In the larger two- and three-bedroom units, this goal can be met by arranging the unit in long, narrow elements in a "T-shaped" configuration. The recommended width for each apartment is 12 to 16 feet. The resulting layout can provide maximum surface area for the units, thereby ensuring excellent ventilation to all rooms even in the larger units.

The overall massing can vary depending on the makeup of the unit types—one-, two-, or three-bedroom. From a design perspective, the largest unit should be located on the lowest level, with the smaller ones stacked above. As a result, the larger units will have direct access to ground level while providing rooftop, outdoor spaces for the smaller units. However, some of the smaller units might be considered for the ground floor to accommodate the elderly and handicapped individuals.

Building Circulation—Halls and Staircases

It is important to eliminate double-loaded corridors whenever possible, as they leave units with only one or possibly two sides exposed to sun and air, thus precluding any chance for cross-ventilation. A preferred layout would be to locate back-to-back stairs between units, which can serve as a main entry stair and a rear one to meet the requirement as a second means of egress. Stairs must be roofed over, but their exterior walls can be left fully or partially open to allow for airflow, while keeping them free of rain and protected from direct sunlight.

REINVENTING AN URBAN VERNACULAR

Unit Plan

Wherever possible, implement an open plan layout with living, dining, and kitchen flowing together, as interior walls tend to obstruct air movement through dwellings. Fortunately, this open plan concept is favored and well-suited to our current lifestyle. Where a door is required between rooms (like for bedrooms and baths), an operable transom window or panel can be added above it to allow for a continued flow of air even when the door is shut.

Ceiling heights should be as high as is reasonable in order to keep the heat that accumulates in the unit up and as far away from the occupants as possible. A 9 foot height would be very desirable.

Roof Type

Generally, roofs should be pitched, but the hipped roof (pitched in all four directions) has a couple of advantages over the end-gable roof with flat ends. The first is that it has an overhang on all sides, not just two, thereby protecting all wall surfaces. The second advantage is that it will prevent hurricane force winds from pushing directly on gabled end walls, which would tend to produce greater pressure on the overall structure.

Wherever possible, roof overhangs are recommended. In addition to being useful by shading the uppermost portion of the building, overhangs are advantageous for keeping rainfall off the building, thereby protecting much of its wood siding from decay and rot. The only disadvantage to overhangs is that during hurricanes the strong winds will put a great deal of uplift pressure on them, which, if too strong, could damage the roof structure. Brackets can be added to the lower edge of the roof to help keep it stable under hurricane conditions. In areas where hurricanes are pervasive and pose a constant threat, the overhang may need to be eliminated to avoid the problem entirely.

The pitch of the roof is best pitched steeply or about 45° to help keep rainwater moving off quickly as well as providing a good fixed angle for mounting solar panels.

Light colored (preferably white) roofs help to reflect solar radiation and help keep the upper floor cool.

Windows and Window Treatments

In the South, glass needs to be protected from exposure to direct sunlight for most of the year except in winter. Overhangs can easily protect south-facing windows and those on the north require no shading, as there is little sun that hits them. However, overhangs do not shade windows from early morning sun in the east or very hot late afternoon westerly sun, as the sun's angles at these times are low, and consequently can enter the building below any overhead shading device. Glass on east and west sides needs to be kept to a minimum or shaded in some other way; glass can be most easily accommodated on either the north or south walls.

If windows are required on walls that are exposed to direct sunlight, some sort of movable covering should be provided to shield them. External shutters that swing, slide, or roll work well in these situations. Those located to the side of windows can be either solid or louvered. Rolling shutters located above windows and doors are another good method for blocking these rays. When shutters are closed, the solid ones will block airflow, but louvered ones still allow for good ventilation. All of these sun blockers are also perfect for protecting windows during potentially damaging storms.

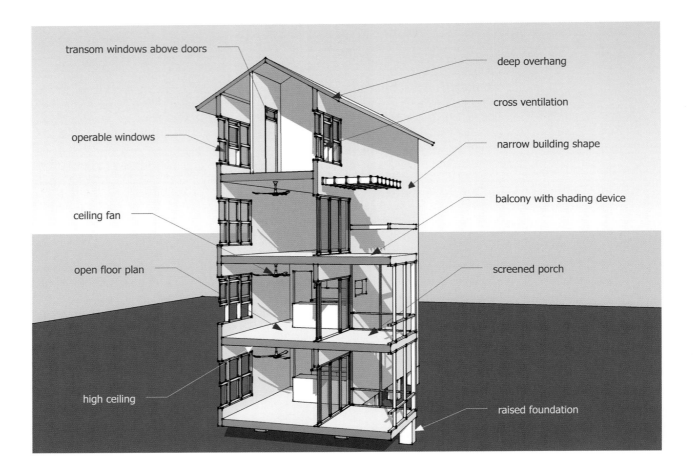

transom windows above doors

deep overhang

cross ventilation

operable windows

narrow building shape

ceiling fan

balcony with shading device

open floor plan

screened porch

high ceiling

raised foundation

Figure 5.16
Idea Drawing For The South

In the southern home, the selection of the proper window and door type is important, as it determines the amount of ventilation a room receives. In order to get the maximum amount of air movement, the windows and doors need to provide as close to 100 percent openness as possible. Double-hung windows and sliding doors and windows allow for only 50 percent openness, as only one panel can be opened at any time. Better alternatives would be the casement and/or the awning types, which do provide for the maximum of air to pass through them. These windows swing outward to open, thereby helping to direct air into the room. In many cases, awning windows are preferable as they shed rainfall, whereas the casement does not protect the opening from the rain. Another option is the jalousie window, which is composed of multiple wood, metal, or glass slats that open simultaneously to give near 100 percent airflow. These windows are useful in tropical areas as they give as much openness as possible and shed rainfall. They have the disadvantage of not closing as tightly as one would require in areas where temperatures drop from time to time and wind can whistle through them during storms. Unfortunately, external shutters cannot cover windows that swing out.

Airspeed is another important criterion when designing for human comfort, as we feel a greater cooling effect as the speed increases. By arranging larger openings on the windward side and the smaller ones on the leeward side, the velocity of the breeze through the unit can be accelerated.

As with the windows, doors, and exterior coverings, interior window coverings need to be thoughtfully selected. They do not keep direct sunlight out of the building, but do help to maintain its coolness by eliminating the sunlight that falls on interior surfaces and the occupants themselves. Curtains block airflow, but Venetian blinds and interior louvered shutters, long favored in the South, let the air move inside with minimal obstruction while providing privacy.

Materials and Construction

Brick or concrete pier foundations are suggested to raise the building up above the ground to help get a free flow of air under it and to elevate it above flood levels. An additional benefit today is that they can, if raised high enough, provide enclosed storage, covered parking, or play spaces.

The vernacular choice for a structural material in the South would most naturally be wood. For a multi-storied apartment building, a heavy timber frame makes sense. There are several good reasons for using this system rather than the more typical "platform frame" with its lighter, dimensional lumber. (1) Heavy timber is considered fire-resistant, as every beam and column is over 6 inches in thickness in both directions. (2) Thicker timbers require less milling, therefore are more economical to produce. (3) In the event that in the future the units need to be renovated, they can be easily reconfigured, as only the infill, non-structural walls can be removed, without affecting the permanent structural frame. (4) The heavy timber frame needs no interior covering or finish. By leaving the wood exposed, one saves on covering materials and/or paint—allowing one to appreciate its natural beauty. (5) This system also provides a greater ceiling height, as the finished ceiling is not dropped down, thus helping to keep the heat up and away from the occupants. (6) The method of mechanically attaching the large wooden members with bolts and metal plates helps to ensure that the structure will better resist hurricane force winds. While this type of construction may be somewhat more expensive at the onset, its long-term virtues will more than compensate for any initial expense.

Along with the heavy timber frame, the floors and roof can be composed of wood planking, which if left exposed, can create a finished ceiling in the unit below. Because noise transmission is a problem between floors in this type of construction, sound-deadening materials must be provided on these floors.

Wood is recommended as the basic construction material in southern construction. Sustainable southern pine is a good choice for the basic structural material of the frame, as its local availability makes it the most economical choice. Roofing and siding built with rot-resistant cypress or cedar shingles, shakes, or clapboard are also a logical choice.

Insulation is a key element in the composition of any exterior wall, floor, or roof to make the southern home energy-efficient and comfortable. Roof insulation can be a ridged type, placed on top of the wood decking. This will allow the top floor to enjoy an exposed, wooden cathedral ceiling by eliminating the attic. Another option is the conventional one of insulating the floor of the attic (ceiling of the top level) with some appropriate material.

The walls can be insulated with (1) organic materials such as cellulose, wool, (2) of manufactured fiberglass batts, (3) blown-in foam, or (4) covered with rigid foam.

Outdoor Spaces

Ideally, every unit should have its own outdoor space, sheltered from sun and rain, in the form of either a screened porch or covered balcony. The upper levels where the smaller units would be typically located could have at least a covered balcony offering shade and protection from rain. The larger units could have screened porches, once a requisite for a pleasant lifestyle in the South, where families can find a cool place to relax in a refuge from mosquitoes. Ground floor units may have direct access to a yard.

It is highly desirable to provide screened porches wherever possible, but certainly for the larger units occupying the lower floors. They inexpensively expand the overall living area by adding essentially an outdoor room to any southern home. Porches might be oriented to face the sidewalk and maintain that southern tradition of contact with the neighbors or the rear where the family can enjoy a shared yard. The lanai, which often encloses a swimming pool, is popular in some areas of the South and has often replaced the screened porch, but it is most commonly found in single-family detached dwellings, not multifamily, urban ones. In the South, either of these open-air rooms are usable most of the year, with the exception of a few of the colder winter months.

Landscape

Shade will always be one of the major concerns when designing for any building in the South. Exterior walkways, screened porches, and arbors can be used to shade a building's lower floors. Additionally, vine-covered arbors can provide even more shade while enhancing the look of the building.

In the South, trees have provided shade, making life more comfortable as well as visually enhancing buildings. They can also serve to provide some of the most reliable shade for the buildings themselves if appropriately placed. Deciduous trees on the south side of buildings can shield them from the harsh summer sun, then in winter after they lose their leaves, the sun can shine on the buildings to provide some added warmth. On the other hand, evergreens are best placed on the east and west sides of buildings to intercept the low sun that is so difficult to defend against. In the South, evergreens such as the live oak and magnolia have reached near legendary status and are found throughout the region and placed on all sides of buildings, without concern for mediating solar impact. This is not to be seen as a problem of any great magnitude, as winters are generally short and mild, and the shade that they cast on buildings during this season has only minimal impact.

Renewable Power and Mechanical Equipment

The South has adequate sunlight to make solar energy a useful source of energy, but the humid atmosphere cuts down on the amount of sunlight that drier regions at the same latitude have available. In order to take advantage of this resource, roofs must be steeply pitched (45° or a 12:12 pitch) to accommodate solar panels attached to them. These panels can be used to generate hot water and electricity as well.

Air conditioning has been used to cool the southern home since the 1950s, but before that time, fans, in particular ceiling fans, were the norm. Fans create a current of air to pass over the body, which dries perspiration cooling the individual. This technique is still relevant and may gain renewed popularity when utility prices rise to make air conditioning unfeasible to a majority of people. It is highly recommend that ceiling fans be installed in all living areas, including screened porches.

Heating, while not the main problem in the South, can be accommodated by means of solar hot water or small unit heaters in living spaces.

The Prospect for Future Urban Development in the South

For the vast majority of southerners, the generally benign climate should continue to support a comfortable and healthy lifestyle well into the future. However, the South is facing severe environmental challenges along its coast, where sea level rise is going to change the map by the end of this century, or sooner. Millions of people who are currently enjoying the benefits of coastal living will need to move to higher, safer ground.

Unlike the Southwest and the Great Plains, normally abundant rainfall supplies an adequate water supply. Despite occasional droughts and a drier climate due to climate change, it should continue to adequately provide for the expected future population growth across the region.

The South is fortunate to have a good source of natural resources such as timber and earth for brick-making. If well-managed, this will provide the region with a continuous supply of construction materials well into the future.

The South is blessed with a wealth of natural resources, a strategic geographic location, a booming industrial and intellectual-based economy, but much of this success hinges on the climate or rather the ability to overcome it. Despite the fact that there is currently plenty of petroleum in the region, as noted in Chapter 1, a decline is likely by mid-century. When this occurs, there will be a need to find alternative fuels to power homes and businesses—specifically to run their cooling systems. If no suitable substitute is found, then it would seem that the greatest future problem facing the hot, humid southern region is the possible inability to air-condition its buildings economically. Before the 1950s, southerners lived without air-conditioning and may be returning to that way of life. If so, our future designers will need to take a lesson from those vernacular examples and again work with the local climate. This is not to be deemed a sacrifice, as life with nature can be a full and comfortable one—a goal that a vernacular tradition can help achieve.

Summary of Suggested Building Practices for the South

Main environmental objectives: Defend against the heat from direct summer sun and humidity.

Orientation

- Living areas should be south- to southeast-facing
- Share as few walls as possible with neighbors
- East and west walls should have few or no openings

Layout

- Buildings need to be spread out with narrow volumes
- Create an open-plan living space to facilitate internal air flow
- Provide shaded areas for living and working outside, such as terraces and decks
- Use screened porches to extend open air, insect-free living
- High ceilings to keep heat up and off occupants

Construction

- Build up off the ground to encourage ventilation below buildings
- Thin, well-insulated walls
- Timber beams for floor and roof structure
- Leave wooden ceilings exposed
- Insulation on the exterior of walls and roofs to expose wood on interior
- Light-colored or pastel exterior walls are preferred to reflect sunlight

Recommended Construction/Structural Materials

- Brick
- Heavy timber and light wood framing
- Wood siding and roof shingles

Roofs

- Wide overhangs to help protect exterior walls and windows (most valuable on south side)
- Steeply pitched with wood shingles or light-colored asphalt shingles

Shading

- Overhangs on the south side
- Exterior solid or louvered shutters, particularly on the west side, less important on the east side
- Covered walkways, verandas, balconies, and arbors

Windows

- Maximum opening for air flow—casement or awning most desirable
- Should be minimal on west- and east-facing walls
- South side can afford more glass (if shaded for summer sun) to warm interiors in winter
- North side can have the most glass

Ventilation and Cooling

- No double-loaded corridors that block air flow between units. Use either single-loaded or separate stairs towers
- Keep the heat out by blocking direct sun from west and to a lesser extent the east
- Cross-ventilation is of major importance, but it must be controlled as it can introduce hot air in when unwanted
- Windows should allow for full ventilation as with awning and casements types
- Use awning windows when it is desirable to keep windows open during rain events
- Fans can be used to augment air circulation within the dwelling and to exhaust hot air build-up
- Roof monitors can be used to exhaust hot air
- Shady walkway—portico and other covered outdoor living spaces
- Shady gardens
- Roof and wall color should be light to reflect sun's rays
- White or pastel exterior wall colors

Heating

- Minimal space heating required in each room
- Fireplaces or wood stoves can help to add warmth in winter

Water

- Channel rainwater away from the structure as quickly as possible
- Collect all gray water for flushing toilets and watering garden plants

Notes

1 Garreau, Joel. *The Nine Nations of North America*. Avon Books. (1981) New York.
2 LandScope America. *East Gulf Coastal Plain*. Website: www.landscope.org/explore/natural_geog raphies/ecoregions/East%20Gulf%20Coastal%20Plain/.
3 Lewis, David C. and Shane C. Kitchens. A Sustainable *House for the Southeastern United States* 2006 SCH Repot 5 Southern Climate Housing, Mississippi State University, MS. Website: http://fwrc.msstate.edu/housing/images/sustainable.pdf.
4 Swartz , Mimi. *New York Times*. As Oil Prices Fall, Houston Shutters. February 28, 2015.
5 National Parks Service, U.S. Department of the Interior. *French Creole Architecture*. Website: www.nps.gov/nr/travel/louisiana/architecture.htm.
6 Louisiana: Pick Your Passion. Website: http://www.crt.state.la.us/cultural-development/historic-preservation/education/louisiana-architecture-handbook-on-styles/french-creole/index.
7 Wikipedia. *Shotgun House*. Website: https://en.wikipedia.org/wiki/Shotgun_house#Characteristics.
8 Wikipedia. *Shotgun House*. Website: https://en.wikipedia.org/wiki/Shotgun_house#Characteristics.
9 Vlach, John Michael. Afro-Americans. In Upton, Dell (Ed.). *America's Architectural Roots: Ethnic Groups That Built America*. National Trust for Historic Preservation, and John Wiley & Sons (1986) New York. p. 44.
10 Vlach, John Michael. Afro-Americans. In Upton, Dell (Ed.). *America's Architectural Roots: Ethnic Groups That Built America*. National Trust for Historic Preservation, and John Wiley & Sons (1986) New York. p. 45.
11 Wikipedia. *History of New Orleans*. Website: http://en.wikipedia.org/wiki/History_of_New_Orleans.
12 *Encyclopedia of Vernacular Architecture of the World*. Paul Oliver (Ed.). Cambridge University Press (1997) Cambridge, UK. Vol. 3 p. 1904.
13 Stoney, Samuel Gaillard. *This Is Charleston*. Carolina Arts Association (1944) Charleston, SC. p. 25.
14 Lewis, David C., and Shane C. Kitchens. *A Sustainable House for the Southeastern United States*. 2006 SCH Repot 5 Southern Climate Housing. Mississippi State University, MS. Website: http://fwrc.msstate.edu/housing/images/sustainable.pdf.
15 The Wood Data Base. *Loblolly Pine*. Website: http://www.wood-database.com/loblolly-pine/.
16 Frank A. Roth II, Extension Forester. *Thinning to Improve Pine Timber*. Cooperative Extension Service Fact Sheet 5001 Arkansas Forestry Service. Website: http://forestry.arkansas.gov/Directory Searches/Documents/thinning_to_improve.pdf.
17 Southern Pine. *Using Southern Pine*. Website: www.southernpine.com/using-southern-pine/.
18 Cypress Wood & Lumber. *About Cypress Lumber*. Website: www.cypresswood.net/content/cypress-wood-and-lumber-product-information.php.
19 The Southern Cypress Manufacturers Association. *Cypress: American, Sustainable, Carbon-Neutral*. Website: http://www.cypressinfo.org/wp-content/uploads/Cypress-American-Sustainable-Carbon-Neutral.pdf.

20 Landscope America. *East Gulf Coastal Plain*. Website: www.landscope.org/explore/natural_geographies/ecoregions/East%20Gulf%20Coastal%20Plain/.

21 E*ncyclopedia Britannica*. Utisol. Website: www.britannica.com/EBchecked/topic/613380/Ultisol.

22 Johnson, Maria. *Our State: North Carolina*. Forged from the Soil. Website: www.ourstate.com/north-carolinas-brick-industry/.

23 National Parks Service. *Timucuan: Ecological & Historic Preserve Florida*. Website: www.nps.gov/timu/historyculture/kp_tabby.htm.

24 U.S. Department of Energy. *Building Energy Data Book. Table 2.1.9*. Website: http://buildingsdatabook.eren.doe.gov/ChapterIntro2.aspx.

25 Wikipedia. *Jacksonville, Florida*. Website: https://en.wikipedia.org/wiki/Jacksonville,_Florida.

26 U.S. Department of Energy. *Building Energy Data Book*. Website: http://buildingsdatabook.eren.doe.gov/ChapterIntro2.aspx.

27 Surging Seas and Climate Central. *Florida and the Rising Sea*. Website: http://sealevel.climatecentral.org/news/floria-and-the-rising-sea.

28 Folger, Tim. Rising Seas. *National Geographic*. September 2013.

29 Folger, Tim. Rising Seas. *National Geographic*. September 2013.

30 U.S. Environmental Protection Agency. *Climate Impacts in the Southeast*. Website: www.epa.gov/climatechange/impacts-adaptation/southeast.html.

31 Lewis, David C., and Shane C. Kitchens. *A Sustainable House for the Southeastern United States*. 2006 SCH Repot 5 Southern Climate Housing. Mississippi State University, MS. Website: http://fwrc.msstate.edu/housing/images/sustainable.pdf.

Chapter 6

The Great Plains: Western Prairies

Figure 6.1
The Flat, Open Prairies Are
Crossed By Long, Straight,
North/South Roads That Connect
One Farm To The Next

The Great Plains, as it is formally called, is also known more colloquially as America's Breadbasket, the Great American Desert, the Dust Bowl, the Heartland, Tornado Alley, and the Saudi Arabia of Wind Power. It is all of those things and a great deal more. While located in the center of the country, the land has a western personality—semi-arid, treeless, and flat. It is vast and open with an overriding feeling of remoteness. The first settlers to the region found it inhospitable, confronted by hostile Indians with a climate that was both capricious and severe. Many could not endure its hardships and either died trying or moved along, leaving abandoned farmsteads and towns in their wake. Now with its economy based almost entirely on petroleum, ranching, and farming the Great Plains has blossomed into a part of the country that is extremely productive, but the land remains rural in character with few major urban centers. The future seems to rest upon a continued supply of those natural resources that have made it so prosperous, as well as the hopeful prospect of harnessing the sun and the wind to generate new and even greater sources of energy.

The Place

Running north to south with the 100th meridian as its approximate centerline, the Great Plains roughly divides our country in two. It spans an enormous swath of land from the Mexican border north, well into Canada, where it encompasses large parts of three provinces. It is hemmed in on the west by the Rocky Mountains. Its easterly boundary is less clearly defined, but as a general rule, lies west of the 98th meridian where the greener, timbered landscapes of the mid-western and southern states begin. It includes all of Kansas, Nebraska, North and South Dakota, most of Oklahoma and Montana, the westerly half of Texas, and the eastern parts of Wyoming, Colorado, and New Mexico.

"The North American Environmental Atlas, produced by the Commission for Environmental Cooperation, a NAFTA agency composed of the geographical agencies of the Mexican, American, and Canadian governments uses the 'Great Plains' as an ecoregion synonymous with predominant prairies and grasslands rather than as a physiographic region defined by topography."[1] According to the U.S. Environmental Protection Agency, "the Great Plains ecoregion includes five sub-regions: Temperate Prairies, West-Central Semi-Arid Prairies, South-Central Semi-Arid Prairies, Texas Louisiana Coastal Plains, and Tamaulipas-Texas Semi-Arid Plain."[2]

This semi-arid heartland presents a broad, open range that normally stretches as far as the horizon in all directions. Marc Reisner described traveling "from South Dakota down into the heart of West Texas ... takes two long days and feels almost like a transcontinental trip, the more so because the landscape is relentlessly the same: the same flatness, the same treelessness, the same curveless thirty-mile stretches of road. All that changes is the crops: sorghum, then corn, then sorghum, then corn, then alfalfa, wheat, cotton—enough cotton, one would think, to clothe all humanity."[3]

Even still, one can find a wide variety of terrain across this broad land, but predictably it is generally, relentlessly flat, morphing at times into gently rolling hill country. There are even low mountains and deeply cut valleys. "The Black Hills of South Dakota and the Wichita Mountains of Oklahoma are examples. These areas are like islands in the prairie and often contain species whose nearest relatives may be hundreds of miles away."[4] A cross-section taken from east to west would reveal a significant rise in elevation from a low in the east of about 2,000 feet above sea level to over 6,000 feet in the foothills of the Rocky Mountains. This rise is gentle, stretched out over such a long distance that it is imperceptible to anyone passing through.

While much of the year the environment is benign, pleasant at times, it has a reputation for being tempestuous. The region is plagued by numerous tornados, long periods of drought, periodic flooding along its major rivers, hail and dust storms. Summers are blazing hot and winters insufferably cold with a wind-chill factor bringing those temperatures down to well below zero. "The annual swing of temperature can be as much as 130 degrees Fahrenheit (~55 degrees Celsius) between winter and summer."[5] Between the northern and southern boundaries of the region, temperature varies even more. As one might expect, the number of frost-free days decreases dramatically, moving across the plain from south to north. The panhandle of Texas can experience about 230 frost-free days each year, whereas along the Canadian border, there are as few as 110 or 120.[6] Snowfall predictably follows a similar pattern with hardly any accumulation in Texas to several feet in the Dakotas. These snowfalls are often delivered with blizzard conditions.

With the exception of some coastal locations, the Plains is the windiest place in the country. "North Dakota alone has wind resources that, if harnessed, could provide about a third of the entire country's electricity demand, and the Plains as a whole could provide

Figure 6.2
A Painting By George Catlin
(C.1839) Entitled *A Bird's-Eye
View Of The Mandan Village
1800 Miles Above St. Louis* Gives
A Clear Impression Of One Such
Village

all the power the country could foreseeably need. However, because of the economics of the electrical industry, wind power is likely to evolve as a largely local institution in the thinly settled Plains."[7]

It is widely accepted that the 98th meridian represents the easterly boundary of the Great Plains, as west of this line rainfall rarely exceeds 20 inches per year, the amount necessary to sustain farming. Along the region's westerly edge, rainfall averages decline to around 10 inches per year. As a result, most of the region is considered to be semi-arid, without the ability to support much more than the prairie grasses that the buffalo once thrived on. Its rivers and streams are fed from this modest rainfall as well as the snowmelt that the Rockies provide each spring and early summer. This water eventually flows into the Missouri, Platte, Republican, Arkansas, and Red Rivers and then into the Mississippi River. However, many of the smaller tributaries are mostly seasonal. "Most of the year, a visitor to a typical Great Plains stream will be almost lost in a wide floodplain dotted with thickets of cottonwood and filled brim to brim with sand," claims Bret Wallach.

He elaborates further by stating: "the rivers of the plains often mock the long blue lines on maps and disappear altogether, only reemerging downstream."[8] If this rainfall and snowmelt were the only source of water for the region, it would still be a modest farming area, not the one that we know it as today.

Native Americans found the prairie a hard place to support agriculture due to its tough sod and lack of dependable rainfall. As a result, few tribes set down roots in one place. For the most part, the Sioux, Cheyenne, Arapaho, Apache, and Comanche led nomadic existences, preferring to follow the buffalo, elk, and antelope across the land. Only a few tribes, such as the Pawnee, Mandan, and Hidatsa, established permanent communities based on agriculture. These villages were usually set along rivers where the floodplain could be use for cropland. Even those tribes considered settled, spent much of the year hunting on the prairie.

During the mid-nineteenth century, wagon trains passed through its emptiness on their way out west in search of brighter futures. Few stayed. Later, the railroads built their tracks across the prairie on several routes. Given millions of acres by the federal government along these rights of way, they opened real estate offices, laid out towns at stopping points, and sold land to tens of thousands of hopeful farmers. Many of these settlements failed due to the lack of dependable rainfall and were abandoned; a few were later resettled. This was to be a recurring pattern on the Plains for some time that coincided with periods of rain and drought. Between 1909 and 1929, farmers aggressively farmed the land with steel plows and steam tractors. They turned over thirty-two million acres of the prairie's sod, making it into wheat fields during what we now know as the "great plow-up."[9] "During the Dust Bowl days of the 1930s, . . . drought, low crop prices, and plowing-induced soil erosion uprooted 2.5 million refugees. Withering multiyear droughts returned in the 1950s, 1980s, and 1990s."[10] It is estimated that in Kansas alone, there are about 6,000 ghost towns.[11]

Despite its location in a semi-arid zone, ironically, it is farming that has emerged as the Great Plains' economic mainstay. The region has become not only the "breadbasket" of the United States, as it produces about half of all wheat grown in this country, but it also supplies the world with two-thirds of its wheat. In addition to wheat, the region grows many other crops such as soybeans, barley, corn, sorghum, and cotton. This fecundity was only made possible by the presence of an enormous, previously untapped reservoir of water, the Ogallala Aquifer, which is estimated to be equal in size to Lake Huron. It was not until after World War II that sustained, large-scale agriculture was made possible with the invention and widespread deployment of modern, diesel-driven centrifugal pumps, which could extract large volumes of water from this gigantic underground lake. It is now the predominant source of the region's water, which has enabled the transformation of the prairie from a parched landscape of native grasses to the verdant, productive farmland that we now have. The Ogallala currently "provides drinking water for more than 80 percent of the prairie's population and irrigates 13 million acres of its land."[12] "Because both the saturated thickness and the areal extent of the Ogallala Aquifer is greater in Nebraska, the state accounts for two-thirds of the volume of Ogallala groundwater, followed by Texas and Kansas, each with about 10 percent."[13]

In addition to farming, ranching has had a long and illustrious history here and played a major economic role. The annual cattle drives from west Texas to the railheads in Kansas that took place for several decades after the Civil War are legendary. Even though those drives are long past, ranching is still a major part of the area's economic base with the Great Plains accounting for nearly 50 percent of the beef raised in the U.S. today.[14]

Figure 6.3
A Map Of The Union Pacific
Railroad's Lands In Nebraska Is
An Example Of The Vast Amount
Of Territory That Congress
Granted To Railroads In The
Mid–Nineteenth Century In Just
One State

Since the early nineteen hundreds, the oil and gas industry has played an important role in the region's economy, and with new discoveries in North Dakota and Texas, there is no doubt that it will continue to prosper. Otherwise, the non-agricultural sector, which has grown over the years, still represents a relatively small part of the nation's manufacturing base. "The region remains a limited contributor to finance, insurance, real estate development, and other service industries as well."[15] Not surprisingly, tourism has never been a significant source of revenue in the region.

During the latter half of the twentieth century, a population shift has been taking place. "Increasing mechanization and farm consolidation continues to drive small farmers off the rural Plains. Though cities have grown and prospered, the farm population is less than an eighth what it was in 1930,[16] 'less than half a million, it's one of the most sparsely populated agricultural areas on Earth.'"[17] "There are 376 counties in the Great Plains and most of them (261) have fewer than 10,000 people. Only 34 have more than 50,000 residents."[18] However, the Plains overall has added population since 1950, but until recently, most of that growth was limited to two states—Colorado and Texas.[19] As a result of the recent oil and gas discoveries in North Dakota, its "economy posted a 13.4 percent growth rate in 2012, according to a report released . . . by the Bureau of Economic Analysis. That's nearly three times as fast as the number two state, Texas, and trounces the national average of 2.5 percent." As North Dakota's Governor Jack Dalrymple told CNNMoney, "There's nothing like an oil boom to get things rolling."[20]

While the overall population of the Great Plains in the U.S. has grown to around ten million people (a small part of the total for a country that is approaching four hundred million), there are virtually no major cities located in this huge area. The largest towns found wholly on the prairie are Oklahoma City, OK, with just over 600,000 people, Tulsa, OK, and Wichita, KA, with populations around 400,000 people according to 2010 census numbers. Smaller cities that actually lay out on the Plains include Lincoln, NE, Lubbock, TX, Amarillo, TX, Sioux Falls, ND, Topeka, KA, and Billings, MT. The larger cities such as Austin, Dallas/Fort Worth, San Antonio, Kansas City, Denver, Omaha, and Minneapolis/ Saint Paul are all located along its fringes or slightly farther away.

As the population has shifted over the last few decades, it is not surprising that the demographics of the region have also changed rather dramatically with regard to both ethnic makeup and age. The young people have been leaving the farms to find better employment opportunities elsewhere. The overall average age for the rural areas has risen from 27.6 years in 1950 to 41.6 years in 2007, well above the 34.9 years average age for the cities and towns of the region.[21]

Another significant change is the influx of migrant workers from south of the border, who have decided to make the Plains their home. This has caused a shift from a largely white majority to one that is now much more diverse. As many whites have left, the Latino population has grown and now represents about a third of the total. Much of this group is located in the southern states nearest the border with Mexico, but many have migrated much farther to the north well into Colorado, Kansas, and to a lesser extent, Nebraska.

As the region experiences significant change, they have brought with them some of the most important economic and ecological challenges in the nation. Currently, oil and water are providing the Great Plains with a thriving economy, but both of these resources are limited and should decline significantly within a few decades. What the future holds for the Great Plains is anyone's guess, but banking on continued water flow from the Ogallala Aquifer is a gamble that may not pay off long term. Likewise, it is unlikely that there will be additional enormous oil and gas finds as the area has been investigated thoroughly. It would seem that at some point the industries that these resources support must wane and change will occur. With a decline in these two areas of employment and revenue, the region will surely continue to lose even more population. On the other hand, it has a wealth of sun and wind, which will go a long way toward relieving the region's future energy needs. Wind power may prove to be a godsend with its potential to produce most, if not all of the power to satisfy the region's needs.

Early Development Patterns

The Great Plains was not settled to any extent until railroads pushed through it. The first transcontinental railway built by the Union Pacific and the Central Pacific Railway companies cut through the center of the plains connecting Council Bluffs, Iowa, with Sacramento, California, and was completed in May of 1869. Subsequently, over a dozen other companies built routes to the north and south. To help these companies finance these ventures, Congress ceded enormous tracts of land to the railroads. The railroad then sold these lands and laid out towns along their tracks at regular intervals.[22]

These "railroad towns" were laid out in the normal grid pattern with streets, not necessarily oriented north and south, but parallel to the railroad. The station became the main focus of commercial activity and development. If the town happened to be a county seat as well, the courthouse was relegated to a secondary position away from the hub of commercial activity. These towns' mainstay and reason for being was to serve as a terminus for the shipment out of agricultural products and livestock and the supply of materials to support the inhabitants. Typically, they were spaced the maximum distance a farmer could transport grain to an elevator. With the advent of the automobile and its requisite highway system, the railroads became less important to farmers and ranchers, who could drive their produce farther to more viable markets. As a result, many small towns that relied on rail transport lost population and their main streets have assumed "a gap-tooth appearance, with a significant number of buildings abandoned or in a state of disrepair."[23] Today, the larger cities and towns in and around the Plains have become more important centers for rural families, as they have the shopping malls and businesses necessary for modern everyday life.

Figure 6.4
This Bird's Eye View Of Childress, Texas (C.1890), With Its Gridded Street Pattern Shows The Railroad Station As The Town's Focus, With The County Courthouse Placed Well Away From The Commercial Activity

Precedents

Due to a lack of plentiful building materials and the inability to farm much of the region, few large-scale, permanent settlements were established on the plains. Some indigenous tribes did build villages along the rivers, but Native Americans were mostly nomadic, following the buffalo. As a result, only limited native constructions can be found on the Great Plains, as they seldom built enduring shelters. For their part, the white settlers of the nineteenth century rarely established anything more than small, farming communities. They constructed their farmhouses with what they could find or afford to import. When possible, these homes were similar to those they lived in previously back East. Jonathan Raban sums it up writing that by 1911, "one could look across a settled country, each farmhouse set a mile apart from its neighbor, the southward drift of coal smoke from their chimneys mingling. The houses themselves were a motley scattered fleet. There were stone bothies from Scotland, shaggy Norwegian sod houses, English farm cottages, vaguely Jacobean in appearance, American log cabins, beetling Swedish clapboard, and far-western claim shacks of wildly various degrees of competence and ambition."[24]

Tipis

The tipi (or teepee) is by far the most familiar of all Indian structures. In many ways, it transcended mere shelter and began to represent the very culture that created it—the

Plains Indians—the Apache, Comanche, Sioux, Arapaho, Cheyenne, and numerous other tribes. It was perfectly designed for a nomadic lifestyle, as it could be quickly erected, disassembled, and easily transported elsewhere. It was warm in winter and cool in summer while providing protection from rain, snow, and wind. It was made from materials that were found locally and at the time in abundance. Through the combination of these characteristics, the tipi represented the very definition of sustainability.

The main structure of the tipi was constructed of straight poles 21 to 25 feet long,[25] stripped of their bark, smoothed with rough stones, and dried in the sun. Longpole pine was the wood of choice, but red cedar was used as well. Construction began when three (four for northern tribes) poles were leaned in onto one another tripod fashion and lashed together about 2 feet from their top ends. Between twelve and twenty additional poles were then added in between the initial structural members, thereby creating the iconic conical shape associated with tipis. The base layout was not a perfect circle, rather it tended to be more egg shape and the cone was slightly skewed with the apex off center. The broader part of the ground plan, which corresponded to the steepest side, usually faced northwest and helped to brace the structure against the prevailing wind. The typical tipi measured between 18 to 20 feet in diameter, depending on the size of family that it was designed to house.[26]

Figure 6.5
Sioux Tipis As Painted By Karl Bodmer In 1833

REINVENTING AN URBAN VERNACULAR

Once the wooden frame was in place, it was wrapped with a covering made of between twelve and twenty tanned buffalo hides sown together. The covering was secured to the poles and came together along the center of the entry opening, where it was held in place with wooden pegs. A hole was left at the upper-most point to allow smoke from the fire to escape. Two flaps were left at the very top and each was attached to a pole. Together, they were used to control the airflow out of the tipi.

The tipi was designed to work well under extreme climatic conditions. Often, an additional layer of skins was added to the interior and secured to the poles. This double skin ran from the soil level to a height of around 5 feet. In some cases, another barrier was introduced above the living space to create a ceiling, which served to hold the heat down near the occupants and to add an extra layer of thermal protection. In extremely cold weather, the tipi was frequently surrounded with a barrier of brush that captured the snow, thus helping to protect the tipi from the wind and hold in the warmth. During hot summer days, the skirts of the exterior and interior coverings were lifted to allow a cooling airflow to move uninhibited through the dwelling.

The tipi could be erected in less than half a day and disassembled in even less time. These jobs fell upon the women. Once the tipi was ready to be moved, it was disassembled and the poles were attached to horses in a manner that formed "V-shaped" sleds. The remaining hide coverings and other household goods were loaded on and dragged by the horses to the next location.[27]

Earthlodges

On the Great Plains, the Mandan, Arikara, and Hidatsa tribes built permanent villages of earthlodges along the tributaries of the Missouri River and the Pawnee in the plains farther south along the Upper Republican River in what is now Kansas and Nebraska. The Native American earthlodge is an ancient dwelling type built with variations found around much of the world in the more northerly latitudes (usually above the 32° north latitude or higher altitudes). Similar constructions can also be found in the American Southwest (see Chapter 7) in the form of the hogan and kiva.

Earthlodges were circular in plan, with a low dome-shaped silhouette. The floor plan could vary from 40 to 60 feet in diameter,[28] with anywhere from 10 to 25 people living in it, and in some cases, with their favorite horses. The Pawnee dug theirs into the ground 3 or more feet, but the more northerly examples were built directly on ground level. The typical structure was composed of four centrally located posts set into the ground in a square pattern. These posts usually measured between 10 and 15 feet in height and the space between them was spanned at the top by beams.[29] Encircling this central area was another structure composed of twelve posts about 5 feet in height, with beams spanning between them as well. Rafters radiated from the center and spanned over the beams to the exterior wall.[30] To complete the enclosure, planks were laid from the earth to the outside ring of beams. This entire structure "was covered with willow mats and then overlaid with a thin coating of earth and sod. At the top of the dome-shaped lodge there was an opening—often two or three feet across—which allowed smoke to escape."[31] In time, native grasses would cover the structure blending it into the earth and its surroundings.

As would be expected, the earthlodge was constructed wholly from locally found materials. The preferred wood for the structure was oak, but cottonwood found along riverbanks was usually more available and made an acceptable substitute. At times, the builders dug into the ground a foot or more to take advantage of the earth as floor and

Figure 6.6
Photo Of A Mandan Earthlodge
Taken C. 1908 By Edward S.
Curtis

the wall of the excavation provided a lower wall. A final layer of earth was used to cover the entire structure, which gave the dwelling a weather-tight exterior coating. Naturally, an earthen coating of this sort can only be used in regions like the Great Plains where rainfall is limited. Buffalo hides were used to cover the floor and some of the walls to give greater comfort.

The men cut and placed the wooden structure, but it was left to the women to finish the work. "It would take a group of women about a week to construct an earthlodge. The lodge would then last about 7–10 years at which time the buried portions of the framework posts would be rotting out. A new earthlodge would then be built at the same location."[32]

The shape, materials, and structure all worked together to create a natural defense from the challenges of this frequently harsh environment. The low, domed silhouette of the earthlodge gave it a minimal exposed surface area and a naturally aerodynamic quality that presented no vertical surfaces to be buffeted by strong winds. The airtight covering of earth served to keep the cold air from penetrating the interior, while the fire set in the center of the circular plan radiated warmth evenly and efficiently around the entire space. Digging into the ground enhanced these attributes and gave the occupants the added benefit of the earth's natural protection and insulation.

Sod House or Soddie

When the Americans and European immigrants arrived on the Plains during the second half of the nineteenth century, they found little material with which to build their homes. Coming from densely forested regions and a tradition of building in wood, they were poorly prepared for the dearth of trees they encountered. These new arrivals were often

Figure 6.7
Mandan Earthlodge

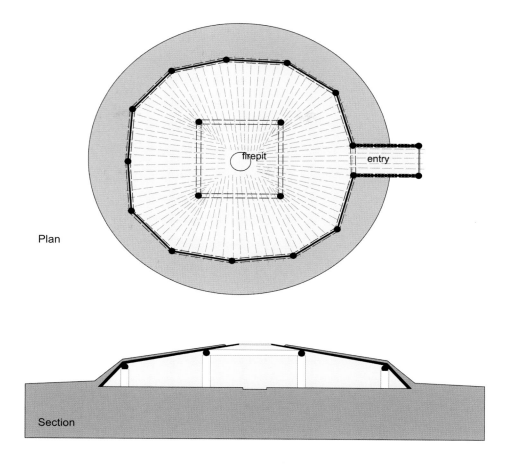

Plan

Section

not financially capable of importing timber and were forced to use those materials that were locally available. In this case, that resource turned out to be the earth under their feet. The prairie was rich in the tough, indigenous grasses on which the buffalo grazed and the fertile soil that nurtured them. It is this combination of grass, their dense root structure, and the soil that they grow in that we refer to as sod.

This sod was dug either by hand or with the aid of a plow in strips of 1 foot or more in width and a few inches deep. As damp sod is heavy and difficult to lift and place, the strips were cut into manageable lengths of 2 or 3 feet. These more or less uniform sections were then flipped over, so that the grass was facing down and placed as one might place bricks, one on top of the other with their joints staggered. Layer upon layer created a rather thick, solid wall, which was generally weather-tight with a high insulation value. "In the late nineteenth century, a modified plow designed specifically for sod cutting was invented: this 'grasshopper plow' replaced the moldboard with a set of adjustable rods, which allowed the operator to cut a uniform strip of sod."[33] These crude building blocks had the notable advantage to the settlers of being virtually free, with only time and muscle required to make them. To save time and labor, many homes were dug into the side of a hill, which could form one or more of the walls of the dwelling.

In time, these earthen homes became known as "soddies." They were usually one-story, rectangular in plan, and composed of only one or two rooms. They had a minimum of doors and windows, as those were expensive because they came from a distance. To make the interiors as livable as possible, many settlers plastered the rough sod interior walls and some covered them with wallpaper.

Figure 6.8
A Nebraskan Farm Family Poses
In Front Of Their Sod House
Surrounded By Newly Planted
Corn. Photographed By Solomon
D. Butcher In 1888

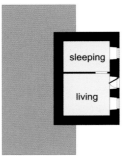

Plan

Section

Figure 6.9
Sod House

Roofs were another problem, as they demanded timber for structure to span over the width of the room. These timbers were frequently covered with reeds and/or brush and a final layer of sod. Unfortunately, the sod roof could not be depended on to be watertight during a long, soaking rain. Even though those occurrences were rare, when they did happen, life was very unpleasant in the soddie. In more advanced examples, canvas or even metal was used as roofing with more predictable and certainly more satisfying results.

More often than not, the soddie was considered to be a temporary building, useful until the time when the settler could afford to construct a more permanent wooden one, but often they ended up being the family's long-term residence.

German Building in the Texas Hill Country

During the first half of the nineteenth century, thousands of German immigrants settled in the Hill Country of southwest Texas. Here, prickly pear cactus and small trees such as live oaks and red cedar sparsely cover the rough, rolling countryside. The climate is usually benign with the temperatures rarely falling below freezing, but climbing to uncomfortably high levels in mid-summer. The land is too rough and dry for farming, so many became ranchers. In this rugged Texas landscape, not at all similar to the European one they left behind, they established towns such as New Braunfels and Fredericksburg, which bear the imprint of their distinctive German architecture to this day.[34]

"The German house is often less elongated than those of the Anglos, being built on a squared plan reminiscent of the Frankish central German house. Typically Teutonic roof profiles such as the Westerwald 'saltbox' and the Frankish 'bellcast' occur frequently; stoves often replaced the open-hearth fireplaces prevalent among Anglos; casement windows are common among Texas Germans, as are cellars; and 'Dutch' doors occasionally appear. For reasons not clear, Hill Country Germans made greater use of outside stairs than did any other group."[35]

Like other groups that settled on the Great Plains, they found only limited resources with which to build. These hills, unlike the plains of Kansas and Nebraska, do not offer much sod for building, but do have a plentiful supply of limestone. Beginning in the 1850s, it was of this rock that so many of the German buildings were constructed. They found that this sedimentary stone was easily worked and broke in relatively flat pieces that could be laid without great difficulty. Durable, impervious, and attractive, it made an excellent exterior wall and was used on both large and small buildings.

The American Farmhouse

Most dwellings that the Anglos and European farmers built in the nineteenth and early twentieth centuries were based on a simple rectangular plan composed of two to four rooms. At times, it was combined with another rectangular room or two, which resulted in an overall L or T arrangement. Usually, the houses were of one, one-and-a-half, or two stories, and the gabled end walls were capped with a pitched roof. The living room (parlor), dining room, and kitchen occupied the first floor, with the bedrooms on the upper floor. The kitchen was the most important room of the house and the center of family activity. It usually had a cast iron cook stove as its only source of heat. The backdoor, which invariably opened out onto a covered porch, was most often used as the entrance, as it opened out to the outbuildings.[36]

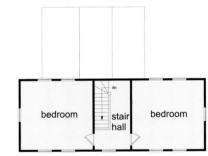

Second Floor Plan

bedroom | stair hall | bedroom

Section

First Floor Plan

back porch | kitchen

parlor | stair hall | dining room

Figure 6.10
Proud Homesteaders Pose In
Front Of Their Home Near
Kearney, Nebraska.
Photographed By Solomon D.
Butcher In 1903

Toward the middle of the nineteenth century, sawmills in eastern states, where forests abound, began to provide uniform, dimensional lumber to settlers on the Plains. As a consequence, their homes were built of milled lumber and framed in the then current balloon method. This technique depended on 2-inch thick boards of varying widths, which were long and straight as are found typically in house construction today. Wooden clapboards covered the exterior walls and wooden shingles the roof.

They stood up straight against the chilling wind. Few had basements, but root cellars dug into the ground for storage purposes provided a refuge from the frequent tornados that ravaged these exposed, unprotected dwellings. When time allowed, trees were planted around homes to provide much-needed shade in summer and a windbreak against winter winds. To this day, these farmsteads are clearly marked against the sky by substantial, encircling groves.

Common Themes Found in the Traditional Buildings of the Great Plains

Without a doubt, climate and traditions on the Great Plains vary more than in any region in the United States. From north to south, one finds conditions of extremely cold winters to very mild ones; pleasant summers to insufferably hot ones; blizzards to hot desert breezes. It is here where the Indian culture is stronger than other parts of the country, but their architecture is little prized and the lessons that it could teach us go unrecognized. The Anglos who settled here in the nineteenth century adapted to the place and built their sod dwellings because of a lack of materials, but once they became more prosperous, they returned to the more conventional and familiar eastern methods. Despite the wide range of conditions and the subsequent lack of architectural continuity, many common vernacular themes can be distilled.

Figure 6.11
Farm House (I–House)

Shape and Placement

The Native Americans revered the round shape as a holy symbol and many of their most prevalent plan arrangements reflected that ideal. Both the tipi and the earthlodge were built around this concept. Beyond their symbolic nature, the round shape had its practical virtues as well. The volume or cross-section of these structures worked in concert with the plan to produce a cone or dome shape, which had worthwhile environmental ramifications. The curved exterior of both the tipi and earthlodge facilitated in channeling strong winds around them, thereby assuring a greater level of structural stability and thermal comfort within.

When tipis or earthlodges were gathered together in either camps or villages, they were commonly arranged in a circle with open community and ceremonial space at the center. When no such formal organization was necessary, the dwellings were most frequently oriented with the entry to the southeast and the rising sun; their back would then be to the northwest and the prevailing winds. While rooted in tradition and based on religious beliefs, it was also a common sense orientation that came from millennia of experience with local climate.

However, the rectangle supplanted the round as the prevalent shape once the American settlers began to dominate the Plains. Square-cornered, boxy-shaped buildings topped with gabled roofs became the norm once the newcomers were well-established.

In most cases, the orientation was to have the front door face the road that abutted the property, not the sun nor with its back against the prevailing wind.

Shelter, Construction, and Materials

Animal skins and earth coverings over posts and beams that composed the Native American structures gave way in the early nineteenth century to all wooden dwellings that relied on construction technologies that the Anglo settlers brought with them from the east. With only a few exceptions, milled lumber with small cross-sections, such as the two by four, became the standard building blocks on the Plains and remains so to this day.

The pitched roof with wood shingles became commonplace in the nineteenth century. The slope had value even in this semi-arid region, as there is enough rain to require the need for swift drainage to keep the building dry. Along with the pitched roof came the gable end wall, which was the cheapest and easiest method of having a roof transition into the vertical, and consequently, became the standard technique. On the other hand, overhangs were not so necessary in this area, as there was little rainfall, lots of sun, and dry air, which meant that there was little need to protect the siding from water damage and rot, as it would dry quickly.

The porch(es) became an important feature to any home as it provided covered, outdoor space for many activities. The back porch, which connected to the kitchen, was used most often, as the family did much of their work there, while they sat in its shade on warmer days and evenings.

Windows were usually of the double-hung type, except in the Texas Hill Country where the German-Russians preferred the casement variety.[37] As might be expected, there were few windows in these houses, as they were expensive and most people bought only those they could afford. In this part of the country, the sun was usually strong and hot, to be avoided during the summer months, so the lack of glass was generally not a great hardship. In winter, they let in the heat of the sun, but unfortunately, after dark, the single-paned glass chilled the air and ill-fitting frames allowed cold air to infiltrate the interior.

Heating, Cooling, and Ventilation

The Native American circular, sunken fire pit in the center of the tipi or earthlodge radiated heat equally in all directions around the interior space. This simple system served to keep these homes relatively comfortable during the worst winter weather. The smoke hole located in the center of the roof above the fire served as a chimney to let the smoke escape. The thick coating of earth that covered the earthlodge absorbed the sun's heat, and its seamless seal assisted in keeping the heat in and the cold wind out. When and where wood could not be found to fuel the fire, dried cowpats (buffalo dung) were used.

The cast iron stove and fireplace provided the source of heat for nineteenth-century ranches and farmhouses. As in the east, coal and wood were often the fuel of choice, but with a scarcity of both, corncobs became a frequent substitute, as they were found in abundance on many farms. After the animals had chewed the nutritious kernels off the cobs and they were dried out, the cobs burned well.

The wood-frame farmhouses were generally uninsulated, and as mentioned previously, exposed on all sides to be battered by winter winds. As a result, they were hard to keep warm because the cold wind penetrated between the cracks in boards and through plaster walls. German settlers in Nebraska and South Dakota filled their wall cavities between the wooden studs with bricks made of mud and dung, which gave them a denser and more stable wall.[38]

Other Considerations

Extreme weather has been a constant concern on the Great Plains from the very first settlers to current times. In particular, tornados that present the biggest challenge due to their unpredictability and overall destructive force. The most effective way of dealing with this problem has been to find shelter below the ground. Native Americans built many of their dwellings either totally below the ground, as with dugouts, or partially so, as with earthlodges. The Anglo settlers sought refuge in root cellars that were also dug into the earth. Rounded building shapes, like that of the earthlodge, were somewhat effective as they presented an aerodynamic form that helped to channel the wind around them. Unfortunately, no building constructed above the ground is safe when hit directly by a tornado's full force.

Natural Resources Available for Construction

Reeds and Grasses

In 1540, Francisco Vásquez de Coronado encountered the Caddoan-speaking tribes living in southern Kansas. He described their grass houses as having thatch that was sown "in and out in such an ingenious manner that each bunch of grass overlaps the bunch below."[39] While the prairie grasses could be useful to construct a comfortable, yet basic house, it is difficult to imagine any important and economically viable use for these grasses in contemporary or future building. Even if there were a good use, the availability of native grass has shrunk and now much of what was once grassland has been converted to crops.

Earth

As in the southwest, earth (including topsoil or sod) is a resource that has served the Great Plains as the primary construction material for millennia. It was first used as a building material by Native Americans, then briefly during the mid-nineteenth century by Anglos to construct their sod houses.

Its virtues are discussed at length in Chapter 7: The West, but to reiterate, its foremost advantage is that it is very economical: (1) there is virtually a limitless supply of it near at hand, (2) it can be mined with relative ease, (3) it can be easily worked, and (4) it requires no refining. Additionally, it is fire- and rot-proof. Thermally, it can act as a heat sink and has the ability to create a tight barrier that keeps the wind out, retaining the interior warmth. It can support heavy loads in compression, and therefore makes good structural walls. It is not suited for rainy or humid climates as it can easily erode, but for an arid and semi-arid place, such as the Great Plains, it works well.

"Buffalo grass (*Buchloe dactyloides*) was one of the most important grasses of the High Plains of Nebraska, Kansas, and Colorado, where it was often found in pure stands. Its sod is extraordinarily dense, with a structure of fine but very tough and wiry roots spreading widely in all directions. Together with the roots of adjacent plants, buffalo grass forms a dense, multidirectional mat with considerable tensile strength. This root system allowed for the cutting of bricks of great dimensional stability."[40] This type of root system that tended to hold the earth together was perfect for making the sod blocks or "prairie marble" from which soddies were built. However, sod is finite, and the process of creating blocks from it is not one that could continue on endlessly. Also, by harvesting the topsoil, one destroys the land's future agricultural value by making it unproductive. This tradeoff between reaping a construction material at the expense of future agriculture is not worth the benefit, so sod should no longer be considered a viable alternative source.

In the nineteenth century, in Kansas, Nebraska, North and South Dakota, German-Russian immigrants "used a material composed of clay mixed with manure, straw and water. This combination produced a durable substance naturally suited to the prairie landscape. Two techniques were used for constructing loadbearing walls; puddled clay, in which clay was layered on a stone foundation, and rammed earth (see Chapter 7), in which an earthen mixture was compacted between wooden forms. One variation of the puddling clay wall used medium-sized stones regularly placed in the lower part of the wall. Another use of clay involved pressing adobe like bricks out of wooden molds, known as *Batsa*." Later, *batsa* was placed between the studs of their balloon-framed houses to help stabilize the structure as well as insulate them.[41]

Historically, adobe was used in the southernmost regions of the Great Plains where the Spanish and Mexican influence was greatest. This technique is still a viable alternative to wood frame construction, as it is cheap and durable, if properly maintained. When interiors and exteriors receive a suitable plaster finish, an esthetically pleasing appearance can result.

Rammed earth was never a major factor in construction on the Great Plains, but it certainly could become one in the future as all the conditions are right: an abundance of material that is easily produced in an area that has little rainfall. Like adobe, rammed earth when fortified with concrete can produce an attractive, long-lasting, and sturdy structural wall. (See Chapter 7 for additional detail.)

Stone

Sources of large quantities of stone are found in the Texas Hill Country and parts of Kansas, North and South Dakota. The stone that is most often used for general construction found in these areas is limestone. Limestone is a sedimentary rock that was produced on the bed of ancient seas like the one that covered the Great Plains millions of years ago. As a result of the process of one layer after another being built up over time, it is stratified. The stone can consequently be broken into neat layers that make it both easier to quarry and to use in construction, as the flat stones stack readily.

Stone requires labor to quarry and to lay up, so it takes time and manpower—two things that builders can rarely afford. "With the completion of local rail service lines, lumber became competitive with stone, and in the late 1920s the use of stone was generally discontinued."[42] Even so, stone may become popular again, if and when transportation cost rises and the pressure on lumber becomes great enough for those prices to rise as well.

Today, we rarely think in terms of permanence, which is a virtue that stone naturally imbues. But the Great Plains is a place with a harsh and unforgiving climate, which can reduce the life of our common modern construction materials significantly. In the future, it may be that coupled with this asset and stone's inherent beauty, it will once again be recognized as worthwhile and find a place in our repertory of commonly used materials. (See Chapter 7 for additional detail.)

Wood

Wood has always been sparse on the Great Plains. Sources of timber have typically been found in limited supply only along rivers and streams and on its eastern margins, which receive more rain. By definition, this semi-arid region finds its identity in this openness and treeless space. To be sure, the earthlodges required a good supply of trees to build, but they were built near the Missouri River and its tributaries. This building type was difficult to perpetuate, as even in these treed locations, the availability of trees suitable for construction was limited and were ultimately depleted.

Across the Great Plains, once the initial, indigenous supply was exhausted, almost all wood had to be imported from the east. Today, it may come from the east, the west, or Canada, but it is still imported. The future of wood construction on the Plains is much like that of the southwest in that it will always be dependent on importation. This fact would argue that smaller members would be most appropriate for future construction, as they are cheaper to ship and most easily handled. This has been the case in the past, and this trend should continue well into the future.

The advent of built-up and fabricated wooden joists, beams, and trusses has meant that less wood is necessary to create a member that can span even greater distances than their natural predecessors. These innovations in lumber design and production make their use more practical in areas where timbers are not found and where lumber needs to be shipped.

Despite its absence from the immediate vicinity, wood has one big advantage on the windy prairie in that it bends well before breaking. Consequently, it can move with the pressure of the wind and then return to its original position. This elasticity can save many structures from destruction. On the other hand, the wooden members must be securely attached to one another so as not to be blown apart. As in the South and South Florida, metal connectors are required to bind the members together to achieve the highest level of strength to resist these forces.

On the Plains, wood has been used first and foremost to span spaces as floor and roof structures, while earth, stone, and brick were employed to create walls. With an increase in the cost of wood, its use may be somewhat reduced and these other more locally found materials may once again replace it in some applications.

Long-term, the need to transport lumber from distant sources to building sites on the Great Plains will mean additional and greater costs. This cost will rise in time as transportation costs rise, which may create an expense that will be increasingly difficult to justify. As a result, it might be argued that lumber will be used more sparingly in the most economical manner.

The Current Approach to Design and Construction

Urban Development Today

The U.S. government passed the first of several Homestead Acts in 1862 motivated by a desire to populate the prairies by giving aspiring farmers land on which they could fulfill their dreams of a better life. As was the custom, the unpopulated landscape was divided into an enormous checkerboard of 160-acre square plots with one-half mile to a side. Originally, each plot represented the site for a family farm. These large plots meant that family homes were widely separated, tending to isolate families. Over the years, the Plains lost population and farms were consolidated into larger units, the separation between homesteads grew even greater in a trend that continues to this day. As a result, the great majority of the region is sparsely populated with only small farming and ranching towns thinly sprinkled throughout. With so few cities and towns of any size in such a large area, sprawl is not a term that applies to most of the region. But in areas where one finds more urban development and growth, such as Austin, San Antonio, Denver, Omaha, Wichita, Oklahoma City, and Tulsa, subdivisions have been creeping farther and farther from the city centers. As elsewhere, these cities are now encountering traffic congestion where none previously existed.

The older housing developments nearer the centers tend to conform to the original grid pattern, while the newer ones have gently winding suburban streets, so commonplace everywhere else in the country. They wind around in picturesque fashion as if there were some topographical reason for doing so, but rarely do any such obstacles actually exist. Streets and yards have been planted with trees and shrubs to give not only some shade from the hot sun, but to emulate those more verdant, wetter climes to the east. Green lawns and fenced yards complete the suburban picture. Spacious sidewalks that line the streets see little use.

Architectural Character

Today, there seems to be little desire to create or maintain a unique character to the region's domestic architecture. Most new homes are designed in much the same way as the majority of the country builds. Housing developers and builders offer a variety of themes from which to choose. There are castles, Tudors, ranches, and any number of unrecognizable hybrids to choose from.

Level, winding subdivision streets are lined with equally spaced, self-contained family homes. Spacious lots guarantee that the abutter is not too close. Sidewalks are legislated by the towns as a necessity for children's safety, but no one uses them as most people drive to where they are going. The backyard is where the family gathers and plays. As a result, there is little or no activity on the neighborhood streets.

Generally, homes are built as split-level, one- or two-stories with a connected two- or three-car garage facing the street. Rectangular rooms are combined in various ways to produce a wide variety of plan arrangements with irregular outlines. Roof pitches vary from shallow to somewhat steep. Siding is any number of combinations of wood, brick, or plaster.

As elsewhere, mechanical heat, cooling, and ventilation have virtually eliminated the idea of opening windows for fresh air. As often as not, curtains cover the windows to maintain privacy or to shield the interiors from too much direct sunlight. Few new homes seek to work with climate and the result is housing developments that resemble those in most other parts of the country.

There are few apartment complexes and those that do exist are usually located at some distance from city centers. Generally designed for young adults, either living alone or with a mate, they typically do not cater to families.

Popular Design and Construction Methods

Construction is generally straightforward, with most new homes built close to the ground on slabs without basements. They are framed with dimensional lumber. Low-pitched roofs with modest overhangs top them off. Windows are usually adequate to let in light and expose what view there might be, but rarely are they designed to provide good cross-ventilation. Air conditioning has usurped that function in almost every case.

The contemporary wood frame house is relatively strong and permanent compared with many indigenous buildings of the past, but the earthlodge had one distinct advantage over it. The earthlodge was built low and sometimes into the ground, and it, therefore, offered little resistance to heavy winds, especially to the most menacing force on the Plains, the tornado. We do not design our buildings in a way to defend from extremely strong wind. To protect people from the devastation of a tornado, the Federal Emergency Management Agency or FEMA advises that safe rooms be constructed in homes to provide shelter from such disasters.[43] Safe rooms are only intended to protect the individual or family, not the building, which could be totally destroyed. Designed of reinforced concrete or concrete block with an extra strong door, they can accomplish their purpose in most cases, but not all families are willing or able to spend the extra money that is required to build them, therefore taking their chances.

Future Environmental Concerns

While semi-arid conditions prevail across the entire Great Plains and give it its most notable climatic character, the region varies thermally from north to south. The north is much colder in winter than the south. It is very likely that they will be even more clearly divided into two very distinct climatic regions by the second half of the twenty-first century. Due to the effects of global warming, the northern half is predicted to become warmer and much wetter with increased rainfall and the southern portion much hotter and drier.

A continued successful economy for the Great Plains is contingent on access to large amounts of water to sustain its agriculture. As the availability of water affected the lives of the region's people over previous generations, the next decades will also be contingent upon it. Fifty years ago, the discovery of subsurface sources took the uncertainty out of farming and its dependence on adequate rainfall, and as a result, the prairies blossomed. Now we are beginning to face the possibility of a future lack of water, which will again change the region's character and development.

Needless to say, the Ogallala Aquifer is finite and if the usages continue at their current pace, it "will begin to give out relatively soon; the only question is when,"[44] contended Marc Reisner in 1993. What would he be saying now? *The Washington Post* supports this point of view as it reports that in a recent study led by David Steward of Kansas State University, "that 30 percent of the Kansas portion of the Ogallala Aquifer has already been pumped out, and another 39 percent will get used up in the next half-century at existing rates. Kansas, clearly, is on the fast track to depletion. As a result, agriculture production is likely to peak around 2040 and decline after that."[45] The consequence of the depletion of this and other aquifers in the region will lead to a dramatic impact on the food supply of this country as well as the world.

Global warming will only serve to make this situation much worse with the southern portion of the Great Plains becoming drier over the next decades. Less precipitation will mean that more water will have to be withdrawn from the ground in order to support current levels of crop production, speeding up the depletion process. When the Aquifer finally gives out, the renewed dependence on rainfall alone will reintroduce uncertainty to famers' lives. As before, it seems likely that many who previously depended on agriculture may leave the southern Plains for other parts of the nation. The ubiquitous grain silos will not disappear, but they will not be filled as fully as before.

Ironically, over the coming century, the northern portion of the Great Plains, which never had access to the Ogallala in the past, is projected to begin receiving more rainfall. This may mean that agriculture will flourish in this area as never before. With the northern plains being more productive than the southern, we may find a greater economic disparity between the two. But it is unlikely that there will be a great population shift to the north, as agriculture can only support relatively small numbers of people.

Design Strategies and Building Components for the Future

Climatic Imperatives

The Great Plains presents a wide range of environmental challenges to resolve for anyone wishing to design a building there. The hot summers and sparse rainfall are reasonably consistent across its full extent. Likewise, strong and potentially damaging winds can be a major problem throughout. However, winters represent different problems depending on one's location, as the northern prairies are much colder than the southern ones. For any region, one must design for the worst-case scenario and on the Great Plains that worst-case would relate to multiple issues—the extreme cold in the north, the intense summer heat, and the strong winds throughout, including the threat of tornados.

When designing for the Great Plains, one finds many similarities with the challenges and solutions found in the buildings of the West. The main exceptions are that there is always the potential for very strong winds and greater rainfall on the Plains. Even still, it is possible to build upon many of the principles and technologies discussed in Chapter 7: The West.

Orientation

As in other regions, one of the foremost concerns is to achieve a direct and appropriate relationship to the specific environment, notably to the sun and wind. Whenever possible, service functions such as kitchens, bathrooms, entries, and closets, that require less sunlight should be located on the north side of residential buildings. They can then serve as something of a buffer on colder days and nights by turning its "back" to the chilling and potentially dangerous winds coming from the north and northwest. Living areas and bedrooms can then be arranged on the south side in order to get the full benefit of tempered sunlight. In order to achieve these goals, the building's long side should face as close to south or southeast as possible. This overall orientation will ensure that the southern sun, which is the easiest controlled, can add welcome solar heating in winter and good day lighting throughout the year.

Unfortunately, tornados, which frequently come from the south or southwest, will confront the most heavily glazed south-facing side, which is most vulnerable. This may not be avoidable. A direct hit from a tornado is usually devastating to any building, no matter the orientation, unless it is one designed in the fashion of a concrete bunker, which is an unacceptable alternative for normal living and consequently for this prototype. However, glass must be protected and a safe place for residents to weather the storm provided.

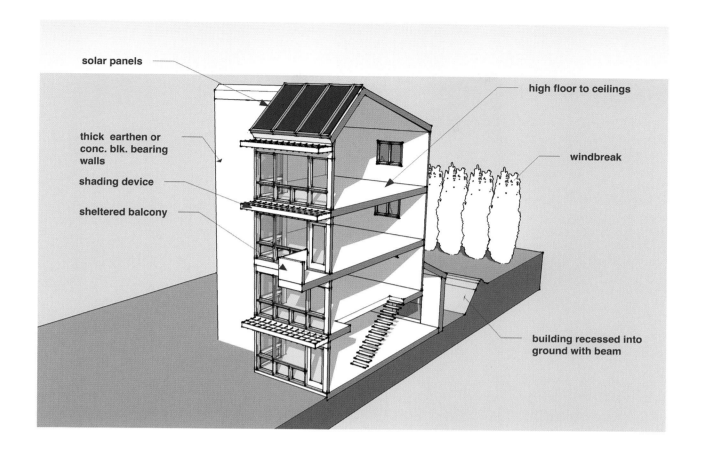

solar panels

high floor to ceilings

thick earthen or conc. blk. bearing walls

windbreak

shading device

sheltered balcony

building recessed into ground with beam

Figure 6.12
Idea Drawing For The Great
Plains

Overall Suggested Configuration and Layout

Buildings in this region should be compact, to reduce the overall surface area exposed to sun and wind. Consequently, a two-room deep arrangement with the unit plans more square in configuration than those of the hot/humid South, but similar to those required for the West.

One further goal in shaping the mass of the building is to make the building as aerodynamic as possible, so that strong winds will not exert excessive pressure against exterior walls, but pass around and over them. Native Americans recognized the wisdom in doing so, and as discussed, many of their structures were rounded as with the tipi and earthlodge. This can be achieved today to some extent by reducing as many of the vertical surfaces that wind would push against as possible.

One method of doing this is by setting the building into the ground as deeply as feasible. Depressing buildings about a half level down (4 to 4.5 feet deep) will result in greatly decreasing their exposure. Under these circumstances, the units on the lowest floor could have partially sunken courtyards, which would be carved into the earth. If a building cannot be set down, then earth berms should be pulled up around the lowest level or solid walls built to accomplish the same result. Either way, this technique has the effect of reducing a building's overall height by at least a half story, which on a four-story building is a meaningful amount.

The second technique is to make the ends of a building more "rounded." To accomplish this objective, floors on both ends (east and west) of the building can be stepped back away from the winds as the building rises. One would start low with a single story, with each subsequent level rising higher and being set back from the one below. This same stepping technique can be used on the north side.

Add to this stepping configuration pitched roofs, which will tend to channel the winds up, over, and around the building, thereby avoiding the pressure that flat, fully exposed walls would need to resist. The sloped roofs will also serve another function by buttressing exterior walls and the building as a whole.

Building Circulation—Halls and Staircases

As many of the units as possible should be entered directly on the ground floor level and only require access by way of a few steps, half a flight up or down. This is particularly important for the larger units where families with children are most likely to reside, so that they have direct access to outdoor play spaces. Each of the upper level units will need a set of stairs.

Single-loaded corridors can be used here as well, but stairs that connect directly to each unit, as is proposed for southern buildings, also work well. This second arrangement eliminates corridors, resulting in a more efficient overall layout. The two stairways required for access and egress to and from the upper floors can be located back-to-back and between the apartments that they serve forming a core. This would also allow them to be entered from either the north or south side of the building, which may have certain advantages when working with site.

In this region, every building should be equipped with a safe haven where residents can find a secure place to protect themselves from tornados. Any such space must be located below grade; therefore, the bottom of stair towers is an appropriate place, as it is quickly accessed by all residents from their apartments. It should be enclosed by the thick stair walls, capped with a timber or concrete roof and have a strong, weather-tight door to seal it.

Roof Type

To achieve the "rounded" effect on the ends of buildings, which was mentioned previously, roof pitches should decrease from the lowest floors to the top. The roofs over the first floor can be a rather steep 6:12 pitch (22.5°), the second to third level roofs can decrease to something in the range of a 3:12 pitch (11.25°), and the final or top one can be flat. This diminishment of roof angle will tend to facilitate the movement of wind up and over the structure with as little resistance to it as possible.

Wherever roof pitches are very low or flat, a green roof can be developed with the addition of a thick layer of soil to support plant life.

Windows and Window Treatments

As in any other region, windows must be carefully selected and placed according to orientation and exposure. On the north side, they should be relatively few in number and of modest size, as cross-ventilation is not as important here as in the more humid South and extremely cold winters mean that too many windows can be a disadvantage due to heat loss. Proper sizing should help to minimize the amount of thermal loss in winter through the glass and by infiltration through their joints. The south side can afford a more generous amount of glazing, as that glass can let in the warmth of the sun in winter and can easily be shielded from the hot, summer sun by overhangs. Little or no glass is recommended on the east or west sides, as the sun hits the building horizontally and is therefore much harder to control.

Good ventilation is still important and an adequate number of operable windows need to be provided. Typically, double-hung and sliding windows and doors will suffice to let in enough air during most of the year, but casement and awning configurations with their ability to open fully are also appropriate.

In any case, glass needs protection from both too strong sun in summer and very high and potentially destructive winds at any time of year. Horizontal shading in the form of an overhang, arbor, or awning will shade the south-facing glass adequately from strong sunlight, if deep enough. Exterior overhead rolling, swing, or sliding shutters will protect the east- and west-facing glass from sun and all sides from high winds and dangerous flying detritus that they may whip about.

Materials and Construction

The need to import wood, which is now the most conventional building material on the Great Plains, requires a re-examination. As is true in the southwest, timber must be brought in, as it does not grow here in sufficient amounts. While this does not preclude its use in the future, it will make it more precious for construction, and therefore limit how often it is used and where. In most cases, lumber is required for floor and roof structure, because of its ability to span over spaces. The best use of lumber is in the form of smaller members known as dimensional lumber. This category comes as two by fours and so forth, and therefore requires smaller trees that take less time to grow and ship more easily. Built-up trusses composed of these smaller members, glulams, and engineered lumber can all span distances commonly found in housing and their production involves less wood to do so. In the Great Plains, these composite pieces will no doubt continue to replace solid wood timbers in future construction, because of the economy with which they can be produced.

Earth is by far the most plentiful and easily obtained construction material found on the Great Plains and sod, cut from top soil, was traditionally the material of choice for the early pioneers. It served well in this semi-arid region where rainfall is usually modest, but it was not a material that one could use over the long term due to its fragility. Soil can be employed more successfully in other ways, such as adobe or rammed earth. These methods use clay sub-soils and are particularly useful for the construction of bearing walls on which the floor and roof structure can rest. As previously noted, where exposed to the sun, the mass of these thick walls can serve as a heat sink helping to regulate the internal temperature in the apartments. Normally, earth constructions should be protected from rain wherever possible, which tends to erode them, so a roof or metal cap must cover the tops of all such walls. They will also require reinforcing with steel bars in earthquake-prone areas.

In addition to earth, stone is found in abundance in many regions of the Great Plains and can be used in much the same way as earth. It is durable and can resist wind, rain, and fire. It has a distinct aesthetic advantage as it is universally accepted as a beautiful material that imbues a sense of permanence and strength when used either inside or on the exterior.

If earth or stone were not used, then a possible substitute would be concrete block made with fly ash and reinforced with steel. This is without doubt a compromise that should be avoided if the other two options are possible.

The basic structure of this type of building may be composed of bearing walls made of either earth or stone, or as a last resort, concrete block, which supports wood floors and roofs. The bearing walls are not only structural, but serve to divide apartment units, guaranteeing acoustical privacy and act as firewalls, which help ensure great safety from the spread of fire within the building. Interior partitions are built with conventional two by four construction.

Outdoor Spaces

The location within the region often determines the type and amount of time spent living outdoors. The most northerly sections, where it is colder longer than southern ones, may offer very few months when it is possible to spend time comfortably outside. By contrast, those living farther south will have the opportunity most of the year. To the north, windbreaks, in the form of evergreen vegetation, earthen berms, or solid walls, may be required to provide shelter from chilling winds, whereas in the southern tier, a cooling breeze may be welcome. In both situations, provision for outdoor living should be a priority. It can be accommodated at ground level with terraces and yards and above ground with balconies. All options should be located on the sunny southern side of buildings and provided with adequate shading devices to give residents the choice of sun or shade depending on the weather conditions and the preferences.

Landscape

Water conservation and retention will become a greater issue in the future as the region's vast aquifers are depleted and climate change brings even drier weather to its southern tier. Wherever possible, buildings should be covered with "green" roofs to capture as much rainwater as possible. It is possible to cover flat roofs with earth and native grasses that require little water to grow. This approach will help to protect the uppermost units from sun and wind while also providing a method for collecting rainwater. All the rain that falls on a flat roof, whether green or not, can be channeled into gutters and then into cisterns below the building. This water can then be sterilized and reused for drinking and all other domestic uses. Functions that do not require potable water, such as toilets and watering of gardens and landscape plants, can use gray water that is captured from those daily uses (except toilets), stored, and recycled.

Trees have functioned as windbreaks and shading on the Plains for the last couple hundred years. Farmers have used them to help keep the soil in place and crops safe from destruction and to protect their farm buildings. The modern apartment building can also benefit from them. Evergreens placed on the north side of a building can help mediate the force of the wind, protecting the building and making life more pleasant overall. By placing deciduous trees on the south, east, and west sides of the building, the direct heat gain from the summer sun can be greatly diminished, while the needed warm winter sun is allowed to fall on the units. Both make the building comfortable and save energy at the same time.

Renewable Power and Mechanical Equipment

From an energy perspective, the Great Plains is blessed with plenty of sun and wind. With normally clear skies, solar power is definitely feasible throughout the region and can find a place on buildings to produce both hot water and electric power. More importantly, this is the windiest region of all, with the exception of some coastal locales, consequently a great place for windmills. The installation of wind-generated power is gaining popularity for good reason, and it appears likely that on the western prairies wind power will be the dominant source of renewable fuel in this century. Unlike solar panels, windmills can be detached from buildings and do not affect their shape.

The only mechanical devices required to help with cooling the units would be fans. Ceiling fans and ventilators could be used to great advantage during periods when there is little airflow, but if the units are well designed and have good cross-ventilation, this need is minimized.

Building Arrangement on the City Block

Under the circumstances described, buildings will not necessarily need to be oriented to the street with a "front" or "back" side, as buildings should always be oriented to the sun. Consequently, the more closed, north side of one building would face the more open, south side of its neighbor. This creates an arrangement similar to that of the Charleston townhouse (see Chapter 5), with one building looking at the mostly blank wall of the one to its south. This might imply a sidewalk not only on the perimeter of the block, but through its center, so that residents and their guests will have access to all units from the north side of the building.

The Prospect for Future Urban Development on the Great Plains

It is likely that there will be fewer people living out on the prairies on small to mid-size farms due to the continued expansion of larger agribusiness there. Likewise, modern, mechanized agricultural methods will only exacerbate the exodus. Little new industry to take its place is likely to be developed here either because (1) it is distant from coastal transportation, (2) there is a lack of natural resources, and (3) there is no available labor force except in the southern precincts where unskilled Latinos could provide it. As a consequence, more people will move into cities and towns or even small farming communities. Most of this future population growth will be at its periphery. Denver, Dallas, Austin, and San Antonio should continue to grow and prosper, as their economies are diverse and come from other sources than exclusively farming and ranching.

It seems that the region will continue indefinitely into the future with agriculture as its mainstay, despite the problem of a dwindling water supply. At some future point, this problem will not be avoidable and must be faced. We are in no position to predict when this will happen, but it might be best to start the process and work toward a solution before it becomes unsolvable.

Figure 6.13
As The Windiest Part Of The
U.S., Wind Turbines Are Now
Becoming A Common Sight
Across The Plains

Oil, gas, wind, and solar power will surely give those that live here more than adequate sources of cheap energy and some employment opportunities as well for some time into the future. Even though it seems that we now have an endless supply of petroleum, it, like water, is finite. Clearly, the great travel distances required to circulate in these farming communities will put added stress on their viability, as gasoline inevitably becomes more expensive toward mid-century. Those communities that remain here will need to consolidate their future urban growth in order to conserve energy.

Like in the West, the intense sun and wind, which creates so many problems on the Great Plains, may begin over the course of this century to provide for most of the region's energy needs. The western part of Texas is now the leading source of wind power in the nation.[46] It is important to reassess the place of these resources and their possible future benefit. The answers to many of our current problems may be found in these technologies discovered long ago, but have been forsaken.

Summary of Suggested Building Practices for the Great Plains

Main environmental objectives: In the southern portions design for mild winters and hot summers; severe winters the farther north one moves. Strong winds and even tornados are another major concern throughout.

Orientation

- Living areas should be south to southeast facing
- Share as many walls as possible with neighbors, particularly in the northern locations
- East and west walls should have only a few or no openings

Layout

- Generally, compact volumes are recommended, but in southern parts of the region, more spread-out arrangements can be afforded
- In the south, courtyards may be used to obtain shade and shut out hot, dry winds
- Wide, overhangs on the south side to protect exterior walls and windows from intense summer sun
- Provide shaded areas for living and working outside, such as courtyards and porches
- High ceilings to keep heat up and off occupants in the south with lower ones (8' maximum) in the far north
- Provide a readily accessible, secure storm shelter below the ground level

Construction

- Build on the ground or into it to keep temperatures stable and avoid strong winds
- Walls and roofs should be well-insulated
- Bearing wall constructed of brick, stone, earth, or adobe—last alternatively is dimensional lumber
- Light wood or engineered lumber is the most desirable framing material and is most appropriate for floor, wall, and roof structures
- Light, reflective exterior wall and roof colors in lower half of the region; in northern areas, this is not so important

Roofs

- Flat or modestly pitched to avoid high wind pressure
- Green and/or usable flat roofs
- Roof covering of baked clay tile or wood shingles on pitched roofs or earth on flat green ones

Shading

- Overhangs, particularly on the south side
- Exterior solid or louvered shutters, particularly on the west side, less important on the east side
- Covered walkways, verandas, balconies, and arbors

Windows

- Maximum opening for air flow—casement or awning most desirable
- Should be minimal on west- and east-facing walls
- South side can afford more glass (if shaded for summer sun) to warm interiors in winter
- North side can have some glass with the most in southern parts where cold is not such an issue

Ventilation and Cooling

- No double-loaded corridors that block air flow between units. Use either single-loaded or separate stairs towers.
- Good cross-ventilation is very important, particularly in the south.
- Cross-ventilation must be controlled, as it can introduce hot or cold air in at unwanted times.
- Window should allow full ventilation when open as with awning or casement types.
- Fans can be used to augment air circulation within dwelling and to exhaust hot air build-up.

- In the south, roof monitors may be used to exhaust hot air build-up
- Roof and wall color should be light to reflect sun's rays

Heating

- Minimal space heating required in each room in south, but central heating is required farther north
- Fireplaces or wood stoves can help to add warmth in winter
- Protect from strong, cold winds by use of vegetative screens, solid walls, and/or earthen berms on windward side of buildings

Water

- Channel rainwater away from the structure and into cisterns
- Collect all gray water for flushing toilets and watering garden plants

Alternative Energy

- Wind and solar are both effective systems, depending on a specific location within the region

Notes

1 Wikipedia. *Great Plains*. Website: https://en.wikipedia.org/wiki/Great_Plains.
2 Wikipedia. *Great Plains*. Website: https://en.wikipedia.org/wiki/Great_Plains.
3 Reisner, Marc. *Cadillac Desert: The American West and Its Disappearing Water*. Penguin Books (1993) New York. p. 435.
4 Mason, Jim. *Flora and Fauna of the Great Plains*. The Great Plains Nature Center. Website: www.gpnc.org/floraof.htm.
5 Wishart, David J. (Ed.). *Encyclopedia of the Great Plains*. University of Nebraska Press (2004) Lincoln, NB. p. 614.
6 Wishart, David J. (Ed.). *Encyclopedia of the Great Plains*. University of Nebraska Press (2004) Lincoln, NB. p. 614.
7 Wishart, David J. (Ed.). *Encyclopedia of the Great Plains*. University of Nebraska Press (2004) Lincoln, NB. p. 437.
8 Wishart, David J. (Ed.). *Encyclopedia of the Great Plains*. University of Nebraska Press (2004) Lincoln, NB. p. 615.
9 *National Geographic*. Great Plains Map. Website: http://ngm.nationalgeographic.com/ngm/0405/feature1/map.html.
10 *National Geographic*. Great Plains Map. Website: http://ngm.nationalgeographic.com/ngm/0405/feature1/map.html.
11 Wishart, David J. (Ed.). *Encyclopedia of the Great Plains*. University of Nebraska Press (2004) Lincoln, NB. p. 15.
12 USGCRP. Karl, Thomas R., Melillo, Jerry M., and Thomas C. Peterson (Eds.). *Global Climate Change Impacts in the United States*. Cambridge University Press (2009), New York. Website: www.epa.gov/climatechange/impactsadaptation/midwest.html.
13 *Water Encyclopedia*. Ogallala Aquifer. Website: www.waterencyclopedia.com/Oc-Po/Ogallala-Aquifer.html.
14 Wishart, David J. (Ed.). *Encyclopedia of the Great Plains*. University of Nebraska Press (2004) Lincoln, NB. p. 38.

15 Duncan, Marvin. Fisher, Dennis, and Mark Drabenstott. *Planning for a Sustainable Future in the Great Plains*. Website: www.iisd.org/agri/nebraska/duncan.htm.

16 *National Geographic*. Great Plains Map. Website: http://ngm.nationalgeographic.com/ngm/0405/feature1/map.html.

17 *National Geographic*. Great Plains Map. Website: http://ngm.nationalgeographic.com/ngm/0405/feature1/map.html.

18 *The Daily Yonder: Keep it Rural*. The Great Plains Since 1950. Website: www.dailyyonder.com/great-plains-1950/2009/07/15/2232.

19 *The Daily Yonder: Keep it Rural*. The Great Plains Since 1950. Website: www.dailyyonder.com/great-plains-1950/2009/07/15/2232.

20 Hargreaves, Steve. *North Dakota Grows Five Times Faster Than Nation*. CNN Money, June 6, 2013, Website: http://money.cnn.com/2013/06/06/news/economy/north-dakota-economy/.

21 U.S. Census Bureau. *Population Dynamics of the Great Plains: 1950 to 2007*. July 2009. p. 15. Website: www.census.gov/prod/2009pubs/p25–1137.pdf.

22 Wishart, David J. (Ed.). *Encyclopedia of the Great Plains*. University of Nebraska Press (2004) Lincoln, NB. p. 184.

23 Wishart, David J. (Ed.). *Encyclopedia of the Great Plains*. University of Nebraska Press (2004) Lincoln, NB. p. 184.

24 Raban, Jonathan. *Bad Lands: An American Romance*. Vintage Departures (1996) New York. pp. 145–146.

25 Horning, Jonathan. *Simple Shelters: Tents, Tipi, Yurts, Domes and Other Ancient Homes*. Bloomsbury (2009) New York. p. 18.

26 Horning, Jonathan. *Simple Shelters: Tents, Tipi, Yurts, Domes and Other Ancient Homes*. Bloomsbury (2009) New York. p. 18.

27 Nabokov, Peter and Robert Easton. *Native American Architecture*. Oxford University Press (1989) New York. pp. 150–163.

28 Horning, Jonathan. *Simple Shelters: Tents, Tipi, Yurts, Domes and Other Ancient Homes*. Bloomsbury (2009) New York. pp. 28–29.

29 National Park Service. *Knife River Indian Village*. Website: www.nps.gov/knri/historyculture/earthlodge.htm.

30 Nabokov, Peter and Robert Easton. *Native American Architecture*. Oxford University Press (1989) New York. pp. 126–143.

31 The Native American Earthroots. *The Earthlodge*. Website: http://nativeamericannetroots.net/diary/1074.

32 The Native American Earthroots. *The Earthlodge*. Website: http://nativeamericannetroots.net/diary/1074.

33 Kampinen, Andrea L. *The Sod Houses of Custer County, Nebraska*. Masters thesis, University of Georgia, (2008) Athens, GA. Retrieved 2011–10–22.

34 Jordan, Terry G. Hill Country. *Handbook of Texas Online* (www.tshaonline.org/handbook/online/articles/ryh02), Uploaded on June 15, 2010. Texas State Historical Association.

35 Jordan, Terry G. German Vernacular Architecture. *Handbook of Texas Online* (www.tshaonline.org/handbook/online/articles/cbg01), Uploaded on June 15, 2010. Texas State Historical Association.

36 PBS film. *Death of the Dream*. Homes on the Prairie. Website: www.pbs.org/ktca/farmhouses/homes_l.html.

37 Koop, Michael. German-Russians. In Upton, Dell (Ed.). *America's Architectural Roots: Ethnic Groups That Built America*. National Trust for Historic Preservation and John Wiley & Sons (1986). New York pp. 130–135.

38 Koop, Michael. German-Russians. In Upton, Dell (Ed.). *America's Architectural Roots: Ethnic Groups That Built America*. National Trust for Historic Preservation and John Wiley & Sons (1986). New York pp. 130–135.

39 Bakeless, John. *America as Seen by Its First Explorers: The Eyes of Discovery*. Dover Publications (1961) New York. p. 100.

40 Wishart, David J. (Ed.). Sod Wall Construction. *Encyclopedia of the Great Plains*. University of Nebraska Press (2004) Lincoln, NB. p. 94.

41 Koop, Michael. German-Russians. In Upton, Dell (Ed.). *America's Architectural Roots: Ethnic Groups That Built America.* National Trust for Historic Preservation and John Wiley & Sons (1986). New York pp. 130–135.

42 Wishart, David J. (Ed.). Stone Masonry. *Encyclopedia of the Great Plains.* University of Nebraska Press (2004) Lincoln, NB. p. 95

43 FEMA. Taking Shelter From the Storm: Building a Safe Room for Your Home or Small Business. (Dec. 2008). Website: www.fema.gov/media-library-data/20130726-1642-20490-5346/fema_l233_v3.pdf.

44 Reisner, Marc. *Cadillac Desert: The American West and Its Disappearing Water.* Penguin Books (1993) New York.

45 Plummer, Brad. How Long Before the Great Plains Runs Out of Water? *The Washington Post* (12/09/2013). Website: www.washingtonpost.com/blogs/wonkblog/wp/2013/09/12/how-long-before-the-midwest-runs-out-of-water/.

46 Forbes. *Texas Set New Wind Power Record.* (30/03/2014) Website: www.forbes.com/sites/peterdetwiler/2014/03/30/texas-sets-new-wind-power-record/.

Chapter 7
The West: Deserts and High Plains

Figure 7.1
The Western Landscape Is
Composed Of A Rich Palette
Of Earthen Hues

A long history marks this part of the country with distinction and character. Successive waves of immigrants invading from different directions, put down roots, reshaped, and melded with the cultures they found. Their stories were largely determined by the land's seemingly endless wide-open spaces and parched environment. The resulting amalgam of people with its desert landscape has given the West its uniqueness unmatched elsewhere in the nation. This process of change continues not only unabated, but accelerated by waves of sun-seekers from the north and job-seekers from across the border, staking out their own parts of the territory. This newest pattern of growth has yet

to meet a limit, but that is not to say there is not one. Many diverse challenges are now becoming more obvious as the region's population increases and resources are stretched. These challenges will, no doubt, give us yet another chapter in the evolution of this very special place.

The Place

The vastness of the landscape is the first thing that strikes a visitor to the American West—the big sky, distant views, and spectacular sunsets. Whether one is driving across these open plains or flying far above, this remarkable terrain tends to inspire great awe. Across this region, the land, which is generally flat or gently rolling, forms seemingly endless, wide-open spaces. Periodically, mesas, buttes, and mountain ranges rise up in sharp contrast to these open plains to punctuate the landscape. To appreciate its beauty, Wallace Stegner suggests that "You have to get over the color green; you have to quit associating beauty with gardens and lawns; you have to get used to an inhuman scale; you have to understand geological time."[1]

This dry, craggy land stretches well over a thousand miles from west Texas to the Pacific coast of southern California. It is bordered in the south by Mexico and runs north to Canada. To a great extent, the Rocky Mountains on the east and the Cascades and Sierra Nevadas on the west bookend the region. Its southwestern portion encompasses all of New Mexico and Arizona, the extreme westerly part of Texas as well as the most southerly part of California. The northerly tier encompasses Colorado, Nevada, Utah, Idaho, westerly Montana and Wyoming, and the easterly portions of Washington and Oregon.

Rivers have cut deeply into the soft, sandstone bedrock that comprises the foundation for the region, creating deep gullies or as the Spanish called them—*arroyos*. In contrast to the parched countryside, wherever rivers run through these channels, one finds their banks green with vegetation. These oases offer cool respites with their welcoming shade provided by native cottonwood, mesquite, live oak, and desert willow trees. Most such watercourses have their genesis from the snowmelt of the Rockies and other more local ranges. Large or small, they all flow either southeasterly by way of the Rio Grande River to the Gulf of Mexico or southwesterly via the Colorado River to the Gulf of California in Mexico.

The region is made up of three primary ecological zones—defined as desert, high dry plains, and Mediterranean. The arid desert zone is composed of the Chihuahua, Great Basin, Mojave, and Sonoran deserts. The Colorado Plateau and parts of west Texas make up the semi-arid high plains. The Pacific coast of southern California represents the moister, more moderate Mediterranean climate. Across these three zones, the constants are: (1) large amounts of sunshine—more than in any other region of the United States, (2) low amounts of rainfall and humidity, and (3) a distinct temperature difference between warmer days and cooler nights.

In the most arid of the desert areas, fewer than 4 inches of rain may fall in a year. The winters can be cold, with temperatures briefly dropping below 30°F, but the summers are always extremely hot with temperatures soaring well above 100°F.

The climate of the semi-arid high plains composed of the "intermountain basin and plateaus are comparatively uniform over a large area of grass lands . . . with cold, windy winters and warm, dry summers."[2] In this zone, temperatures can fall to below zero in winter and rise to highs over 100°F in summer. Strong winter winds can make already low temperatures feel much colder.

The Mediterranean climate found on the Pacific coast of southern California is normally dry, yet more moderate in temperature. In major cities of the area, such as Los Angeles and San Diego, temperatures do not vary much and are usually "in the 60s°F (15.6°C) from December through May, and in the 70s°F (21.1°C) from June through November. What passes for a rainy season here generally lasts from November to February, but an entire month's rainfall often comes in one day."[3]

In higher elevations, the "monsoons" can deliver sporadic, yet copious amounts of rainfall from July to September. When the rain comes fast and in large amounts, flash flooding can be the result, swelling deeply cut arroyos and sweeping away everything in its path. However, the West is best known for long periods of drought, without any significant rainfall. During such times, brush and forest fires are commonplace and dust storms can easily be whipped up by the high, dry winds.

This sometime inhospitable climate became the home to the earliest peoples who crossed the land bridge from Asia over 25,000 years ago. These first settlers evolved into various Native American groups. Some were nomadic, while others settled in one place and began farming. The pueblo peoples, such as the Navajo, Hopi, and Zuni, built cities of stone and mud, which housed tens of thousands of inhabitants. Farther to the north, the Great Basin tribes, such as the Shoshone and Ute, who were more nomadic hunter-gatherers, built less substantial brush shelters, lean-tos, and wickiups.

The Spanish were the first Europeans to settle here, quickly subjugating the native peoples, imposing their religion, and making their own distinct mark on the land. They came from a place thousands of miles away, but one that shared with their new homeland a similar landscape and climate. They easily adapted to this new, yet familiar environment. They laid out numerous towns with gridded street patterns and central plazas, built Catholic missions, and took up ranching and farming.

The Mexicans, upon gaining their independence from Spain in 1821, occupied and governed much of the territory in their turn. However, their hold on it was weak and their tenure a relatively short one. Texans overthrew them in 1836 and established their own republic. In 1848, the American troops defeated them and annexed the rest of Mexican lands north of the current border. Americans had been settling in the territory since the early nineteenth century, but they began to swarm into it in much larger numbers once gold was discovered in California. Later, the railroad ensured a steady flow of American immigrants to the region, solidifying their place in its development. Anglo prospectors, ranchers, and farmers contributed to creating legends of the "old west" that live on today as a part of its collective heritage.

Due to its desolate nature, during its early history, most of this vast region remained largely unsettled. As a result, the federal government or Native Americans now control at least half of the overall land area. 85 percent of Nevada, two-thirds of Utah and Idaho, and most of California, Wyoming, Arizona, and New Mexico are not controlled by the states themselves.[4] Today, there is great pressure being brought to bear by large corporations, ranchers, and farmers wanting to develop the mineral wealth, to graze and lumber federal lands, creating conflict with environmental groups wanting to conserve it.

Most recently, the warm climate and employment opportunities have contributed to the overall attractiveness of the southern part of the region. During the latter half of the twentieth century, large numbers of retirees retreating from the harsher northern climes settled here. The shared border with Mexico makes it a natural entry point for large numbers of Latinos seeking employment and opportunity in the U.S. Today, this group represents approximately one-sixth of the total population in the U.S., but in a belt from Central California to the Rio Grande Valley, it is much higher. The demographics

of the region continue to evolve in this way to create a very diverse, yet stratified socio/ economic mixture.

Figure 7.2
Downtown Phoenix, AZ, Shines At Night, But Lacks Activity

The West is growing more quickly than the rest of country, except for the South. Its major cities are Albuquerque, Phoenix, Tucson, Salt Lake City, El Paso, Reno, Las Vegas, and San Diego, with Los Angeles being by far the most populous. Some have questioned the wisdom of building major cities in a land with so little water, but their growth continues unabated.

Early Development Patterns

The basic layout of western cities and towns has developed over a long period of time through the influence of several cultures. The first of these, the Native American pueblo builders focused their developments first and foremost on the sun. The sky with its celestial bodies had great religious and symbolic meaning, dictated the timing of rituals, determined planting times as well as the overall physical shape and orientation of their communities. These mega-buildings varied in numerous ways from one to the next, but maintained through design a common thread of multistoried, compactness that helped perpetuate a strong sense of community.

In the late sixteenth century, the Spanish encoded in the *Law of the Indies* the manner in which all newly established towns in their territories in the New World were to be laid out. It prescribed in 148 individual sections where the most appropriate land for such development was to be found, how they were to be divided, laid out, used, and maintained. The focal point of any town was to be a centrally located square or rectangular, main *plaza*. A measurement of 600' by 400' was suggested as a good general size. Furthermore, towns were to be oriented with their corners to the prevailing wind(s), in order to avoid much "inconvenience," which could result in a street grid oriented at a

REINVENTING AN URBAN VERNACULAR

45° angle from the cardinal north/south axis. Roads were to be wide in cold climates to let sun in and narrow in hot ones where shade was desirable. Around the main plazas were to be located the important buildings of the town. Despite this lengthy set of rules, many early western towns established under Spanish authority began with these intentions, but later deviated and derived their forms from the local physical context of topography and natural features. In time, these strict guidelines evolved into barrios with tightly packed housing centers with small roads networks through. The cluster housing created shaded streets for easy walking.[5]

When the Americans took over, their traditional north/south grid was implemented and prevails in most cases to this day. Blocks are large, carved from the mile-square sections laid out in the nineteenth century. As in many other places, cities developed in a rather independent way as blocks of farm or ranch land were given over to development. With few obstacles in the open flat land, streets could be made wider here than elsewhere and straight with few variations for miles.

Precedents

Since the very first settlers put down roots in the West, each successive wave of newcomers brought with it a unique way of life and its own particular architectural approaches. Since little construction took place in the northern portion of the region before the end of the nineteenth century and most of it occurred in the area we commonly refer to as the Southwest, it is here where the following precedents are found. Most of them were imported building traditions that were gradually transformed by local culture and the climate into yet another unique regional typology. As with other vernacular architecture, early builders of the region were led by the necessity to find practical solutions to meet their needs. The Native American Hogan and pueblo as well as the Spanish missions and homes clearly exemplified this process. The last wave of settlers, the Americans, added their craft in woodworking to the mix. The results are an intriguing mixture of practical solutions developed from greatly diverse cultures and traditions in response to the requirements of this new land.

The Hogan

It is surmised that when the Navajo Indians migrated from Canada about 1400 AD, they brought with them the concept for a primitive shelter built of earth and wooden poles, which evolved into what we now know as the Hogan. The earliest versions, while simple, served as basic protection from winter weather and the summer's searing sun. It was little more than a circle of poles leaning in to one another, teepee fashion, which were then covered with leaves, bark, and earth. Over time, this basic form evolved into a more spacious and permanent dwelling.

Hogans were built in three basic ways—the conical forked-pole Hogan (male), the four-sided leaning log Hogan, and the polygonal, corbelled roof Hogan (female). Whereas the first two were built with logs standing on end, the polygonal Hogan was composed of logs stacked one on the other. Usually based on a hexagonal or octagonal plan, walls rose vertically to head height where they began to step (corbelled) inwardly to create a dome-shaped roof. This last iteration developed most fully as a result of having an adequate supply of railroad ties for wall material.

Figure 7.3
A Reconstruction Of A Typical
Navajo Hogan Of The Southwest

All three types shared several basic elements to their makeup. A fire was located in the center with a smoke hole directly above it. The doorway openings faced the rising sun in the east, which was usually away from the prevailing wind. A portico was often erected in front of the entrance and an outer and an inner curtain hung to keep out the stronger and cold winter winds. Walls and roof were covered with boughs and sealed with mud after which a thick layer of earth was added.

Most Navajo families had two or more Hogans—one in the desert and one in the mountains as they moved seasonally in search of fresh pastureland for their sheep. During pleasant days, they lived outside of the main building in the open air or in a smaller, less well-made summerhouse.[6]

The Pueblo

In the early sixteenth century, when the Spanish first encountered these impressive Native American megastructures, they gave them the modest name of pueblo. The title pueblo, which can be translated as simply village or town, does not adequately capture the uniqueness or beauty of these settlements. Southwestern pueblos are dense urban developments that were created in response to local ecology and specific social forces. They are collections of multiple units placed side by side and one on top of another. As they rise from one floor to the next, they also stepped back in a stair step fashion, with the lowest to the south and the tallest usually to the north. They were frequently three or four stories in height, and at times, reached five stories. Some of the oldest of these "big houses" as they are called are found in Chaco Canyon. Each of the 14 major buildings in the canyon was composed of no less than 100 rooms, ranging up to nearly 700 rooms.[7]

South-facing units opened out onto a public plaza "that connected their settlements to the forces of the cosmos, represented in the form of the celestial sphere and the

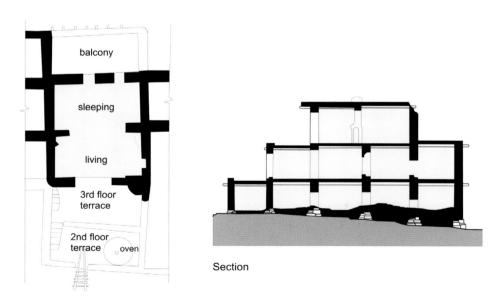

balcony

sleeping

living

3rd floor
terrace

2nd floor
terrace   oven

Section

Figure 7.5
Pueblo   Plan

mountainous horizon. Such plazas both accommodated public festivals and rituals and symbolized the spiritual connections of its inhabitants to the divine. This kind of plaza became both the crucible of daily life and the axis mundi of the pueblo people."[8]

The ground floors of the original pueblos had no doors or windows, thereby creating a protective one-story wall around the entire town. Pueblo dwellers used external ladders to access each level, so during times of attack, they raised their ladders and fought their enemies from above. The windowless units on the first floor and others buried below the upper units were normally used for storage, while the ones exposed to the southern sun were for living. "Rooms were often organized into suites, with front rooms larger than rear, interior, and storage rooms or areas."[9]

"The basic room was approximately 12 feet wide, 14 feet long, and no more than 7 feet from hard-packed floor to ceiling rafter."[10] These living units had very small openings for windows and doorways, which let in only a limited amount of daylight, while the thick exterior walls blocked most of the sun's heat. Originally, there were no doors or glass windows, but hides were used to shield the unit from outside weather. As openings existed only on one wall, there was no cross-ventilation within the living unit. This lack of air movement was not considered a disadvantage, as the air temperature was often too hot for comfort and its movement over the skin would only make one hotter. The result was cool interiors that gave one comfort during the heat of the day.

Much of the Indians' time was spent outside on the roof terraces where they dried their produce, worked, socialized, and held community events. To make these exposed areas more comfortable, they often built overhead stick frameworks, or *ramadas* for

Figure 7.6
Zuni Terrace Houses, As Photographed By Edward S. Curtis In 1903

REINVENTING AN URBAN VERNACULAR

shade.[11] Interior and exterior spaces were used for both living and working, so to maximize comfort, one moved to an area that was most suitable for the task. On warm evenings, they slept outside on the rooftops where it was coolest, but when it became colder outside, they moved indoors. During cold weather, the internal living areas were warmed by small fireplaces, which provided adequate heat to keep the occupants comfortable.

The stone or earthen walls were thick, with the lowest parts measuring over 3 feet at times, gradually getting thinner with each ascending story. Stone walls were usually dry-stacked or chinked with an earthen mortar. The mud walls were built by means of a freeform "puddling" method, which the Indian builders had developed. It was not until the Spaniards arrived that molded adobe bricks were introduced.

These thick walls served to moderate the heat and cold by acting as "heat sinks." That is to say, the walls absorbed the heat of the strong sunlight during the day, while keeping the interior cool. Then at night, as the outside air cools, the warmed walls radiated some of the day's absorbed heat into the interior spaces, helping to keep them comfortable. Additionally, by sharing walls with adjoining units, the overall surface area of the structure was reduced "by some 60 percent, and those exposed walls were very carefully oriented."[12] This reduction of exposed wall surface and generally southern orientation ensured the full climatic benefit of the layout. Additionally, the higher, north-facing walls shielded the residents from the harsh winter winds that blew down upon them from that direction.

Rooms were spanned over with a structure of exposed, rough-hewn wooden beams. Once the roof beams were in place, the wall was built higher to create a low parapet above the roof. Over the beams was placed a layer of smaller poles, then a layer thatch of straw. Finally, this built-up roof structure was covered with layers of mud and earth nearly 1 foot thick. As the pueblo builders lacked iron tools to shape and craft the wood beam, they frequently did not trim them to proper length, but allowed them to protrude beyond the outside wall. One additional benefit to this detail was that the wooden beams wicked moisture out of the earthen roof structure to help maintain a drier condition. The resulting extensions (*viga*) became a common feature in the southwestern adobe architecture. Once the structure was complete, the walls received a coating of mud plaster.[13]

To expedite drainage, the roof was slightly pitched to scuppers of hollowed-out logs, which projected out beyond the walls. Fortunately, rainfall was not usually so significant that it would soak through the roofing, but yearly maintenance and replastering was required to keep the roof watertight.

The pueblo represents a masterpiece of vernacular architecture. While providing protection from enemy attack, it offered its inhabitants a setting for communal events and social interaction. It offered relative comfort and shelter in a very harsh environment. It had a minimal negative impact on its natural environment, as their builders used the locally found resources for construction with amazing efficiency. The overall result was a beautiful and greatly admired urban form.

The Spanish Mission

Despite the Spanish reputation for seeking riches and exploiting the indigenous peoples in the New World, their primary, stated goal was to spread the Christian religion by converting the native population. The earliest Catholic friars to "found missions among the Indians came up the Chihuahua Trail with Juan de Onate and the first Spanish colonizing expedition in 1598. During the seventeenth and eighteenth centuries, Franciscans built roughly 100 mission churches across the Southwest, including more than two dozen in Texas, nearly four dozen in New Mexico, a handful in Arizona and more than 20 in California. Many missions decayed and fell into ruin over time. Some took root and endured."[14]

The focus of any mission compound was always the church, which dominated the complex due to its large mass, bell towers, and greater level of detail on its façade. Looming over the rest of the complex, it was designed to impress skeptics and the newly converted and to show the power that the Spanish god possessed. Beyond the obvious religious function, the church gave cool shelter to the faithful, and in times of war it provided a safe haven. In 1834, the Texans' defense of the Alamo makes this point very clear. The thick stone walls of the compound provided a sturdy, defensive haven from the Mexicans' bullets and cannon balls—at least for a time.

The grand monasteries of Europe with their elegant cloisters certainly served as prototypes for these simpler, frontier examples. A typical southwestern mission was laid out with one or more courtyards or quadrangles behind or to the side of the main church. Around the courtyard was a series of rooms that varied in function. This central space was called the *patio* or *plaza*, which was usually quite large. The Mission San Fernando Rey de Espana in southern California encompassed "a quadrangle of buildings around a patio that measured 295 feet by 315 feet, and included storage, living quarters for the Tongva Indians (later called Fernandeños), a flour mill, and workshops for making wine and brandy, candles and soap, for carpentry, weaving, and saddlery."[15] These open plazas served as focal points for large community and religious events and activities.

Figure 7.7
This Photograph Taken By Walter Smalling, Jr. Of The Mission Church At Taos, NM, Reflects The Power And Simple Elegance Of Its Adobe Forms

The buildings were constructed with essentially the same basic techniques that the pueblo used. All walls were composed of either adobe brick or stone. They could be quite massive, with the mission church having walls up to 7 feet in thickness at their base. Massive wooden beams accommodated the roof structure of the main church building, which required a long span. Openings in the walls were few and only of very minimal size designed to let in an adequate amount of light, but exclude the heat of the mid-day sun.

There were rarely any overhangs on these buildings, but porticos attached to them connected the rooms surrounding the quadrangles. The portico served to shade the adjoining rooms from the sun as well as to provide additional out of doors living and work areas. As with Indian dwellings, the roofs of most buildings were flat and could be used for sleeping as well as various other practical functions.

The Courtyard Houses

The courtyard house is an ancient concept that is found in many arid parts of the globe. Most likely, the Moors brought this building idea to Spain with them from the Middle East and the Spaniards subsequently imported it to their new territories in North America. It clearly fit the needs of both cultures as they equally valued privacy and security, which its inwardly focused layout made possible. Upon arrival in the New World, the Spanish found an environment much like that of their homeland and one where the courtyard could be readily adapted.

Figure 7.8
Martinez Hacienda, Taos, NM

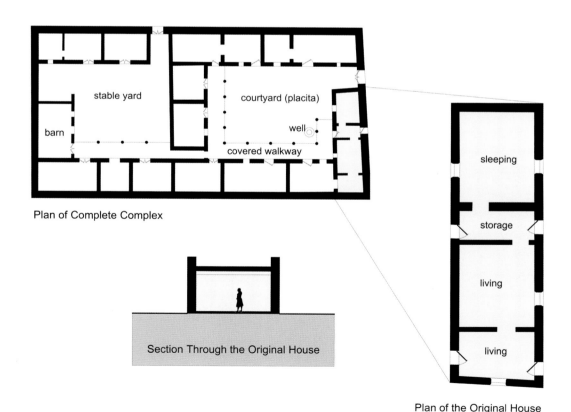

Plan of Complete Complex

stable yard

barn

courtyard (placita)

well

covered walkway

Section Through the Original House

sleeping

storage

living

living

Plan of the Original House

In addition to its other virtues, the courtyard has certain environmental characteristics that make it work particularly well in hot, dry climates. The walls of the courtyard provide a cool shade over a great deal of the interior during the day, while those walls exposed to the direct rays of the sun absorb its heat. At night, the cool evening air descends into the courtyard as the day's heat rises from it. As a result, the courtyards are cool by morning. This cycle continuously modifies the climate within the courtyard, keeping it within a narrow temperature range, which results in a much more pleasant environment here than elsewhere even on the hottest days.

Aside from protecting oneself from the sun and introducing a flow of air into the dwelling, the courtyard can contain fountains and pools and be filled with plants to create the next best thing to a beautiful oasis within. Water from the pools evaporates and the plants transpire adding humidity to the dry air, which can make a noticeable difference in improving one's level of comfort.

The first structures that the Spanish (and later the Mexicans) built around courtyards were mission complexes, military compounds (*presidios*), and ranch houses (*rancheros* or *haciendas*). As the Spanish were not always welcomed conquerors, they were most useful as defensive structures; with its environmental advantages a secondary consideration. In the case of the *presidios* and in some of the missions, the courtyards were rather large, as they needed to accommodate communities of people and could be better regarded as quadrangles.

While the Spanish–Mexican *rancho* or *hacienda* was designed as a combined frontier home and ranch/farm compound, it also served as a fort to defend against hostile Indian attacks. Built with thick adobe walls, flat roofs, and few or no exterior openings, they had similar defensive advantages as the missions. The rancho was normally only one-story tall and encompassed one or two large courtyards (*placitas*). Typically, one courtyard was surrounded by the living quarters, while the other was used to house the livestock—mainly sheep, cattle, and horses.

They were built with walls of adobe brick, often 2 feet thick, which resulted in cool interiors on hot days. Open air corridors were frequently attached to their exteriors to protect the building and window openings from the sun and to provide outdoor spaces where the residents could escape the interior confines on pleasant evenings.

Figure 7.9
The Severity Of Design Of Martinez Hacienda Near Taos, NM, Reflects The Need Of The Earliest Hispanic Settlers To Defend Themselves From Marauding Indians

Figure 7.10
Old Fisherman's Wharf In
Monterey, CA, Is One Of The
Few Remaining Examples Of The
Influence Of The Yankee
Craftsmen On Hispanic Building
In The Early Nineteenth Century

The Monterey House

Until nearly the mid-nineteenth century, the typical Spanish/Mexican home was built of thick adobe walls, which were capped with either a flat or low-pitched tile roof. Often they grew by the addition of one or two rooms at a time as the family's size or fortunes grew. Because there were few connections between rooms, most were entered from the outside off of covered walkways. As weather conditions were usually pleasant, a lot of family living and most cooking was done outside, frequently under shade-giving arbors. In towns, houses often shared a party wall with their neighbor, making a continuous row along the streets. In describing such streets in Santa Fe in 1840, an American, Matthew V. Field, wrote, "A very pleasant effect produced by the grass growing on the tops of the houses, and as all dwellings are connected it is not uncommon to see children chasing each other the whole length of a street along the house tops."[16]

It was in the southern California town of Monterey that this Spanish-Mexican dwelling type merged with new American techniques and traditions. An American from the Boston area named Thomas O. Larkin is credited with these innovations. In 1835, he built the first two-story adobe home in California "with massive redwood timbers providing heavy structural frames and long-spanning rafters . . . The large square posts and beams were put together in much the same manner used in traditional timber framing on the East Coast. Horizontal and vertical members were joined with pegs, spikes and various methods of joinery to create a sturdy skeleton. This solid frame supported the second floor and roof, and held the adobe wall elements upright from within. The adobe walls created an exterior envelope around this internal frame, and were tied to it by the horizontal members that pierced the walls, holding wood frame and adobe walls together."[17] This wooden frame helped to stabilize the overall structure in times of earthquake, which adobe alone would not.

By projecting the second floor joists through the adobe wall, Larkin was able to add a balcony that ran the length of its street façade, thus creating the most distinctive feature of the new type. In future iterations, floor plans consisted of three, four, or more rooms arranged in a row along the front in the normal Hispanic pattern. Each of these upper rooms had at least one door onto the balcony, which also served as a hallway. In many cases, a second balcony was added to the rear of the building as well. In some instances, the overhanging balcony was supported by slim wooden pillars and used to cover a long veranda.[18] In the larger examples, low, one-story wings extended from the rear of the main house to enclose a pleasant garden reminiscent of attractive Mexican precursors.

Along a similar line, in 1850, Anglo settler, Louis Dorrance, built the first pitched-roof building in Santa Fe where the flat roof prevailed. "The building had a simple gable roof with wood shingles and a two-story porch across the front. The local population dubbed it 'Casa Americana' because it represented a new architectural style imported by the Americans sometimes referred to as 'territorial style.'"[19] Even though the pitched roof was not required in this semi-arid southwest, it did have the advantage of shielding the tops of adobe walls from any moisture infiltration, thereby reducing wall maintenance.

The New England ship-builders who settled in and around Monterey, California, brought advanced woodworking and carpentry skills to the area. "The many decorative wood details the ship carpenters gave to the houses provided their unique New England appearance."[20] To augment the New England feel to the basic house form, one could add a "decorative chimney cap or chimney hood; double-hung wood-frame windows with mullions; often, window shutters; occasionally, full-length windows opening onto the balcony; a relatively simple paneled entry door."[21]

Common Themes Found in the Traditional Buildings of the West

The homogeneous nature of the climate and traditions of the West are striking. Indian culture is still strong and influential in this part of the country and their native architecture has been widely adopted as an iconic style. Unfortunately, it now has little of its original substance or meaning. The lessons that the people of the West developed over centuries through trial and error are clear and deserve our attention as they can go a long way toward resolving many of the region's future problems.

Shape and Placement

The basic western building is cubic in form, a shape that tends to mitigate the worst effects of that hot/dry climate. Rooms are small due to a lack of long timbers to span larger spaces. Ceilings are as high as feasible to keep the heat up above the occupants. Buildings share party walls with neighbors, thereby reducing exposure to the sun. Whenever possible or desirable, units are stacked one upon another not only for economy, but also to consolidate the structure into a more cubic mass. Parapeted roofs were flat and meant to provide a place for living–work, social interaction, and relaxing, as well as a viewing platform of the community's daily life and frequent public ceremonies. Overhangs were rare, as they were difficult to build, and given the fact that rain was sparse, there was little need to shelter walls from the water.

Most living was traditionally spent outside with only cold or stormy weather requiring one to take shelter indoors. Winter living was usually done on the south side, which offered protection from north winds and where sun can reflect off walls to provide additional warmth. In summer, shade was desired during the day for most activities and was often provided under shade-giving structures, called *ramadas*. *Ramadas* were arbor-like structures composed of posts and beams of rough tree trunks and covered with reeds or cactus sinew. They were often located out in the open, away from buildings, so that cooling breezes could flow more freely. The use of landscaping for shade, while desirable, was not always practical, as there was rarely enough rainfall to sustain trees large enough to create an adequate amount of it.

As mentioned previously, many traditional urban homes in the West were arranged around courtyards. These were normally single-family dwellings of only one story. The courtyards provided not only privacy, but shade in the shadow of the building's walls, assuring both a refuge from public view and the searing, summer heat.

Shelter, Construction, and Materials

A very dry, nearly rain-free, environment allowed for the use of the area's most abundant construction resource, earth, which has been used since earliest times. Thick adobe and rammed earth walls with earth-covered roofs were the most common methods of construction. They were desirable for their low cost and their ability to mediate climate by acting as heat sinks.

Heating, Cooling, and Ventilation

In the West, "since humidities are very low, cross-ventilation is not mandatory: indeed, at midday in mid-summer, air temperatures are so high that a breeze passing across the skin would add more heat by conduction than perspiration could dissipate. Thus the typical desert form is closed, centripetal, uses a very limited number of small openings to cut down heat and glare."[22] Therefore, in many cases, traditional buildings, such as the pueblos, did not rely on ventilation for cooling, as any opening could allow hot air in, which might then prove difficult to exhaust.

However, there are many instances when a steady flow of air can be cooling. In the border town of Ures, New Mexico, there are many examples of houses with a central hall or breezeway that connects the street to the interior patio known as *zaguán*. Furthermore, they usually "open to adjoining rooms, (and) draws fresh air into the interior of the house by means of natural convection."[23]

Natural Resources Available for Construction

The West is rich in sustainable building materials such as earth, stone, and to a lesser extent, wood. These resources have served the people of the area well since the first arrivals set down roots millennia ago.

It is extremely fortunate that stone and earth are both found in such abundance, thereby meeting the first test for sustainability. Additionally, they require no energy other than muscle power to build them into thick, thermal-absorbing, load-bearing walls. Nor are either of them subject to rot, insect damage, or fire. On the negative side, they are subject to earthquake damage. Fortunately, with the exception of southern California, the region is not prone to these events. Another negative is that they are very labor-intensive to put in place, and therefore could be expensive, where labor is not cheap. While stone is impervious to the elements, earth can be damaged by wind and water.

Native Americans did not have the technology of the vault or the dome, which used stone or brick, to span over their spaces. Consequently, wood was traditionally used to complete their structures by spanning between the masonry-bearing walls. Unfortunately, wood is relatively scarce in this region. While renewable, it must be transported from distant sources, which tends to compromise its claim to sustainability.

Stone

Native American groups, such as the Anasazi, built some of the most beautifully constructed stone buildings in the southwest. It is the most durable on the list of natural building materials, as it does not burn or rot, and it can withstand millennia of weathering with no ill effects. In the West, stone is found in abundance either on the ground ready for use or in exposed rock faces where it can be easily extracted.

In the region, sandstone and limestone make up the preponderance of the rock used in construction. While somewhat different from one another, they share many of the same characteristics, as both are classified as sedimentary rock. This type of stone is created from the accumulation of small particles, which are compressed over a very long period of time. These particles may be derived from either wind-blown sand, sediment deposited from ancient rivers, streams, or lakes, or tiny marine creatures. In the case of sandstone, the elements are usually small bits of sand, whereas limestone is composed of crustaceans from long-receded oceans.

Colors vary greatly between the different types of stone. Limestone frequently has a gray to yellowish hue. Sandstone comes in a wide range of colors with pink to dark red predominating as the result of the presence of iron oxide. Other minerals, such as manganese, which gives a purplish hue, add to the wide variety of subtle shades, imparting great character to the rock.

Both sandstone and limestone are extremely durable, lasting for all intents and purposes, forever. Even though they can be eroded under freezing and thawing conditions, if water is allowed to saturate them, the most severe weathering, which the deserts and high plains can muster, rarely reach these extremes. Stone buildings of ancient origins have fallen into disrepair and their walls have collapsed, but the stones have not suffered noticeable deterioration and are ready to be reused.

Because the sediment that created the stone was put down in layers, the excavated rock often comes out as neat, flat slabs suitable for construction. Even though the pueblo Indians did not work these slabs, but used them in their natural state, the stone broke off in such neat blocks that they could lay it in a consistent manner that gave the impression of being shaped.

Traditionally, Native American builders often mortared the stones together with mud. This gave some limited structural value to the wall and helped fill the gaps left between the stones, thereby making the wall more cohesive. These walls depended for their strength on their great thickness or mass. In some early mission churches, where the walls could reach 50 feet in height, the base of the wall might exceed 7 feet in width. In some cases, these walls were further strengthened by the addition of massive, tapering buttresses. Naturally, the thickness of the walls was reduced as they ascended.

With some notable exceptions, such as the structures in Chaco Canyon, the native stone construction was more primitive than that of their European counterparts. The arch, vault, and dome are all techniques for using stone or masonry to span an opening or space that were not used in the West until the Spaniards introduced them in the missions of southern California in the early seventeenth century.

Though stone can often be easily quarried, it is labor-intensive to place, consequently expensive. Frank Lloyd Wright used stone extensively at his own home, Taliesin West, in Scottsdale, AZ. To reduce labor cost and the amount of concrete needed in a wall, he in-filled standard concrete forms with large and small loose stones and filled around them with a dry concrete mix. This technique could be useful in future building projects due to its sustainability and lower cost.

Earth

Earth is most likely the oldest building material known to man. It is probable that nearly one quarter of the world's population still live in dwellings composed of earth. It has certainly been the predominant construction material in the southwest until the twentieth century. Due to the abundance of easily excavated earth and clay soils, the region has developed a long tradition of earthen buildings that started with the Indians, later the Spaniards and Mexicans, and lastly the Americans. Many examples of these earthen structures are now several hundred years old and still in use.

Earth does not have the tensile strength that would allow it to span over openings (wooden or stone lintels have traditionally been used for this task), but it does well in compression and can be stacked for multiple stories as has been demonstrated in any number of pueblos.

As previously mentioned, earthen construction's main nemesis is water, and to a lesser extent wind, both of which can compromise its structural integrity and erode its mass. Also, any shifting of the earth that an earth structure rests upon can cause cracking, so building with this material in an earthquake zone would not be advisable.

On the positive side, earthen structures can be cheap (or even free) depending on the availability and cost of materials and labor. The technology is simple and not dependent on industrial processing, such as steel or concrete, avoiding those costs and negative environmental effects. Once constructed, it provides a wall that stores and releases energy slowly.

Adobe

Marc Treib in his book *Sanctuaries of Spanish New Mexico* clearly defines adobe as "a carefully balanced product of clay, soil, and a binder such as straw, all blended in proper proportion. Although the straw does not increase the tensile properties of the brick, during drying it helps modulate evaporation in different parts of the block. Too much clay in the mix causes the bricks to shrink and crack while drying; too much sand causes them to become brittle and fall apart. An ideal composition is required, a balanced mixture derived in any locality only through a process of trial and error."[24]

When the proper balance is struck, these sundried bricks make durable construction units as long as they are not exposed to moisture for an extended period of time. If protected, adobe masonry can last indefinitely. The Spanish built many of their mission churches with adobe and placed these walls on a stone foundation that extended 18 inches above the level of the ground to keep water away from the adobe walls.[25] Pueblo builders channeled rainwater off of roofs by way of hollow logs that extended well beyond the buildings' adobe walls. Most importantly, it was common practice to seal the vulnerable adobe brick with a thick coat of mud or lime plaster.

"The Indians built their pueblos on the basis of puddled construction: with or without a form, they piled up heaps of mud in layers to make walls. Piled up one or two feet at a time. But extensive time was needed for each layer of the walls to season properly, drying slowly to retard cracking."[26] The Spanish implemented the use of molds to form standard size blocks. They would lay up a couple of feet of these dried adobe bricks with adobe as mortar, making a homogeneous wall. As with the puddling technique, the adobe wall needed to dry out completely before the next layer commenced, which could take an extended period as construction had to be done when no rain was anticipated. Needless to say, the whole construction process could be very lengthy.

Rammed Earth

Rammed earth is an ancient construction technique that is used to build walls by compacting earth within a movable form. It has been heavily employed around much of the world, with the notable exception of the Western hemisphere. Large sections of the Great Wall of China were made in this way. The English, French, Germans, and other northern Europeans have produced many examples of multistory, domestic architecture that are several hundred years old that were made in this manner. Africans used this approach in all parts of the continent in various ways and continue to do so.

While perfectly suited to the desert regions of the southwest, it was never used by the indigenous peoples or by succeeding cultures. However, it has begun to gain popularity with many contemporary architects, who have used it with great success.

Rammed earth is traditionally constructed with essentially the same mixture of soils as adobe. The mix is placed in formwork, which is usually made of wood, akin to that used

Figure 7.11
Architect Rick Joy, In Tucson, AZ, Has Helped To Promote The Use Of Rammed Earth As A Modern Alternative As Shown Here In The Façade Of His Firm's Offices

in concrete construction. The sides of the form, which can be any workable height (most typically 18 to 24 inches) are usually widely set apart. The soil mix is added in layers of about 8-inches deep and then compressed to about 5 inches. Traditionally, this is accomplished by pounding the soil by hand with mallets. Once the form is completely filled and compressed, it is then removed and repositioned above the just completed wall and the process begins again. This results in a series of deep layers, which are stacked one upon another to the desired wall height.

Some of today's building codes require the addition of Portland cement to the soil mix to give the wall greater strength and weathering capabilities. Now, as a standard practice, some builders "mix cement with structural road base used in road building, commonly known by the name of 'ABC (aggregate base course)' with small hydraulic loaders . . . and compact it using pneumatic soil backfill tampers. This engineered soil is sometimes mixed with iron oxide or other agents to tint the soil to a desired color. The resultant strength of the soil mixes compacted in this way generally range between 300–800 psi, and building code requires that soil samples generally be tested by a certified engineer prior to the beginning of construction."[27]

The question is: Do these additives make the earth structure that much better than their predecessor, which were constructed of all natural products and have lasted centuries? In 2005, a group of MIT students constructed a test wall of rammed earth in Cambridge, Massachusetts, to explore its potential in a northern climate and developed innovative techniques for its construction. They used a conventional soil mix without any added cement, protected it with a metal cap, and raised it above the ground on concrete foundation system. Upon a recent examination, it still stands much as it did upon completion over a decade earlier.

Rammed earth walls share most of the advantages and disadvantages with those of adobe brick, but they can have an added bonus—a bold look of multicolored, wavy striations. For this reason, many rammed earth walls are left unplastered to reveal their intrinsic beauty both as an interior and exterior finish.

Clay Tile

Even though clay tiles are not used structurally, they represent another major construction resource. Mainly used as roofing or flooring, these are frequently handmade and sun-dried and/or kiln-baked. Flooring tiles left to cure on the open ground can frequently be embossed by a stray cur walking over them, thereby augmenting their uniqueness with a footprint. These products seem never to lose popularity. In some areas, metal roofs have supplanted the traditional tile ones and tile floors have given way to a wide range of petroleum-based products such as vinyl. Regardless, the industry remains strong. In Mexico, Saltillo "tile has been made using the same methods that were brought from Spain hundreds of years ago. The area around Saltillo has the proper mix of clay, climate and dedicated workers to produce one of the world's most popular tiles."[28]

To their detriment, clay tiles have the disadvantage of being brittle, and therefore breakable and subject to cracking. They are porous, so in some cases, floor tiles may need to be sealed for easy maintenance. On the more positive side, they are very sustainable and they elicit a soft beauty that imbues a traditional feel to any structure. Equally important, in an arid region subject to frequent, raging brush fires, they are fireproof. They have been the roofing and flooring material of choice for many generations and certainly are likely to serve well into the distant future.

Timber

In the West, timber is a precious commodity and a necessary one for the basic structure of any vernacular building. It is precious because the normally dry climate of the region does not support a large number of tall, fast-growing trees. They are found to a limited extent in the mountainous areas that interrupt the flat, dry plains and deserts of the region, where snow and rain are more likely to fall. The Native Americans used small trees, such as mesquite, which were more readily available, but could only span over short distances. This lack of size limited the width of their rooms of these very early domestic buildings to usually no more than 14 feet. The tree trunks were minimally worked as the Indians lacked iron tools. They stripped the bark but left the rounded shape intact, which resulted in an appealing, organic appearance.

The Spaniards and Americans cut larger trees in the mountains and dragged them down to their building site usually with the help of oxen. The Spaniards brought with them the tools necessary to shape wood into more useable rectangular forms. Later, American skilled carpenters arrived with even more advanced woodworking expertise and were able to add even finer detail to their buildings.

Mesquite, pine, and cottonwoods represent traditional species that were often used in construction. Mesquite, while dense, does not grow tall and is often twisted, making it a difficult wood to use in construction. Cottonwood grows fast, but it is not satisfactory for major structural pieces.[29] Today, evergreens, such as Douglas fir, Ponderosa pine, and Engelmann spruce, make up the preponderance of the species used in construction in the West.[30]

A heavy timber structural frame has many advantages that have been covered previously, but some relate more closely to the architecture of the southwest. When timber beams are left in a rounded, unworked state, they harken back to the Native American construction techniques, which give the structure a western look and feel. Another practical advantage is that heavy timber is fire-resistant, which is important in this dry, fire-prone region.

Unfortunately, the lack of locally significant quantities of large trees means that heavy timber must come from a distance. The transportation adds to their expense, and by definition, makes it less sustainable. As a consequence, much of the floor and roof structure must be built with thinner pieces of dimensional lumber, such as two by fours. Long spans therefore need to use engineered lumber or be prefabricated of numerous small, individual pieces into trusses.

Hay Bale

More recently hay bale construction has gained a degree of popularity with some of the more alternative builders of the region. This form of construction provides a well-insulated wall that is relatively cheap to build. It does have limits however; it is not load-bearing and needs to have a structure built over and around it. Additionally, hay bale walls must be encased in plaster on the outside to keep rainwater away from the straw, insects out, and to make it fire-resistant. On the inside, plaster or gypsum board is required to provide a finished surface. If not properly installed, mildew can become a problem in these walls. It is for these reasons the method does not seem appropriate in multifamily urban dwellings of several stories.

Figure 7.12
The Use Of Refined Concrete Block In The Walls Of These Modern Apartments Demonstrate How They Can Create An Elegant Exterior Surface

Concrete and Concrete Block

Concrete is not a sustainable material, as its manufacture contributes significant CO_2 emissions, but it seems that some concrete will always be a factor in construction because of its strength, durability, and fire-proof qualities. To limit the amount of concrete, but to get the best qualities that it offers, hollow concrete block presents a reasonable compromise. A hollow concrete block wall has most of the desirable qualities that a solid one does, but less concrete is involved as the blocks have voids in them. The result is that a typical concrete block contains about half the concrete of a solid wall. With the addition of steel-reinforcing bars, it is capable of resisting earthquake forces. A double concrete block wall composed of an inner and an outer layer of block can be filled with earth to obtain a wall that has the same mass and thermal qualities of traditional earthen ones. This has the added advantage of not using synthetic insulation made from petroleum.

Concrete is made from limestone, which can be easily quarried in abundance in the West, thereby making the transportation costs somewhat less than they would be otherwise. The basic environmental problem is one of refinement from the raw material into a usable form as a great deal of fossil fuel is required. Currently, the need to use concrete seems inescapable, but it should be minimized whenever possible.

The Current Approach to Design and Construction

Urban Development Today

Over the twentieth century, the region's development occurred in much the same way as it has in other parts of the United States. The automobile coupled with cheap, flat open land, enabled flight from cities and towns to increasingly distant suburbs. Long, straight streets, wide enough for five to eight travel lanes lined with drive-up stores extend outwardly without constraint into the desert. As elsewhere, the original centers of the western cities have developed with central business districts punctuated by a few tall buildings and very little housing to keep them lively after working hours. Until recently, there have been few attempts to make these urban centers walkable, as most people today consider the climate too hot to be out on the street during daylight hours. As a result, the parking garages are closely connected to office buildings and little activity takes place on the downtown sidewalks.

Figure 7.13
This New Housing Near Downtown Phoenix Demonstrates How Low-Rise, Multifamily Housing Can Be Built Near The Center Of Our Cities And Still Have A Connection To The Street And Help To Create Healthy Neighborhoods

REINVENTING AN URBAN VERNACULAR

Architectural Character

The unique character of southwestern vernacular architecture, as previously demonstrated, was created from fundamentals relating to climate, materials, and tradition, but current practices rarely take these values into account. Often, modern buildings appear as recreations of various historic styles, but are constructed by an array of modern techniques in lieu of traditional ones. Released by air conditioning from the need to rely on pragmatic determinants, some architects and builders now focus their designs on superficially re-creating the look of the past. Traditional building elements such as projecting *vigas* and softly rounded plastered adobe walls that evolved over centuries are being imitated in other less appropriate materials. A pastiche of styles—Pueblo, mission, Mediterranean, Spanish Revival, and Santa Fe—to name a few popular ones is currently the norm. This reliance on style to perpetuate the regional character is proving counterproductive, as this attempt to cloak new uses in traditional garb is creating monotony and Disneyesque neighborhoods and towns. When banks are designed to look like pueblos and shopping centers like frontier trading posts, little of substance is left of vernacular practicality. These current attempts to cling to traditional shapes and details reveal a rather desperate struggle to find a regional identity through past forms.

Popular Design and Construction Methods

Thick stone or earthen walls that once absorbed the sun's heat and released it slowly during the cool of the night have now been replaced with thin, well-insulated ones. The insulated wall is intended to keep the interior temperature stable with the help of mechanical systems, such as central heating and air conditioning.

These thinner walls are built with a variety of construction techniques. The majority of them are composed with wood or steel-stud framing with fiberglass and/or polystyrene insulation. It is typically covered on the outside with sheets of plywood or oriented strand board (OSB), metal or fiberglass lath and then plastered to resemble adobe. Alternatively, the siding might be covered by rigid expanded polystyrene insulation using a method called exterior insulation finishing system (EIFS). This is then stuccoed over as in the frame method. A concrete block wall is at times substituted for the light frame wall, resulting in a more substantial structure, which is also covered with insulation and plastered.

Another method of construction that is gaining some limited popularity is one called insulated concrete form (ICF). This method employs blocks of ridged insulation, which stack in brick fashion, and are used as forms for steel reinforced poured concrete. One company touts the product as follows: "Insulating Concrete Form (ICF) technology is a green and sustainable building system that delivers a foundation or wall that is highly energy efficient, structurally tough and has superior fire resistance and sound suppression. ICF construction is fast, easy and cost effective. ARXX ICF structures average 44 percent less energy to heat and 32 percent less energy to cool than conventional construction methods."[31]

These products are not perfect. "While older, traditional stucco walls were designed to get wet and readily dry out, the newer synthetic systems are less permeable to moisture. If trapped water cannot readily drain away or dry to the exterior, the underlying structure is more vulnerable to moisture damage."[32] The result of poorly installed modern walls as described earlier can be water damage to the frame and mildew in the wall itself. Expanded polystyrene has virtues, but it is difficult to think of it as a

Figure 7.14
This Project In Santa Fe, NM,
Shows How Current Construction
Practices Of Steel Studs Covered
By Rigid Insulation Form The
Basis For Pseudo-Adobe
Buildings In The Southwest

"green" or "sustainable" material. It must be considered first and foremost a long-lived, petroleum-based product, which throws off large amounts of carbon dioxide during its manufacture and uses limited resources in its production.

Western builders have, for the last century, adopted the conventional construction materials and methods used by the rest of the country, but with a southwestern overlay. This overlay is one of style, where traditional forms are imitated in looks alone—not substance. Thin, insulated walls have taken the place of thick heat-absorptive ones. Natural materials have been replaced with petroleum-derived products such as polystyrene.

The question for the future is: What can we do to regain a sense of place in the southwest while building in a sustainable manner that is both environmentally responsible and that can accommodate a comfortable, modern lifestyle?

Future Environmental Concerns

In general, the region is getting hotter and drier. Water is and will remain the main concern for the West as it "is prone to drought. Southwest paleoclimate records show severe mega-droughts at least 50 years long. Future droughts are projected to be substantially hotter, and for major river basins such as the Colorado River Basin, drought is projected to become more frequent, intense, and longer lasting than in the historical record."[33] Ramifications of a hotter, drier climate involve public heath, drinking water availability, loss of timber and crop production, insect outbreaks, and a greater frequency of devastating wildfires.

Water conservation is of special concern in this region, as this resource is so precious and limited. The implications of the prolonged lack of rainfall can be seen historically in the Anasazi experience of a 150-year drought from which they never recovered. Scientists discovered this phenomenon "by looking at tree rings (a study called dendrochronology) in the Sand Canyon area. In the period between A.D. 1125 and 1180, very little rain fell in the region. After 1180, rainfall briefly returned to normal. From 1270 to 1274 there was another long drought, followed by another period of normal rainfall. In 1275, yet another drought began. This one lasted 14 years."[34]

In 2008, the city of Tucson estimated that 45 percent of its water usage was dedicated for outdoor purposes.[35] This use of water is only possible while it is in reasonably good supply, but it must be remembered that this source is limited. Most of the water that is used in the southwest today now comes from its underground aquifers that are vast, but finite and being depleted quickly.

The region's current population of about 56 million people is expected to increase to 94 million by 2050. A severe and "sustained drought will stress water sources, already over-utilized in many areas, forcing increasing competition among farmers, energy producers, urban dwellers, and ecosystems for the region's most precious resource."[36]

Because water will become too valuable to waste, cisterns might be included in all new buildings and purified by use of a solar distilling process to make it potable. Unfortunately, many state and local regulations prohibit their use and "HUD Handbook 4150.2 Section 3–6 indicates that properties served by cisterns are not acceptable for mortgage insurance. However, the HOCs have the authority to consider waivers in areas where cisterns are typical."[37] These regulations must be changed, and no doubt, will be when supplies of water begin to run low.

Yet another concern with direct consequence to the construction industry is the potential loss of timber in the region due to global warming, which will increase the likelihood of forest fires and the invasion of damaging insect pests. We began to experience this phenomenon between 1970 and 2003, when burned areas in western U.S. mid-elevation conifer forests increased by 650 percent. In addition to this, the warmer winters have "exacerbated bark beetle outbreaks by allowing more beetles, which normally die in cold weather, to survive and reproduce."[38] Both fire and insect damage will have a severe and devastating effect on regional lumber production, which will in turn increase construction cost by reducing the availability of wood, one of our most desirable building materials.

As in other regions, western buildings need to be designed to work with the current and future local climate and provide a place where people can live full lives at one with their environment. One ought to try to go beyond construction methods, sustainable materials, and efficient layouts by incorporating our known passive technologies to produce some or all of the buildings energy requirements. The West, particularly the southwest, is in one of the more enviable positions to capitalize on their geography and climate to reach this end. There is no place in the United States where the sun shines brighter or longer than here. Solar collectors and photovoltaic units could grace every rooftop. Hot water, heat, and even electricity are all possible products of solar technology. Low-tech solutions such as the use of clotheslines to air-dry clothes work better here than anywhere else in the country in this arid climate with full sun all day.

Design Strategies and Building Components

Climatic Imperatives

In the hot/dry West, staying cool throughout the day is the greatest challenge for most of the year. Even though winters can be cold and windy at times, it is summer that presents the most severe extremes of temperature.

Orientation

Generally speaking, a south-facing orientation is a favorable one for buildings in all climates, as it is here. The typical living unit benefits from a south to southeast exposure, as the sun will be available to heat the units in winter and overhangs can more easily control the summer's stronger rays. Any walls with a western or to a lesser extent the eastern exposure should have few openings. North-facing walls will not benefit from warming winter sun, but do have the advantage of avoiding direct heat gain during the summer months.

Overall Suggested Configuration and Layout

Vernacular examples can be particularly helpful in determining the overall massing of future urban buildings. Traditionally, one-, two-, and even three-story urban buildings shared common walls with their neighbors, and many focused inwardly on private

Figure 7.15
Idea Drawing or The West

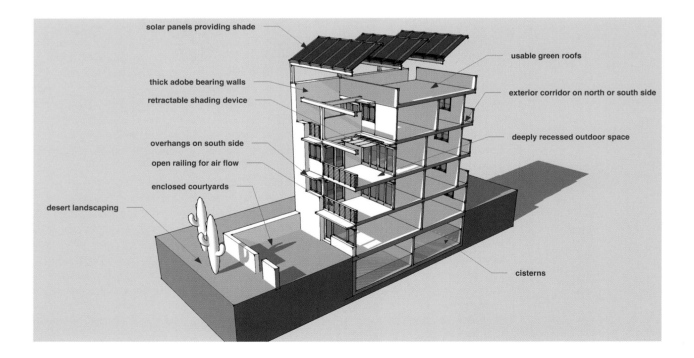

solar panels providing shade

usable green roofs

thick adobe bearing walls

retractable shading device

exterior corridor on north or south side

overhangs on south side

deeply recessed outdoor space

open railing for air flow

enclosed courtyards

desert landscaping

cisterns

courtyards. Pueblos typically stepped back from south to north in order to allow sunlight to reach outdoor spaces on every level. By adapting the traditional pueblo to more modern building forms, one can get the use of rooftops for outdoor space in the same way Native Americans did. Both of these arrangements, the courtyard and the stepping pueblo, help to save energy, materials, and buildable land while providing adequate, private outdoor living space. Some first floor one-bedroom units might be included in order to provide direct access for those challenged by stairs.

If floor areas diminish as they go up each level, so too will the size of units and the number of bedrooms in them. Therefore, it is suggested that the one-bedroom and studio units could occupy the top floors and two-bedroom units between the ground floor and the upper ones. The lowest floor could be composed of the largest units of three or more bedrooms. This arrangement gives the large families the advantage of ground floor living, where children can have direct access to open space, be it public or private.

Traditionally, in Latin societies, privacy is of major importance and the courtyard provided for this is nicely suitable, as it was hidden within the home. In more modern examples, where the outdoor space is more exposed, privacy can be maintained through the use of party walls and screens between abutting units and overhead, shading devices to shield them from neighbors' view.

Building Circulation—Halls and Staircases

In this region, units on the upper floors can be connected to the ground level by either stairways that serve a set of units exclusively (see Chapter 5: The South) or by open air corridors connected to stairs as shown. The more economical method is to use the latter, as it can serve many more units. It is recommended that these passageways have units on one side only (single-loaded), be roofed, but unenclosed and located on the north side of the building. By doing so, the corridors will be protected from the elements, but open to the fresh air. Also, the open hall on the north side will allow air to flow freely through the apartment units, without the interference that a double-loaded corridor would create.

Unit Plan

Individual apartments can be deeper in the West than in the more humid South, as constant air exchange is not as imperative and on very hot days can be considered a disadvantage. Consequently, the plan for the larger units can assume a squarer plan in lieu of a long rectangular one of the South.

The single-loaded corridor arrangement aforementioned should not result in the loss of privacy if entries, vestibules, kitchens, closets, and other spaces that require little or no privacy can be placed on the corridor side of the unit. Bathrooms can be located along them as well, if they are windowless with venting to the outside. Two-bedroom units, which require a good amount of window space, can benefit from being arranged in two-stories with the corridor only on the lower floor where semi-public living space occurs. This layout will allow upper-story bedrooms to face out in both directions. Three-bedroom units located on the ground floor level avoid any conflict, as no corridor is needed, due to the fact that these units have direct access.

Roof Type

Roofs in the southwest were traditionally flat until the Anglos arrived in the nineteenth century and promoted the widespread use of pitched ones. In the past, flat roofs made of earth had a problem with leakage as rainwater could seep into spaces below and compromise earthen walls supporting them. The pitched or sloped roof solves these problems by creating an impervious surface that channels the rainwater quickly away. Today, we have products that can offer a complete seal from the infiltration of water and allow us to use a flat roof, without worrying of leakage.

With the addition of a thick layer of sand and gravel over a waterproof membrane, a green roof planted with native vegetation is not only possible, but also highly desirable. Such a roof has several advantages. First, a green roof like this acts to further protect upper units from solar radiation by reflecting it due to its light color. Furthermore, it can serve to filter any rainwater that falls on it, which can then be channeled through drains into basement cisterns for future use. Finally, these roofs are ideal for outdoor living as in prior times. The sand/gravel layer can be partially covered with loosely laid baked clay or concrete slabs or flagstones to provide a hard, walkable surface suitable for most outdoor activities. These advantages tend to make the argument for this type of flat roof a powerful one.

Where flat roofs are not chosen, a pitched roof can be covered with traditional clay tiles. Whether flat or pitched, the roof color should be light so as to reflect as much solar radiation as possible, which will serve to help keep the upper floor much cooler.

Windows and Window Treatments

Traditionally, windows in the southwest were small and deeply set into thick earthen walls. This arrangement kept the heat out by reducing the exposure to the strong summer sun while allowing some fresh air in when needed. This goal is as relevant today as it ever was; however, today's needs and our windows are very different, and therefore require a somewhat different approach. Contemporary Americans, with the availability of inexpensive glass, prefer large windows for taking in views, additional warming from the winter sun, and simply the pleasure of having bright, sunny spaces.

As in some parts of the West, the temperature differential from hot summer days to much cooler nights can be 30° or more, a dwelling is quickly cooled when windows are opened in the evenings. The double-hung window, sliding windows, and door afford no more than 50 percent ventilation, but can be adequate in most situations. Casement and awning-style windows offering nearly a 100 percent airflow are also desirable options.

As in the past, windows benefit from sun protection. The larger glass areas of our modern structures certainly need to be shielded, which presents something of a new challenge. This protection is most effective when the shading device is located outside the building rather than inside, as with curtains. South-facing windows (and walls) can be easily shaded through overhead devices such as roof overhangs and trellises. Those facing the east and west, where low-rising or setting sun can be brutally hot, require vertical screening—either solid or louvered. Exterior shutters, which can be opened and closed or adjusted, either throughout the day or seasonally, offer the greatest degree of protection for these locations.

Materials and Construction

"The main requirement for thermal comfort in this region is a building material with a very high heat-holding capacity—i.e., one which could absorb solar radiation all day and release it slowly all night. The mud-walled, mud-roofed constructions, which desert people all over the world have evolved, accomplish this task most admirably."[39] If all things were equal, the first choice for the wall construction would be either adobe or rammed earth. Both are cheap, easy to put in place, and they are sustainable. However, this form of construction is not earthquake-resistant, and is therefore, unsuitable for multistory buildings in areas prone to them.

A second choice, which is more practical but less sustainable, would be a double layer of hollow-core concrete block, in-filled with earth and reinforced periodically with steel bars. This wall can be used effectively as a heat sink, which was so effective in traditional structures. The materials are readily available and reasonably inexpensive. Similar to adobe walls, they need only a modest amount of skill to build, they are fireproof, and their thermal qualities are excellent.

While the early adobe and rammed earth structures had foundations of stone, current circumstances dictate that they must be of concrete. While not a sustainable material, it is required to provide a stable base for the earthen and concrete block walls that rest upon it and to make watertight cisterns.

The Native Americans left their walls unplastered at times, and certainly unpainted. It was the Spanish who introduced the concept of whitewashing them. "One of the most widespread and economical techniques for arid climate modification is the coating of walls with a reflective surface . . . whitewash reflects 80 percent of solar radiation . . . the frequent overpainting further increases the density of the reflective area and contributes to its efficiency."[40] It is highly desirable to plaster interior earthen or adobe walls to help

Figure 7.16
Casitas De Colores Apartments By Dekker, Perich, Sabatini Architects In Downtown Albuquerque, NM, Demonstrate How Some Architects Are Beginning To Address The Need For A Regional Character To Their Architecture

maintain a clean, dust-free interior environment. Painting exterior walls exposed to the sun white or a light color would most certainly help to deflect the sun's radiation.

Floors can be made of a concrete slab either finished and left exposed or covered with clay tiles. Either flooring choice is durable and long-lived. They have a degree of mass that allows for the collection and slow release of any solar radiation that falls on them, which serves to maintain a consistent interior temperature during winter's colder days.

Outdoor Spaces

Courtyards and balconies need to be protected from the sun, so wherever possible, walls on the east and west sides as well as overhangs are useful toward achieving this end. Rather than hanging them off multifamily dwellings of several stories, these spaces can often times be set into the building to minimize exposure to sun. This may also mean that both the living room and a bedroom can be located to face it.

Overhead shading devices are very useful to keep strong direct sun off people and surfaces. The traditional *ramada* can still be a useful device when placed over contemporary courtyards and terraces. Likewise, canvas awnings can be extended out to shade these same spaces in summer and be retracted in winter to allow the sun to shine on and heat up the building's earthen walls. These devices play an important role by giving the residents the ability to control their environment, thus making their exterior space much more pleasant throughout the day, year round.

As previously mentioned, flat rooftops can provide additional outdoor space for residents at little additional cost. Solar collectors can be placed high enough above these roofs to do double duty by acting as a *ramada*, shading the roof surface and any activities that may take place on it.

Landscape

Landscaping is yet another way to use low-cost, environmentally friendly resources to enhance the overall comfort and quality of life for residents. Trees, shrubs, and vines can effectively screen buildings from the sun, create pleasant shady areas, and add cooling humidity to the air. Plants must be chosen carefully, so as not to use too much water. Indigenous plants will be most suitable, as they are well-adapted to the environment, consequently their water needs will be minimal.

Plantings, fountains, and pools of water can provide additional humidity to the atmosphere in a localized area, such as a courtyard, which will tend to cool anyone nearby. This is an age-old principle that one can still find in many hot/dry locations around the world and is still of great merit today.

Renewable Power and Mechanical Equipment

Up until the mid-twentieth century, people living in the West used evaporative coolers to help mediate the climate by adding humidity through mechanical means. These were units that, more often than not, were mounted on roofs or through an outside wall and supplied a mist of water vapor, which helped to cool interior spaces. Often referred to as "swamp

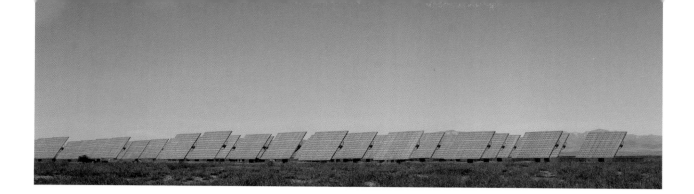

Figure 7.17
The Southwest Is By Far The Best Place To Take Advantage Of The Sun To Generate Power And Solar Installations Such As This One Are Becoming A Common Sight On The Landscape

coolers," they operated quite effectively, but when houses were not well-ventilated, they could produce unwanted odor, mold, and mildew. The advent of modern air conditioning replaced these rather primitive devices with a more convenient and comfortable option, but one that is hardly sustainable. A more earth-friendly approach is to use ceiling fans or even whole house fans to increase airflow when desired.

The western region is the best location in the country for solar collectors, whether for hot water or the generation of electricity through photovoltaic panels. Therefore, the payback on these units will be more rapid than elsewhere and make them a good investment. A secondary advantage that can be obtained at no additional cost is that these panels can save energy by shading roofs, helping to keep them cool. If mounted high enough above a flat roof, they can also shield outdoor activities from the sun.

The Prospect for Future Urban Development in the West

The western region will be facing some unique challenges over the course of the twenty-first century. Like much of the world, any number of construction materials will become more scarce and consequently more expensive—perhaps prohibitively so. However, the lack of water may be the region's major problem. If development continues at the pace that it has over the last few decades, shortages will result. While politicians are reassuring, nothing should be taken for granted in this regard and we must begin to plan accordingly.

Air conditioning, which made residents of the southwest feel more comfortable since the 1950s, may become too expensive for many people to operate. If electricity costs become so high that only a few can afford them, some of our current luxuries will need to be eliminated. Air conditioning may be one of the first to go. If so, then our buildings must once again be designed and built with more concern for natural methods of climate control.

Despite its environmental issues, the southwest is blessed with a vast amount of traditional building materials, which may at some point regain their former popularity. Earth may once again become a material of choice due to its availability and appropriateness to the region's climate. As a substitute in part for steel and concrete, the use of earth may enable the southwest to continue to grow and prosper in a much more sustainable manner than presently.

Likewise, the sun that parches the plains and the wind that blows so fiercely at times may come to the rescue and provide a steady source of energy adequate to power the region's future needs.

Summary of Suggested Building Practices for the West

Main environmental objectives: Defend against the heat from direct summer sun, cold winter temperatures, and high winds at higher elevations and farther north.

Orientation

- Living areas should be south to southeast facing
- Share walls with adjoining units wherever possible
- East and west walls should have only a few or no openings

Layout

- Compact and cubic volumes (centric)
- Courtyards may be used to obtain shade and shut out hot, dry desert winds
- Provide shaded areas for living and working outside, such as verandas, courtyards, and porches
- Medium to high ceilings to keep heat up and off occupants

Construction

- Build directly on the ground
- Thick walls of earth or masonry for thermal mass
- Dimensional or engineered lumber, or built-up trusses for floor and roof structure to minimize use of wood
- Insulation not required except in the roof due to mass in walls and roofs
- Reflective wall colors (white, pastel, silver)

Recommended Construction/Structural Materials

- Stone or concrete foundations
- Earth wall (adobe or rammed earth), stone/concrete or concrete block for bearing walls
- Baked clay floor tile
- Light frame (dimensional or engineered lumber) for roof and floor structure
- Plaster (lime) interior walls and partitions

Roofs

- Either flat, covered with sand and gravel and accessible to residents for outdoor functions
- Pitched with covering of clay tiles or light-colored, reflective metal

Shading

- Overhangs, particularly on the south side
- Exterior solid or louvered shutters, particularly on the east and west sides
- Add shade coverings over exterior livable spaces, walkways, verandas, balconies, etc.

Windows

- Most configurations work well—double-hung, sliding, casement, or awning

- Minimal number of windows on west- and east-facing walls
- South side can afford more glass (if shaded for summer sun) to warm interiors in winter

Ventilation and Cooling

- Keep the heat out—small openings to exterior
- Cross-ventilation is of secondary concern as it can introduce hot air into dwelling
- Ceiling fans are useful within dwellings and whole house fans can exhaust hot air build-up at night
- Evaporative cooling may be useful
- Use shady gardens to introduce humidity into the air through plantings, pools, and fountains

Heating

- Minimal space heating required in each room in the south, but central heat in the north
- Fireplaces or wood stoves can help to add warmth in winter

Water

- Collect rainwater in cisterns for all uses—including drinking
- Collect all gray water for flushing toilets and watering garden plants

Notes

1   Stegner, Wallace. *Where the Bluebirds Sing to the Lemonade Spring.* The Modern Library (2002) New York. p. 54.
2   AIA Research Corporation. *Regional Guidelines for Building Passive Energy Conserving Homes.* U.S. Department of Housing and Urban Development (1978). Washington, DC. p.65.
3   California, Dream Big. *Weather: San Diego.* Website: http://archive.visitcalifornia.com/Travel-Tools/Weather/.
4   Congressional Research Service. *Federal Land Ownership Overview and Data.* December 29, 2014. pp. 4–5. Website: https://fas.org/sgp/crs/misc/R42346.pdf.
5   Veregge, Nina. Transformations of Spanish Urban Landscapes in the American Southwest, 1821-1900. *Journal of the Southwest 35*(1993) pp. 371–460. Website: http://jsw.library.arizona.edu/3504/veregge/veregge.html.
6   Nabakov, Peter, and Robert Easton. *Native American Architecture.* Oxford University Press (1989) New York. pp. 322–336.
7   Sofaer, Anna. *The Primary Architecture of the Chacoan Culture: A Cosmological Expression.* (1997). Webpage: www.solsticeproject.org/primarch.htm.
8   Polyzoides, Stefanos. *The Plazas of New Mexico.* (2002). Website: http://www.mparchitects.com/site/thoughts/plazas-new-mexico-0.
9   Wikipedia. *Ancient Pueblo Peoples.* Website: http://en.wikipedia.org/wiki/Ancient_Pueblo_peoples.
10 Nabokov, Peter and Robert Easton. *Native American Architecture.* Oxford University Press (1989) New York. p. 370.
11 Treib, Marc. *Sanctuaries of Spanish New Mexico.* Ebook. Website: http://publishing.cdlib.org/ucpressebooks/view?docId=ft72900812&chunk.id=d0e797&toc.depth=1&toc.id=d0e199&brand=ucpress. p. 24.
12 Fitch, James Marston. *American Building: The Environmental Forces That Shape It.* Houghton Mifflin Company (1972) Boston, MA. p. 271.

13 Noble, Allen G. Wood. *Brick, and Stone: North American Settlement Landscape*. Vol. 1: Houses. University of Massachusetts Press (1984) Boston, MA. p. 83.

14 DesertUSA. *The Spanish Franciscan Missionary: Principal Missionary Order in Spain's Vast Colonial Empire*. Website: http://www.desertusa.com/ind1/franciscan.html.

15 Social Studies Fact Cards, California Edition. *Mission San Fernando Rey De Espana*. Website: http://factcards.califa.org/mis/sanfernandorey.html.

16 Spears, Beverley. *American Adobes: Rural Houses of Northern New Mexico*. University of New Mexico (1945) Albuquerque, NM.

17 Harvey, Caitlin Paige. *Thesis—Vernacular Significance in Monterey Colonial Style Architecture*. Chapter III: The Monterey Colonial Style. Mexican and American Design Influences. Graduate School of the University of Oregon. (August 2004). Eugene, OR. p. 47.

18 Noble, Allen G. *Wood, Brick, and Stone: North American Settlement Landscape*. Vol. 1: Houses. University of Massachusetts Press (1984) Boston, MA. p. 86.

19 Ibid p. 45 with footnote 4.

20 McMillan, Elizabeth. *California Colonial: The Spanish and Rancho Revival Styles*. Schiffer (2002), Atglen, PA.

21 Kasparowitz, Lawrence. *A Style of Architecture called "Monterey"*. Blog Post, October 16 2009. Website: http://kasparowitz.blogspot.co.uk/2009/10/style-of-architecture-called-monterey.html.

22 Fitch, James Marston. *American Building: The Environmental Forces That Shape It*. Houghton Mifflin Company (1972) Boston, MA. p. 269.

23 Vint, Bob and Christina Neumann (Eds.). *Southwest Housing Traditions: Design Materials Performance*. U.S. Department of Housing and Urban Development: Office of Policy Development and Research (May 2005) Washington, DC. p.36. Website: https://www.huduser.gov/portal//Publications/pdf/SouthwestHousing/SW_Housing_Traditions.pdf.

24 Treib, Marc. *Sanctuaries of Spanish New Mexico*. E-book. University of California Press (1993) Berkeley, CA. p.35. Website: http://ark.cdlib.org/ark:/13030/ft72900812/.

25 Treib, Marc. *Sanctuaries of Spanish New Mexico*. E-book. University of California Press (1993) Berkeley, CA. p.33. Website: http://ark.cdlib.org/ark:/13030/ft72900812/.

26 Treib, Marc. *Sanctuaries of Spanish New Mexico*. E-book. University of California Press (1993) Berkeley, CA. p.34. Website: http://ark.cdlib.org/ark:/13030/ft72900812/.

27 Dahmen, Joe. *Rammed earth*. MIT. Website: http://web.mit.edu/masonry/Rammed/unitedstates.html.

28 Saltillo Tile. Website: www.trinitytilesupply.com/saltillo.htm.

29 Vint, Bob and Christina Neumann (Eds.). *Southwest Housing Traditions: Design Materials Performance*. U.S. Department of Housing and Urban Development: Office of Policy Development and Research (May 2005) Washington, DC. p.115. Website: https://www.huduser.gov/portal//Publications/pdf/SouthwestHousing/SW_Housing_Traditions.pdf.

30 Wikipedia. *Agriculture in the Southwestern US*. Website: http://en.wikipedia.org/wiki/Agriculture_in_the_Southwestern_United_States.

31 ARXX ICF. Website: www.arxx.com.

32 Inspectapedia. *Stucco Wall Methods & Choices – Best Practices Guide*. Website: http://inspectapedia.com/BestPractices/Stucco_Wall_Method_Choices.php.

33 Global Change. *Southwest*. Website: http://nca2014.globalchange.gov/report/regions/southwest.

34 Annenberg Learner. *Collapse: Why do Civilizations Fall? Chaco Canyon*. Website: www.learner.org/interactives/collapse/chacocanyon.html.

35 City of Tucson Ordinance 10597. Website: www.tucsonaz.gov/files/water/docs/rainwaterord.pdf.

36 Global Change. *Southwest*. Website: http://nca2014.globalchange.gov/report/regions/southwest.

37 Gaston, Todd L. *Rainwater Harvesting in the Southwest United States*. Research Paper, (May 6, 2010).

38 Global Change. *Southwest*. Website: http://nca2014.globalchange.gov/report/regions/southwest.

39 Fitch, James Marston. *American Building: The Environmental Forces That Shape It*. Houghton Mifflin Company (1972) Boston, MA. pp. 268–269.

40 Oliver, Paul. *Dwellings: The Vernacular House World Wide*. Phaidon Press (2003) London. p. 143.

Chapter 8

The Pacific Northwest: Marine Forest

The Place

Occupying one the most spectacularly beautiful swaths of land in the United States, this region developed late and quite uniquely into an economic powerhouse with an Asian connection. Historically isolated from the rest of the continent by mountains and wide deserts, it has adapted to its environment independently. Stretched out along the Pacific Ocean, it has always relied on the sea for its livelihood and connection to the rest of the world. Reaping the ocean's bounty and plentiful natural resources that the land provided gave it prosperity. A mild, rain-filled coastal climate has made it verdant and a pleasant place to live year round. In sum, these factors dictated the development of this region with its distinct identity and personality. Joel Garreau in *The Nine Nations of North America*[1] drives the point home with little ambiguity when he writes that it is "the only place in the West with enough water. Everything else for a thousand miles in any direction is basically desert. It's no wonder that essentially different civilizations have grown up on the Pacific coast as a result."

Figure 8.1
The Picturesque Northern
California Coast Is Relatively
Undeveloped

Composed of the westerly portions of Washington and Oregon as well as the northwestern quadrant of California, it is confined to a narrow band between the Pacific Ocean and the Cascade ranges. With San Francisco Bay area near its southern boundary and the Canadian border as its northerly extreme, it stretches about 900 miles. Yet, at its widest, it is never over 90 miles.

A naturally stunning rugged coastline and spectacular mountains that appear to erupt from the otherwise low-lying countryside define it. The Commission for Environmental Cooperation has classified the ecoregion as *marine west coast forest*, where "mountainous topography dominates, cut through by numerous fjords and glacial valleys, and bordered by coastal plains along the ocean margin."[2]

Its mild temperatures and plentiful rainfall marks another noteworthy feature of the region's identity. Here the ocean tempers the climate with only relatively small temperature variations throughout the year. For example, in Seattle, the average high in August is a rather cool 73°F and the average low in January is a chilly 36°F—a modest 47°F spread. In San Francisco, the average low in January is 46°F and the average high in August is 68°F—a spread of only 22°F.[3] Some might call this chilly: as did Mark Twain when he claimed that the "coldest winter I ever spent was a summer in San Francisco."

In addition to modifying temperatures, the Pacific Ocean contributes a great deal of moisture to the environment in the form of a gentle or "soft" rain, along with a good deal of fog and mist. "The weather loves to hang in a difficult-to-dress-for balance of wetness that is moister than mist but drier than drizzle,"[4] as Joel Garreau puts it. The preponderance of the rain falls from mid-October to early spring, with little over the summer months. The amount of rain can vary significantly from place to place. The foothills of the Coastal and Cascade ranges can receive over 80 inches in a year. In Seattle, it rains on average 152 days a year for an average accumulation of 34 inches. Although farther south drier conditions tend to prevail with San Francisco receiving on average only 23.64 inches. This plentiful moisture makes the countryside exceedingly verdant and covered with dense forests, but the dampness can make the air "feel raw and less comfortable than the thermometer might suggest."[5] The dank, often foggy conditions cut out the sunlight and can contribute to a somewhat depressing atmosphere throughout the winter months. In addition to the rain, at times, the winds along the region's coastal margin can be fierce, exceeding 80 miles per hour. Fortunately, "the coastal mountains provide some protection and winds are generally lower in the summer."[6]

As a result of this normally hospitable climate, when the first white men arrived, they found a large population of prosperous Native Americans living in permanent settlements along the shore in a land of plenty. The long growing season ensured an abundant food supply throughout most of the year. Wild berries, acorns, various types of fruit, and a wide variety of grains and vegetables composed much of their harvests. The ocean and numerous rivers supplied fish, shellfish, and sea mammals, which provided protein for a well-balanced diet. In addition to a plentiful food supply, the vast forests that covered the adjacent mountainsides supplied a bountiful stock of wood, which was put to use in multiple ways, most notably the construction of substantial, permanent lodgings.

Separated by some 3000 miles from the earliest European settlements on the east coast, this region was the last place in the contiguous states to be settled in great numbers by Anglos. Before the nineteenth century, most of the contact with the outside world came from the sea. Sir Francis Drake explored San Francisco Bay in 1579. In 1778, Captain James Cook first mapped and recorded details of the northwest coast of North America for his English sponsors. Spanish, Russian, French, and English ship captains explored it during the eighteenth century, claiming it for the nations under whose flag

Figure 8.2
A View Of Seattle's Skyline
As One Approaches From
The Bainbridge Island Ferry
On Puget Sound

they sailed. Beyond simply exploring the coast, during the late eighteenth century, a small number of Russian fur traders settled along it and up the rivers where they traded with Indian trappers. Their hold on the area was tenuous and brief. It was Yankee seamen in their clipper ships who established the most enduring relationship to the area. In addition to trade with the indigenous peoples, they brought their fellow New Englanders, who established their own settlements, which later became the region's first major cities.

It was not until the beginning of the nineteenth century that the United States became interested in claiming the territory. The Louisiana Purchase in 1803 and the Lewis and Clark expedition in 1804–1805 both firmly established the U.S.'s claim to the Pacific shore. The Treaty of 1818 with Great Britain finally defined its northern border with Canada at the forty-ninth parallel north, where it remains to this day. However, up until the latter half of the nineteenth century, the region's physical connection with the rest of the country was distant and arduous. It was either by sea around the southern tip of South America through the Straits of Magellan or overland by way of the Oregon Trail. This did not change significantly until 1869 when the Transcontinental Railway successfully linked San Francisco with Saint Louis and the rest of the East. In 1883, the Northern Pacific Railway did the same for the northern tier of the region by linking Puget Sound to the Great Lakes. Today, the interstate highway system and air connections make travel to and from the region easy and fast, helping to erase this sense of isolation.

Even though the region is small in area, it has three substantial and thriving metropolises. San Francisco, today with over 4.5 million people in its metropolitan area, is the largest of the region's cities, but only ranks eleventh in the country. Seattle-Tacoma-Bellevue with nearly 3.7 million people ranks fifteenth. Over 2.3 million people inhabit the Portland-Vancouver-Hillsboro statistical area, which ranks twenty-fourth.

With the exception of San Francisco, which was founded in 1776 by Spanish settlers, the others were established in the mid- to late nineteenth century and as such can be considered new arrivals. Each site was selected because of its protected harbor and first

developed around trade. However, San Francisco's growth was accelerated dramatically by the discovery of gold in 1848. The ensuing gold rush took the population from a scant 1,000 to over 25,000 by the end of 1849.[7] Seattle benefitted in a similar way when it served as a staging area for the Yukon gold rush of the late 1890s.

The cultural influences on the region came from both east and west. In his book *American Nations*, Colin Woodard refers to this region as the "Left Coast" noting "the coast blended the moral, intellectual and utopian impulses of a Yankee elite with the self-sufficient individualism of Appalachian and immigrant majority." The resulting culture is one that is "idealistic but individualistic."[8] Politically, it is liberal. Environmentally, it is sensitive.

In addition to the Anglo influences, it owes a great deal of its personality to a long and close relationship with Asia. Russians were some of the first people to occupy the territory during the eighteenth century, but the Chinese who immigrated from 1849 to the 1890s to work menial jobs gave their Asian culture a significant place in the region. Today, strong economic ties through trade continue to closely link the two sides of the Pacific.

Trade has been a natural outgrowth of the region's proximity to the Pacific Ocean and the numerous rivers that offered a connection to the world beyond. Native Americans were known to have traded with each other up and down the coast as well as inland for centuries before the white man arrived. The Russians and French and later the British—seeking beaver pelts—opened the door to this remote land in the eighteenth century. Its exposure to the Orient made west coast cities the obvious port of entry for Asian goods and for export of raw materials.

Since the land was first settled, the forests and the sea have provided plentiful natural resources, which have created the economic basis for lumbering and fishing. The natural scenic beauty has produced a robust tourist industry "The lowlands of the Puget Sound, Willamette Valley, Fraser Valley and the southeastern tip of Vancouver Island

Figure 8.3
The Ports Of Seattle And Tacoma Have Formed An Alliance Making Them The Third Largest Marine Cargo Complex In North America. They Handle Most Of The Lower Forty-Eight States' Waterborne Commerce With Alaska And A Large Portion Of Asia

REINVENTING AN URBAN VERNACULAR

possess the area's main expanse of highly productive agricultural soils, as well as urban lands."[9] More currently, light industry and technology have become major economic generators—Silicon Valley is synonymous with computing and Seattle with Microsoft.

Upon entering the twenty-first century, the coastal Pacific region remains a desirable place to live and its population continues to grow at a rapid pace as its economy thrives. Its main revenue sources remain vigorous and its cities are maturing in a sophisticated and sensitive manner. It has embraced the concepts of a sustainable and active lifestyle while enjoying the area's beautiful natural landscapes.

Early Development Patterns

From northern California to Alaska, the majority of Native Americans built their villages in protected coves near the ocean or along rivers where they had easy access to fishing. These settlements were normally laid out with their wooden buildings in one or more rows following the water's edge. In front of each tier of buildings, they built a boardwalk of wood that connected one to another with a dry walkway.

When the Anglos arrived in large numbers in the mid- to late nineteenth century and laid out their coastal cities, like the Native Americans they oriented them to the water's edge. The initial grids in some of the major coastal cities, such as San Francisco, Seattle, and Portland, were laid out before federal government surveyors arrived to enforce the

Figure 8.4
A Currier And Ives Rendering Of An Aerial View Of San Francisco, Which Shows The Convergence Of Separate Gridded Street Patterns

official orientation to the cardinal directions (north/south), which allowed the founding fathers to do as they saw fit. As a result, multiple grids with their streets running at various angles to one another with oddly shaped intersections were created. Some of the streets that ran between intersecting grids often became major streets of the city such as San Francisco's Market Street, West Burnside Street in Portland, and Yesler Way in Seattle.

Over the course of the second half of the nineteenth century, the entire Northwest Territory was divided into the then typical pattern of square mile *sections* discussed in Chapter 4. A land rush ensued and the Oregon Trail was the avenue to this Promised Land. Newly arrived individuals and families were given claims to properties with 320 acres each, according to the national Donation Land Claim Act of 1850.[10] The arable valleys, such as the Willamette, were settled first and agriculture blossomed there, while the mountains that enclose and clearly defined them remained as timberlands.

This division between the mountains and valleys holds true to this day with the major difference being that housing has sprawled out from the cities into this flatter, fecund landscape. Oregon has introduced groundbreaking legislation to limit sprawl by defining urban growth boundaries, but no other state as yet has followed their lead. Across the region, the people have maintained a strong relationship to nature and the outdoors, resulting in a desire to conserve their remaining undeveloped land and to create parks and open space within city boundaries.

Precedents

The aboriginal peoples that settled the northwest coast of the Pacific came to the area thousands of years ago, and over that time developed sophisticated and unique construction technologies and building designs. By contrast, the Anglos settled the area in the mid- to late nineteenth century and brought with them from the east coast Victorian methods and prototypes for building. As a result, we have a wonderful assortment of Native American building types for precedents, but few unique recent Anglo ones.

Plank Houses

Because the people of the northwest coast had relatively easy access to food sources nearly year-round, they were able to create and live in permanent settlements composed of durable, long-lasting buildings. Their structures, commonly referred to as plank houses, were built all along the northwestern Pacific coast from Northern California to Alaska. They were built in a variety of configurations and sizes, but were always made from the trees, usually cedar or redwood, that grew prolifically nearby. Some were built into the ground and others on it. Roof shapes varied considerably from place to place. They used the common shed, gabled ones that shed in two directions, mansards, hips, and those that were nearly flat.

Lewis and Clark wrote one of our first records of them in 1805 when they came upon a Chinook village just east of what is now Portland, Oregon, on the banks of the Columbia River. They described the houses as being "comodious" and built on an artificial mound about 30 feet above the natural terrain. They were sunk about 6 feet into the ground with another 18 inches extending above it. Each house measured about 20 by 30 feet and had a gabled roof with a small door at one end. Their roof structure was composed of stout timbers and lighter beams covered with the bark of white cedar and arbor vitae. The walls

REINVENTING AN URBAN VERNACULAR

Figure 8.5
A Typical Tanaktak House Once
Found On Harbeldown Island In
British Columbia Was
Photographed In 1914 By
Edward Curtis

were made of split boards that held back the surrounding earth. A small opening in the roof allowed light in and smoke to exhaust. The half nearest the door was the living space that several families shared. They slept in raised beds on either side of a central fire. To the rear of the building was storage space for their main source of food, dried fish, and berries that had been preserved for winter use.[11]

Along the northwestern coast, the Indians built even more significant structures than their inland counterparts. These were above ground and to a large degree resembled the Iroquoian longhouses (see Chapter 4) in their basic layout and size, but were more substantial in their construction. Rather than saplings for structure and tree bark for the covering, these Pacific coast houses were built of large cedar logs and thick wooden planks. Houses varied in size, but they usually sheltered several families. Some were extremely large and housed an entire village. Captain George Vancouver reported in 1792 one such structure, dubbed the "Old-Man-House," that sheltered over 600 people. The long side was parallel to the shore and measured more than 380 yards or nearly a fifth of a mile in length.[12] These very long structures were actually a series of dwellings strung together, townhouse fashion, with the chief's unit in the middle.

Every family occupying the building was allocated its own space, with rush mats hung from the rafters to form a separation between each group. For greater comfort, rush mats also covered the hard-packed earthen floors. "At the center of the house was the communal fireplace, where all of the members of the house could gather to socialize, eat, and work during long winter evenings. Sleeping platforms were set up along the walls, and food hung from the rafters to dry."[13]

The typical Salish house of the Seattle area had a single shed roof with its high side facing the coastline. It was typically between 25 to 50 feet from front to back. They stretched out along the shore as their lengths were unconstrained and could be expanded as needed. Its structure was composed of a series of posts and beams set 12 to 14 feet apart. The posts were rectangular measuring 3 or 4 inches thick and 2 to 3 feet wide. The round roof beams could be as much as 2 feet in thickness and spanned across the full width of the dwelling. Smaller rafters spanned between the beams and supported cedar planks that made up the roof covering. The roof planks were often 3 to 4 inches thick and

Figure 8.6
Salish Plank House

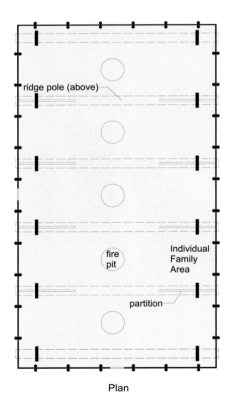

Plan

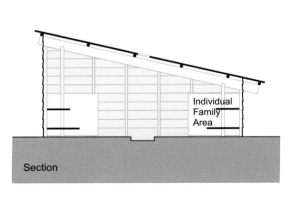

Section

REINVENTING AN URBAN VERNACULAR

Figure 8.7
This Reconstruction Of A Yurok Plank House Is Found At Patrick's Point State Park, CA, And Gives A Clear Impression Of Those Indigenous Dwellings

3 or more feet wide and ran from the high end to the low and overlapped one another to keep rain out. They were often secured with cedar rope, and in some cases, even weighted down with heavy stones to keep the roof in place in the event of high winds. Holes were left in the roof or in the roof planks to allow smoke to exhaust from the fires below.

The walls were composed of cedar planks similar to those on the roof. These were placed horizontally with the lower one overlapped by the one above, shingle style. They were held securely in place by pairs of vertical poles that tightly sandwiched them together.[14] In some cases, sidewalls were raised slightly off the ground to allow air to enter to feed the fire and to help keep the ground inside dry.[15]

Even though these buildings were considered permanent, in summer, many of the tribes moved inland to fish the rivers, gather berries, and to hunt in the forests. They built temporary shelters from planks that they removed and transported from their "permanent" dwellings, leaving only the main post and beam structures behind until returning after colder weather set in. The first Europeans to see these skeletonized structures assumed them to be abandoned.

The Yurok tribe of northern California built a somewhat different type of plank house from those built by the Chinook or Salish. Here, the roofs were composed of three pitches with the middle one almost level. These houses were nearly square in plan with the front measuring between 17.5 to 21.5 feet wide and the depth only about 3 feet deeper. Planks

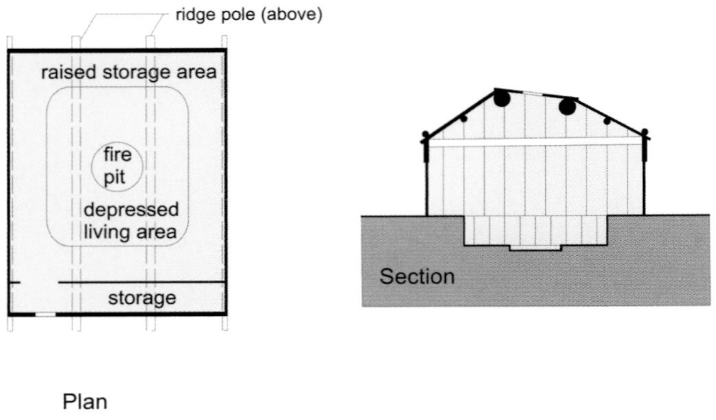

ridge pole (above)

raised storage area

fire pit

depressed living area

storage

Plan

Figure 8.8
Yurok Plank House

Section

were set into the ground vertically to compose the exterior walls. The gabled front and rear walls were made of thicker planks than the sides, with some being notched to support four roof beams. These beams spanned the entire interior space, eliminating the need for interior columns.

The typical house was set into the ground with the sidewalls emerging only a few feet above the soil level. The center of the house, which was dug down another yard or so and surrounded by horizontal planks to hold the earth back, was where the fire was placed. This two-level arrangement provided an upper level for storage and a lower one near the shared fire for living. The entrance was small, circular, and carved through one of the wider support planks in the front of the building. It was located at the ground level, which required that one crawl through on hands and knees to enter. This inconvenience put an intruder at a serious disadvantage, allowing the women to protect themselves when the men were away by using flaming logs from the fire. A sliding plank or animal hide covered it and acted as the doorway. To help control the wind by keeping it from blowing directly in on the occupants, a wooden partition was erected between the entrance and the living space.[16]

The Yurok built their homes of the redwoods that grew in nearby forests. By only harvesting planks from dead or fallen trees or by stripping slabs off living trees in a manner that allowed the tree to survive, they made only a slight impression on the ecosystem of the forests.

Because they were built within a wide temperature range from northern California to Alaska, the need for tightness varied considerably. The more southerly Yurok homes were composed of rather loosely fitting planks that allowed a flow of air in all seasons. Out of necessity, those in the northern extremes tended to be smaller, more finely built with tighter joints to seal the cold and wind out. Furthermore, they also had wooden floors to keep the inhabitants comfortably up and off the colder earth that was acceptable farther south.[17]

Houseboats (Floating Homes)

Houseboats are found along the coast of the Gulf of Mexico and Florida, but they are most prolific and notable along the Northern Pacific coast. From San Francisco to Vancouver, British Columbia, they can be found in significant numbers dotting sheltered waterways. The trend began during the second half of the nineteenth century when makeshift housing of every nature was built to accommodate the hordes of new settlers. Houseboats answered the need for modest, affordable shelter for some of them. "At the turn of the century, discarded tramcars set on floating rafts made pleasant houseboats for the arty."[18] Later, during the first part of the twentieth century, more affluent families attracted by the romance of living on the water built recreational houseboats for vacationing, which assumed the pet name of "arks."[19] By the time of the Great Crash of 1929, there were thousands of houseboats along the northern Pacific shore in communities or scattered about inlets and wetlands. After the Crash of 1929, they once again satisfied a pressing need for cheap housing.[20]

Since World War II, the majority of houseboats found in the Northwest were inhabited by people seeking an affordable alternative to land-based housing. Many of them were hippie dropouts, artists, and fishermen, who began to assemble their own unique floating structures. Drawing from whatever cast off resources that were to be had, they created rather unconventional assemblages. When amassed in colonies, they might have "looked more like a wrecking yard" to some people used to orderly, landside residential developments. But it is hard to dispute that these architectural follies have a romantic quality that is difficult to match elsewhere or in other ways.[21]

The basic houseboat or more correctly in today's official parlance, "floating home," is composed of three parts—the hull, the superstructure, and the roof deck. The hull sits

Figure 8.9
Houseboats Such As These Found On Lake Union In Seattle Are Connected To Unique Neighborhoods By Floating Docks

in the water and provides the flotation that supports the whole and may have some living space partially below the waterline, the superstructure rests on the hull and contains living quarters and the roof deck is used as outdoor recreational space.

Types of hulls have varied significantly over time in their composition. "During the Great Depression, poor fishermen living in the tidal mud flats of the Skagit River Estuary in the state of Washington built floating small houses called *floatbacks* on large logs that gave the house buoyancy during the 2 or 3 hours a day that the tide was in."[22] Later, hulls were created from discarded artifacts, such as barges, tugboats, ferryboats, schooners, scows, and surplus military vessels such as landing craft and lifeboats—anything that floated and could support a light structure. A flat bottom was most desired, as it was more stable than a keeled hull, could enter shallow waters, and was most easily towed.

The typical superstructure was compact, efficiently laid out as on a ship, and low to avoid tipping over in rough weather. Built from the "flotsam and jetsam of the waterfront," they create a "nostalgic and nautical imagery." Inspired by the free-spirited hippie movement, they imbued an idiosyncratic look and feel that represented clearly the desire for independence and self-expression of their builders. Some were painted in pastel colors, while others were sided with cedar shingles and left to weather naturally.

The roof deck, located over the superstructure, provided an outdoors space high above the water with good views and an abundance of sun. Here was where one could enjoy being outdoors on the water, relaxing or entertaining. It could be left totally open, partially enclosed, or covered by any number of shading devices, most often canvas. These roof decks could run the full length and width of the superstructure, which it covered.

Aside from scavenged materials, western red cedar was frequently used in their construction due to the fact that it is one of the lightest softwoods and weight is always an issue on watercraft.[23] Current practices are to build with materials that are commonly used in ordinary residential construction, such as dimensional lumber. Ironically, today, hulls are often made of concrete, as it resists the destruction that sea worms can cause to wooden ones.

During the 1950s and 1960s, these communities came under greater scrutiny by local government authorities, who wanted to bring them in line with modern standards of health and safety as well as popular aesthetics. Today, neighborhoods of floating homes can be found in large cities such as Portland, Seattle, and San Francisco as well as the Bay area towns of Sausalito, Alamenda, and Richmond. They now function as town-regulated communities, which have connections to water, sewer, electricity, and gas—utilities making them more permanent than many of their predecessors. Docks that stretch out into the water, serve as sidewalks that link floating homes on both sides into neatly organized neighbor units. Moored within a few feet of one another, residents have little privacy outside and are obliged to live in relative harmony.

Victorian Townhouses

San Francisco developed as one of the nation's densest cities as a result of the division of blocks into very small increments. The street frontage for the typical house lot is only 25 feet and the depth 100 feet to 125 feet, making the average lot size 2,713 square feet (third smallest of all U.S. cities after Baltimore, MD, and Jersey City, NJ).[24] Due to this small amount of street frontage, zoning eventually allowed homes to be built across the full width as townhouses. While they occupied the lot's entire width, they did not need to fill their entire depth, which allowed for generous gardens at the rear.

Figure 8.10
The Traditional Victorian Bay
Windows Such As These Are
Found Throughout San Francisco

As the gridded street pattern cut across the hilly terrain with no notice given to the topography, many of San Francisco's streets were by default quite steep. As a result, these two- and three-story townhouses that lined them needed to adjust to the contours. The transition naturally took place at the lowest level, which was often used as a garage or storage basement. The first floor level where household living began was connected to the sidewalk by a long set of steps. This transitional layer gave buildings an even more distinctive and individual aspect, which the Victorians prized and took full advantage of the opportunity.

They were constructed with wood, specifically redwood and Oregon pine, which grew nearby. It was abundant, therefore inexpensive, and was easily crafted into intricate detailing and ornamentation that the Victorians valued so highly. Wood has an added advantage as it is resistant to damage from earthquakes, as it will bend rather than break.

These single-family homes were built near the centers as well as farther out in the then newly developed streetcar suburbs. They were designed in a wide array of styles—Italianate, Gothic Revival, Queen Anne, Stick/Eastlake, and Second Empire—creating an exuberant mélange along neighborhood streets.

The Victorians loved a wide variety of shapes and were likely to add cylindrical towers with conical roofs, balconies, porches that wrapped around on two or more sides, and bay windows, resulting in rather fanciful imagery. However, it was the bay window that was distinctive and proliferated in San Francisco and to a lesser degree elsewhere in the region. Not one, but often two were added to the façades of even narrow townhouses.

Color was employed to augment and accentuate these details and lines of the building. Choices of color could be wide-ranging and exuberant from maroon, Pompeii red, olive green terra cotta, blacks and browns, to many others. These richly colored houses were consequently nicknamed "Painted Ladies" to reflect their presence in the city.

The floor plans were laid out in a rather conventional manner of the day. The first floor had an entry, a hall that ran front to back and a staircase, which occupied about a third of the width and living space occupying the rest. A parlor, dining room, and kitchen were normally on the first floor with bedrooms above.[25]

It is thought "that some 48,000 wooden houses were built in San Francisco in the 65 years between the Gold Rush and the Panama Pacific Exposition of 1915."[26] Some were built to replace housing destroyed by the Great Earthquake and Fire of 1906, when over 400,000 people were left homeless. The result of all of this construction is a uniquely San Franciscan housing type that resulted from local conditions. Zoning law, topography, the availability of lumber, and the then current construction practices all contributed to it. In addition, a desire to relate to the street and the activities taking place there, as well as a need to bring in the sun and air, led to the adaptation of a ubiquitous element in their architectural makeup—the bay window.

Common Themes Found in the Traditional Buildings in the Pacific Northwest

Shape and Placement

The Native Americans oriented their windowless buildings toward the water, whereas the Americans, following tradition placed theirs facing the street. More recently, wherever a scenic view is possible, it becomes the overriding factor and often times that too is toward the water. Rarely, it seems, was any generation of the region's builders overly concerned with facing the sun and capitalizing on its energy until more recently.

Buildings in the region were often elongated as in the case of the Salish longhouses, which were always one-story structures and could stretch out any distance required. During the latter half of the nineteenth century, the Anglos often opted to build two-story homes, as it is the most efficient use of the land and a more economical approach. However, the twentieth century saw the advent of massive numbers of bungalows and California ranches built. They tended to be low, single-storied with a desire to cling to the landscape, and a more casual lifestyle tied to nature and the outdoors. Throughout the region, the single-family home became the most common housing type chosen by the white settlers, except in San Francisco where townhouses were also popular. Sharing common walls, the two- and three-story townhouse might be considered the only true urban building type until the early twentieth century ushered in the more massive and taller apartment building.

Shelter

The Native Americans chose low-sloped roofs pitched in one or more directions. In the early days, the Anglo builders chose their complex roof layouts as they related to the then

Figure 8.11
This Iconic Barn At Sea Ranch With Its Sloped Roof And Weathered Wooden Siding And Structure Has Served As An Inspiration For A Generation Of West-Coast Architects

current Victorian style. The Victorians had pitches that varied from the near flat Mansard roof that transitioned to a rather vertical one to flat ones as seen in the Italianate style. Dormers often broke the line of the roof to offer greater detail and interest. The depth and detail of overhangs varied from type to type. Throughout the last century, the most common house types, bungalows, and ranch houses were sheltered with low-pitched roofs. Few, if any of these roof arrangements found their genesis in the climate as one might expect, as the rarely used steep roof could shed the copious amounts of rain the region receives more quickly. Nor was there any consistent use of deep roof overhangs to help protect buildings from strong sun or driving rain.

The mild west-coast climate has always allowed for a great deal more outdoor activity than in many other regions of the country. With this said, one needs shelter in the more northerly, colder, and rainier areas than in the San Francisco Bay area where there is less precipitation. In both environments, porches were frequently the answer during the Victorian era and later with the common bungalow. These porches or verandas added to the overall aesthetic quality and charm of the home, but more importantly, they tended to serve several useful functions, such as a family gathering place or informal, exterior living room and a place to socialize with passing neighbors. In the region's more southerly locations, where the sun shone more predictably, the terrace or patio became a popular adjunct in Spanish homes and in the later twentieth-century house.

Construction and Materials

Due to the surrounding abundant forests, wood has always been the material of choice for construction in the region. The Indians used unsawn, whole logs or carved slabs from living trees into thick planks for their sturdy, post and beam structures. Up until the twentieth century, Anglos also constructed their large industrial and commercial buildings

Figure 8.12
Victorian Homes, "Painted
Ladies," Line One Of Portland,
Oregon's Shady Streets, Much
Like Those Of Other
Northwestern Cities

of heavy timbers due to their strength and resistance to fire. Today, many of these buildings remain, exhibiting flooring systems composed of massive timbers supported on masonry bearing walls. However, since the Americans only began to build in earnest during the mid-nineteenth century, light wood framing, which had become the framing method of choice across the nation, was adopted in the region as well. Consequently, the Victorians milled large logs into much smaller ones for home construction and subsequent generations have followed suit to this day. With this construction technique, they built both single-family homes and townhouses in all of the major cities of this region.

Throughout most of the nineteenth century, the more substantial commercial and apartment buildings located in cities used stone and brick bearing walls as their main structure. Under most circumstances, masonry provided the stability and fireproof structures that these larger buildings required. But these bearing walls often collapsed in earthquakes, as they were not reinforced with steel, which was needed to hold them together and is now required.

Heating, Cooling, and Ventilation

Winter temperatures across the region rarely go below freezing and usually only briefly. Consequently, Native Americans made do with a campfire in their uninsulated plank houses, which were not particularly tight and prone to infiltration of outside air. The Victorians had the advantage of tighter wood frame dwellings equipped with wood- and coal-burning fireplaces as well as more modern cast iron stoves. While neither culture's houses were insulated, wood with its cellular composition, inherently provided a certain amount of insulation in both situations.

Ventilation has never been a prime concern expressed in the architecture of the Pacific Northwest, as summers were rarely too hot for comfort. The Indians lived all winter in lodges with no windows and only one door, an adjustable smoke hole in the roof and cracks between the siding for ventilation. In summer, they camped in temporary shelters that rarely provided more than shelter from the rain. Anglos in tight, permanent housing relied on their traditional double-hung windows to let in outside air when they wished it. Townhouses relied on the bay window to introduce as much light in as possible.

Natural Resources Available for Construction

Wood

With abundant forests found nearby, the indigenous peoples and the first Anglos to settle the northern Pacific coast relied exclusively on wood for construction. These lush forests that supplied our antecedents continue to thrive. Plentiful precipitation (averaging 40 to 60 inches per year across their range), mild winters, foggy summer days, and good soil all contribute to the region's dramatic tree growth.[27] As a consequence of these favorable environmental conditions and modern forestry management techniques, wood products are now produced in greater quantities than ever before. Northern California, Oregon, and Washington together supply more than half of all timber cut in the United States, as well as a great deal of the nation's pulp and paper production. Even though they are considered the region's primary economic resource, they did not become available nationally until the early twentieth century when adequate transportation facilities were developed that allowed for their exploitation. Large-scale logging operations using clear cutting as the favored technique are now the norm. As a result, many thousands of acres of land have been accumulated by large lumber companies. Also, huge parts of Washington and most of the land in Oregon and northern California are government-owned and much of this land is leased out to private logging operations.[28]

In a very narrow strip along the Pacific coast from southwestern Oregon to beyond the San Francisco Bay area, one finds some of our most magnificent trees—the spectacular **redwoods** (*sequoia sempervirens*). Some of these trees have been dated to be over 2,000 years old and well over 350 feet in height.[29] The average redwood takes over 200 years to fully mature at which point they can reach from 200 to 240 feet in height, with diameters of 10 to 15 feet. However, over the last century and a half, mankind has devastated their numbers by logging over 95 percent of the old growth redwood forest for its timber. Today, most old growth redwoods survive mainly in national or state forests (200,000 acres), where they are protected for future generations to admire. Fortunately, they are fast growing and 20-year-old trees may average 50 feet in height and over 8 inches in diameter.[30] As a result, today, there are over 640,000 acres of second growth forests that are being commercially cultivated and harvested.[31] Aside from the beauty of its color and grain, redwood lumber is popular in construction due to its resistance to rot, insect damage, and fire. Used today for exterior siding as well as interior trim and finish, it

commands a premium price and only makes sense when used sparingly or on high budget building projects.

Second only to the redwoods in size is the coastal **Douglas fir** (*Pseudotsuga menziesii*), which is the major lumbering tree of the region. Douglas fir is not a true fir, but a separate species. It grows throughout the west, but is most abundantly found along the coast of Washington, Oregon, and northern California. The Western Wood Products Association claims that it "is North America's most plentiful softwood species, accounting for one fifth of the continent's total softwood reserves." Mainly due to its high yield per acre, the most productive in the U.S., Oregon is ranked number one in the production of softwood lumber. Typically, these trees take only 30 years to regenerate. Douglas fir is known most importantly for its strength, and is therefore used commonly as structural members. But it is also a beautiful wood that can be used for interior finishes, flooring, doors, and plywood.[32]

After Douglas fir, **Hem-fir** is the next most abundant group of trees logged in the region. It is a combination of Western Hemlock (*Tsuga heterophylla*) and five true Firs, which grow intermingled in coastal forests. They are classified together as their characteristics are nearly indistinguishable from one another and can be used for similar purposes. The Douglas fir is the only species that can surpass their production volume, strength, and versatility of end use. As a result, they are frequently used in the construction of homes and other small-scale frame buildings.[33]

Figure 8.13
Loggers Proudly Display Their Handiwork On One Of The Many California Redwoods That Were Felled During The Nineteenth Century

Figure 8.14
Douglas Firs Such As These
Planted On A Hillside In Oregon
Represent One Of The
Northwest's Major Industries

Among the various cedar species found in the region, the only native one, **western red cedar** (*thuja plicata*), is the largest and most abundant in the managed forests. Historically, it was found in abundance and was frequently the favorite of aboriginal people in the construction of their plank buildings and boats. Like other cedars, it is non-resinous and has a strong spicy scent. It is perhaps best known for its resistance to rot and insect damage, which is due to a compound called tannin found in their bark, wood, and cones. Consequently, its most common usages today, as in previous times, are for applications where it is exposed to weather, wet locations, or where it comes in direct contact with the earth. It is also favored as shingles and shakes on both roofs and siding due to its attractive appearance, durability, lightness, and superior insulation qualities.[34]

In addition to the plentiful softwood species, there are large stands of hardwoods such as **alder**, **maple**, and **oak**. Alder, a member of the birch family, is the most abundant hardwood found in the forest of the costal northwest. It can grow well over 100 feet tall with trunks of 2 to 3 foot in diameter. Due to the fact that it can be easily worked, finished, and has an attractive appearance, it has a wide range of uses from veneers and plywood to furniture and cabinetry. Lower grades of it can be used to make pallets or pulpwood.

Stone

Even though the area has a great deal of stone that underlies it and can be seen in outcroppings along the coast and on mountainsides, it has never become a major building material. At times, Native Americans used rounded river stones to build perimeter walls to protect the base of their buildings and to fence compounds to keep animals either in or out, but little more. Settlers employed them as foundations, but rarely siding or structure. Builders of multistory commercial and industrial buildings made the most of stone for bearing walls, as it could support heavy loads and was fireproof. Many such buildings are being retrofitted with steel to help them resist earthquakes. The very fact that wood was and still is so plentiful and easy to use made the need to work with the heavy, more cumbersome stone less desirable and even unnecessary on small-scale projects.

The Current Approach to Design and Construction

Urban Development Today

The twentieth century found the cities of the Northwest, like others across the country, beginning to expand outward with the advent of the streetcar and later the automobile. Large tract developments covered surrounding hillsides with thousands of standard developer model homes. With little land left within a desirable commuting distance, cities are now building housing nearer or in their downtown centers at an amazing pace. Many of these new developments are mid-rise buildings of six floors, bumping up against height restrictions of 65-feet, but many others are unrestricted and consequently much taller. These new apartment buildings are created to serve single people and couples or a couple with one young child, but rarely families with more than one school-age child. It would seem that families are still expected to move to the suburbs.

Architectural Character

Built in the international style, the taller buildings are constructed of steel and/or concrete and sheathed with glass. On the inside, floor to ceiling expanses of glass offer wonderful views of the city and its surroundings. However, these glass sheets face all directions and there is no attempt to shield them from the sun or provide natural ventilation, which can lead to overheating, and therefore require air conditioning. Usually, only a very small portion of these window walls can open for fresh air and often those openings are too small to provide much ventilation.

Rarely is there any outdoor space saved around the building as they take up most of the lot. Outdoor space on balconies, if offered, is usually tiny with only enough room for a couple of chairs and a small table. In most of these buildings, there is a long list of amenities that the residents expect, which include common social areas, with game rooms, outdoor kitchens, pools, and gyms. However, rarely is there play space provided for children.

Popular Design and Construction Methods

The taller apartment and condominium buildings are made of steel or concrete and glass with concrete block and/or steel studs making up the interior partitions, as one sees in other parts of the country and beyond. Parking is usually placed below grade under the main floor or occupying the street level. Mid-rise buildings with as many as six stories may be structured of steel as well, but they are frequently built with light wood frame. If parking is located on the ground floor of these lower buildings, it is made of concrete to safeguard the upper structure from fire.

Future Environmental Concerns

Even though the climate is mild and the region is not considered to be often visited by major storm activity, it faces its own set of challenges. According to the EPA, "in the coastal zone, the effects of sea level rise, erosion, inundation, threats to infrastructure and habitat, and increasing ocean acidity collectively pose a major threat to the region."[35] Each of these brings with it the potential for the loss of human life and the destruction of buildings, infrastructure, and the loss of natural resources.

While forest fires routinely plague the area east of the Cascades, the coastal forests are usually left unscathed due to the region's wetter conditions. This has begun to change and forest fires are becoming more commonplace and destructive, as global warming brings less rain and snow and rising temperatures to the region. In addition to affecting human life, they destroy both structures and the very forest from which the lumber for their construct is produced. Millions of acres of potentially profitable forests have been incinerated, resulting in the loss of billions of dollars to the lumber industry.

On the other hand, global warming is predicted to bring more severe weather events, which have the potential to bring too much rain and high winds. "Although the Pacific Northwest escapes the threat of hurricanes and powerful tornadoes due to the cool water to its west, the region is no stranger to strong, damaging winds. Each winter season, several Pacific low-pressure centers (or cyclones) make landfall upon the Northwest and British Columbia coasts, resulting in winds strong enough (40 to 60 mph) to produce power failures and modest damage west of the Cascades. Less frequently, perhaps two or three times a decade, windstorms of considerably greater magnitude occur, with winds gusting to 70 mph or more, extensive power failures affecting hundreds of thousands of homes, and damage reaching the tens or hundreds of millions of dollars. But, once every 30 years or so, the region experiences far more powerful storms, with hurricane-force winds and massive damage. The greatest windstorms occur in neutral (neither El Nino nor La Nina) years."[36] In 1962, "the Columbus Day Storm, official wind gusts reached 127 mph in the Willamette Valley. Many stations had gusts between 75 and 100 mph, and this includes quite a few locations that were inland."[37]

More ominous than flooding, high winds, or forest fires is the geophysical potential of a major, devastating earthquake. The northern coast occupies a section of the *Pacific Rim of Fire*, where the world's most powerful earthquakes occur, including its more notorious neighbor, San Andreas Fault in southern California. The fault that lies below the northern Pacific coastal region is known as the Cascadia Fault. It was unknown until the 1970s, since it has exhibited no recorded activity in modern times.[38] It is considered by some experts that there is a one in three chance that, by 2065, there will be a major, devastating earthquake in the region with the loss of thousands of lives and innumerable structures.[39] As it possesses a serious potential danger to the region, all construction must be mindful of it and structures should be designed accordingly. The consequences of a major earthquake are not simply the destruction that it will wreak, but in all likelihood, it will be accompanied by a tsunami that will do much more damage. Low-lying, coastal areas are in grave danger under the circumstances. This is not news to them and there are designated evacuation routes in place, but these preparations may not be enough to save hundreds or more, not to mention all the structures in its path.

Design Strategies and Building Components for the Future

Climatic Imperatives

In some respects, the Pacific Northwest is the easiest region for which to design, as its cool temperate climate with a narrow temperature range requires less concern for heating and almost none for cooling. However, its "soft" rain that creates many foggy or overcast days calls for a need to increase natural lighting. Likewise, its hard rain that can drop large amounts of precipitation in a short amount of time deserves serious consideration as well. In addition to the wind and lack of sunlight, frequent strong winds along the coast need to be given greater than normal consideration.

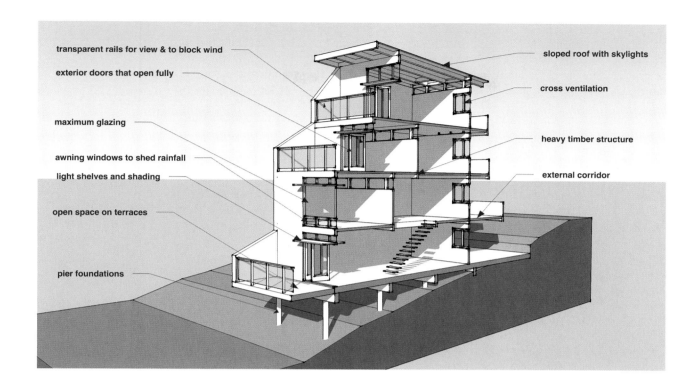

transparent rails for view & to block wind

exterior doors that open fully

maximum glazing

awning windows to shed rainfall

light shelves and shading

open space on terraces

pier foundations

sloped roof with skylights

cross ventilation

heavy timber structure

external corridor

Figure 8.16
Idea Drawing For The Pacific
Northwest

Orientation

As elsewhere, the long side of these buildings must be oriented to south, southeast, or southwest to capture as much sun as possible. A good southern orientation will go a long way toward passively heating apartments even though the sun is frequently hidden.

Topography can be a major consideration in building sitting and planning due to the hilly nature found in many cities and towns of the region. The way the building meets the land must be carefully considered. In some cases, buildings or parts thereof may step down the slopes to provide a more harmonious relationship to the terrain. External stairs may play a bigger role here too than in many other parts of the country. Wherever possible, buildings should be sited above fog zones, but not on ridgelines where wind can be a problem.

Overall Suggested Configuration and Layout

An open-plan layout for living spaces can be advantageous in most cases in order to facilitate the unobstructed flow of air through a unit. The fewer partitions and other obstacles the better.

Ceiling height is not as important here as in the other regions that can have extreme temperature variations throughout the year. Ceilings can be low, as the build-up of heat in the upper part of rooms will not be too great. Likewise, they can be high because it is not necessary to keep the hot air down near the occupants in winter. Good cross-ventilation can exhaust heat from ceilings in summer.

Entries, baths, kitchens, storage, service functions, and interior stairs are best located on the north side of the building, as they require the least amount of direct sunlight. All living spaces would benefit from some exposure to the sun for both psychological reasons as well as thermal comfort. As in other regions, westerly-facing spaces must be placed judiciously and with concern for excessive amounts of low-angled, direct sunlight that is difficult to control or temper.

With regard to massing, there is greater opportunity for variety here than elsewhere in the country due to the milder climate. Still, a compact building mass is the most effective way to mediate even these modest environmental demands. Row houses and clustered housing where party walls are shared work well to this end by limiting the amount of surface area exposed to wind and weather.

Building Circulation—Halls, and Staircases

If units are separated from each other or there is a great deal of topography to account for, then exterior walkways and steps can be useful to connect units to each other, parking, and to public sidewalks. Coverings are desirable over these exterior features due to the high amount of precipitation.

Circulation between units within the building may be achieved by way of covered, yet open halls and stairs. In some cases, these elements need to be protected not only from the rain, but also seasonally from wind. In such cases, retractable vertical barriers made of canvas can be installed to cover these openings by rolling up and down.

Double-loaded corridors with units on both sides are discouraged, as they do allow the opportunity for cross-ventilation through units. It is suggested that a single-load corridor arrangement be used or direct access to upper units by way of a dedicated staircase, without the need for halls.

Roof Type

As snow is rarely an issue, just about any roof shape or type will suffice. To shed rainfall, low- or highly pitched roofs, whether they be hipped, gabled, or shed work well. The low-profile roof does have a certain advantage, as it allows the wind to flow over it more easily. Flat green roofs are also a good option and have additional advantages over the other traditional solutions, as they can be made usable and can blend in better with the landscape.

In order to help protect and preserve building walls and siding, roofs with overhangs—preferably deep ones—can shed rainwater away. Gutters can further help to channel it off and away from buildings. The region has adequate water, so there is no need to capture it in cisterns or other storage containers.

Roof color may be either light or dark, as the amount of sunlight is not so necessary to reflect or absorb.

Windows and Window Treatments

Sunlight is rarely so strong that extra treatment is required to block it in most cases. Still, thoughtful consideration to orientation can make a difference to overall comfort and energy consumption. Overhangs on the south and a restrained number and size of windows facing west and east can make a difference here as elsewhere. There will be little heat loss through windows placed on the north side, so having glass face this direction is not as much of a problem due to heat loss as in colder climates.

Because of cloud cover during much of the year, there is less natural light than might be desired. Large glass areas can help to increase the amount of natural light available in each unit. Also, they will allow one to take advantage of views when available. Skylights, particularly on north-facing roofs, may be a suitable way to augment daylight to upper floor units.

Overhangs on the south side can shield unwanted direct sunlight. Light shelves above windows that reflect sunlight up onto the ceilings and therefore deeper into rooms are very useful and should be a consideration in all designs.

Most of the year, the outside temperature is within a comfortable range, so a large portion of the window area can be operable to facilitate the introduction of fresh air. In some cases, entire walls can be folded or slide away to make the outdoors totally accessible and integrated with the interior. Insects may be a problem, but not nearly as troublesome as in some other regions. Even still, screens may be desirable, and in some cases, required.

Where needed, interior window coverings can be selected from a wide variety of options. Curtains, shades, or blinds all are acceptable alternatives and need to be selected based on their ability to block sun and/or let air flow through them. Exterior window coverings are not required in this climate.

Materials and Construction

Wood is the clear preferred choice for construction material. It is found in large supply locally, making it relatively inexpensive. It comes in a wide range of shapes and sizes from beams, studs, planks, and shingle to mention a few. Its applications include structure, roofing, siding, interior wall coverings, trim, and flooring. It is the region's traditional choice as seen in the plank houses of the Salish and Yurok as well as the Victorians. Likewise, modern architects since the mid-1950s have embraced it for economic reasons as well as aesthetic ones.

The post and beam method of construction is an appropriate and practical way to structure Northwestern mid-size buildings. Because this method requires less refinement of timber, goes together quickly and easily, requires less interior finish, and creates flexible interior space when change is required, it saves time and money. Interior partitions can be composed of dimensional lumber, such as two by fours, with a covering of wood plank, paneling, or gypsum board.

Exterior siding and roofs can also be made of wood where codes allow. Planks, clapboards, shakes, and shingles all work well for wall coverings, but benefit from the protection of an overhang, as rot is their major enemy. Roofs can be made of wood shingles or shakes, where fire is not a problem.

Foundations are normally composed of concrete and run around the perimeters of the buildings. However, for sloped sites, the response is often to place the building on piers. This strategy allows the builder to work on uneven or sloped sites with little disruption to the natural contour of the land, thus saving money and time while building more lightly on the land. It also helps to keep buildings above flood waters caused by excessive rain or a tsunami. Where parking is required, many architects choose to raise the building on piers and place the parking below the first floor level. While this approach is cost-effective, it has the disadvantage of removing all apartments up and away from direct access to the grounds.

Outdoor Spaces

With such moderate temperatures most of the year, denizens of the Pacific Northwest consider access to the outdoors one of the great benefits to living there, and most tend to take advantage of the opportunity whenever possible. In addition to many great national and state parks close at hand, cities offer excellent parks and waterside promenades for this purpose. Multifamily buildings can augment these public amenities by offering pleasant and functional places where one can enjoy nature beyond the confines of their homes.

Balconies and rooftop terraces are recommended for upper stories where direct access to ground level is not feasible. These spaces should be ample in size, allowing for more than a mere table and couple of chairs as is typical today. They can be a place to relax and enjoy the sun when it is shining and sheltered when raining. Solid railings are recommended here, not only for safety, but to give added privacy and to cut down on unwanted wind.

Lower units with direct access to ground level can offer private courtyards or yards. It is here that children can feel more freedom to run and play in this additional space.

Due to the dampness, which can be incessant at times, outdoor spaces, such as terraces, can benefit from partial coverings that shed water. A roof or awning serves to keep one dry while still enjoying the fresh air.

Landscape

Landscape can be useful to shade in summer and protect from wind in the Pacific Northwest as in other regions. Evergreens planted as a hedge on the windward side can provide an effective windbreak. They can also offer effective shade from the harsh, low westerly sun. Deciduous trees and shrubs work well on the south side for shade in summer, but allow sun in during colder months. Vines grown on arbors attached to the building's south side can serve as an effective overhanging shading device.

In some coastal or mountainous locations, protecting buildings from strong winds may be a priority. Earthen berms are an effective technique for sheltering structures, but in hilly areas where there is already a certain amount of terrain variation, this may not be necessary or even possible. Where space is limited, solid walls of wood, stone, masonry, or concrete block may be used to the same end. Both techniques have the added advantage of providing more privacy from streets and/or neighbors.

Renewable Power and Mechanical Equipment

Ceiling fans, and to a lesser extent, whole house fans are an effective mechanical means for regulating inside comfort. However, if units are designed with good cross-ventilation, they will not often be required.

Solar panels will be less effective here than in many other parts of the country because of the region's large number of cloudy days. Wind power along the coast and in the hills may help supply some energy to neighborhoods, but the reliance upon hydropower is most likely to persist for a long time into the future.

The Prospect for Future Urban Development in the Pacific Northwest

When the early explorers first charted its coastline, the region was rich in natural resources and it remains so to this day. Food, water, energy, and lumber are all available in quantities large enough to sustain growth for the foreseeable future.

The region is a rich source of food for not only itself, but for export around the country and the world. Today, there is still an abundance of fish and shellfish taken from the sea and local rivers as it has been for millennia. A wide assortment of agricultural products are grown in its fertile river valleys such as the Willamette, Napa, Sonoma, and others. These fertile croplands, vineyards, and orchards are watered from rain and snowmelt, requiring little irrigation unlike many of the nation's other productive regions. Additionally, the growing season is a long one (8 months or more) due to the mild climate where freezing temperatures last only briefly.

Rivers filled by snowmelt from the Cascade Mountains and abundant rains not only provide the water that all civilizations rely on for their existence, but today, these rivers

Figure 8.17
An Apartment Complex In San Francisco, CA, Demonstrates Modern City Living, With The Benefit Of Traditional Bay Windows And Common Open Spaces

have been dammed to supply electrical power, which our modern societies rely on to function. Its largest dam, the Grand Coulee on the Columbia River, was built in 1933. Since then, no fewer than ten other dams have been built downstream from it. Furthermore, the United States and Canada have agreed to build three additional dams in Canada "to store water during periods of heavy flow and then release the water when flow was low to guarantee consistent power generation."[40] Hydroelectric generation in the region produces "enough electricity to meet the needs of 13.6 million homes. And because hydropower is one of the lowest cost forms of energy, most Northwest residents have a significantly lower electric bill than residents in other parts of the country."[41] This lower energy cost has helped to attract "manufacturers that are heavy power consumers; most notable is the aluminum-smelting industry."[42] "But peak water flow is typically a seasonal event driven by snowpack melt, so the price-reducing effect of hydropower normally lasts only a few months each year, typically in the spring and early summer."[43]

Even with these advantages, the region is still reliant on natural gas and oil to generate additional power, fuel vehicles, and heat buildings. Fortunately, as noted earlier, the need for electrical power is greatly reduced due to a good supply of hydroelectric power and the need for heating and air conditioning is comparatively small as a result of the mild climate. The need for gasoline to power cars, trucks, and buses is being addressed by the installation of good public transport and a concerted effort to make biking a priority in cities.

Add to these points the fact that the forests can provide a reliable flow of timber for future construction. Known as the "timber basket," the northwestern region is governed by some of the world's toughest environmental laws, which provide protection for habitat, watersheds, soils, and biological diversity. Reforestation and management practices are not voluntary, but are enforced by law, and systematic replanting has been going on since 1912. "Each year, more than 1.5 billion tree seedlings are planted in the U.S.—some five new trees for each American. Nationally, annual forest growth has continually exceeded harvest since the 1940s."[44]

In the long run, it appears that the Pacific Northwest will have adequate resources to sustain continued growth if it uses these gifts wisely; even with farsighted urban planning, it still is left with many of the same problems as other cities around the country. One of the most obvious problems is traffic congestion. The cities along the northern Pacific coast, despite effective long-range planning and controlled growth, are not immune to the lingering problem of traffic congestion that plagues most of the world's metropolises. Commuting times in its largest cities are long and rush-hour traffic jams are normal, but there is a concerted effort to tackle the problem on a long-term basis. Oregon, through its urban growth boundaries legislation, has started to put the brakes on sprawl and loss of valuable farmland. Seattle, by way of their urban village strategy, is doing much the same thing as are other cities. All of the cities of the region seem committed to developing an efficient rapid transit system and biking lanes to make their cities more car-free and walkable. Hopefully, their examples will encourage others to follow suit in the years to come.

In total, the northern Pacific coast has more positive elements for growth than negative ones and is active in preserving these assets for future generations. Its citizens as a whole are probably more sensitive to environmental issues than anywhere else in the country and they tend to act on them. This proactive stance will go a long way toward maintaining a healthy physical environment despite expected dramatic future growth.

Summary of Suggested Building Practices for the Pacific Northwest

Main environmental objectives: Defend against rain and wind. Provide additional natural lighting.

Orientation

- Orientation is less important here, but living areas should normally be south to southeast facing
- Share walls with neighbors as with row houses or cluster buildings
- East and west walls can have a few openings, but they should not be excessive
- Covered, open stairs for unit access

Layout

- Narrow volumes with open living areas
- Deep overhangs to help protect exterior walls and windows from rain (most valuable on south side)
- Ceilings height can be either low or high, as heating/cooling demands are less important
- Single-loaded corridors when horizontal corridors between units are required, but direct access via stairs between units is most desirable

Construction

- Build on piers off the ground where terrain is sloped
- Wood post and beam frame is preferred
- Maintain exposed wooden roof and floor structure on interiors to save cost of interior finish
- Insulate well all walls, roofs, and exposed floors

Recommended Construction/Structural Materials

- Timber and/or light wood structural framing is appropriate
- Wood plank, shingle, or shake siding for roofing and siding

Roofs

- Flat, green roofs where advantageous
- Low- to steeply pitched roofs are all acceptable
- Wood shakes or shingles roof covering where code allows

Shading

- Overhangs to protect glass from excessive sunlight on the south side
- Exterior solid, louvered shutters or rolling doors particularly on the west side, less important on the east side
- Provide covered areas for living and working outside, such as terraces, decks, porches, and balconies

Windows

- Provide maximum opening for airflow—casement or awning most desirable. Folding or garage doors, which open spaces up entirely to exterior are possible

- Glass exposed on west- and east-facing walls should be minimal
- South side can afford to be fully glazed (if shaded for summer sun) to warm and help light interiors
- North side can have as much glass as desired to provide additional light and view
- Skylights may be used to introduce more light on top-floor roofs

Ventilation and Cooling

- Good cross-ventilation is desirable
- Encourage air movement with ceiling fans, and in some cases, whole house fans
- Windows should allow full ventilation when desired
- Skylights in roofs may be used to exhaust hot air build-up on top floors
- Provide covered outdoor areas, such as terraces and balconies, for summer living

Heating

- Dark floors where sun enters through south-facing window walls can retain warmth
- Fireplaces or wood stoves can provide minimal space heating to add warmth in winter

Water

- Channel rainwater away from the structure as quickly as possible through guttering
- Collect all gray water for flushing toilets and watering garden plants

Notes

1 Garreau, Joel. *The Nine Nations of North America*. Avon Books (1981) New York. p. 4.
2 *The Encyclopedia of Earth*. Marine West Coast Forests ecoregion The Commission for Environmental Cooperation (CEC). Website: www.eoearth.org/view/article/154464/.
3 U.S. Climate Data. *San Francisco*. Website: www.usclimatedata.com/climate/san-francisco/california/united-states/usca0987.
4 Garreau, Joel. *The Nine Nations of North America*. Avon Books (1981) New York. p. 260.
5 Embassy of the United States in Japan. *About the USA*. Website: http://aboutusa.japan.usembassy.gov/e/jusa-geography-15.html.
6 Embassy of the United States in Japan. *About the USA*. Website: http://aboutusa.japan.usembassy.gov/e/jusa-geography-15.html.
7 Richards, Rand (1992). *Historic San Francisco: A Concise History and Guide*. Heritage House (2011) San Francisco, CA.
8 Woodard, Colin. *American Nations: A History of the Eleven Rival Regional Cultures of North America*. Penguin Books (2011) New York.
9 *The Encyclopedia of Earth*. Marine West Coast Forests ecoregion. The Commission for Environmental Cooperation (CEC). Website: www.eoearth.org/view/article/154464/.
10 City of Portland. *Donation Claims*. Website: www.portlandoregon.gov/transportation/article/65586.
11 Clark, William and Meriwether Lewis. *The Journals of Lewis and Clark, 1804-1806*. E-book (2005). Website: http://www.gutenberg.org/ebooks/8419?msg=welcome_stranger#link12H_4_0048.
12 Nabokov, Peter and Robert Easton. *Native American Architecture*. Oxford University Press (1989) New York. p. 233.
13 Finney, Dee (Ed.). *Native American Housing*. Website: www.greatdreams.com/native/nativehsg.htm#PIT.

14 Nabokov, Peter and Robert Easton. *Native American Architecture*. Oxford University Press (1989) New York. p. 236.

15 Nabokov, Peter and Robert Easton. *Native American Architecture*. Oxford University Press (1989) New York. p. 235.

16 Kroeber, Alfred L. Yurok: Arts Houses. *Handbook of the Indians of California*. Dover Publications (1976) New York. p. 78. Website: https://books.google.com/books?id=YDdn0WNMQMYC&pg=PA134&lpg=PA134&dq=takimitlding&source=bl&ots=fF-OfarEnc&sig=SCOpcOH6evnTn5gstRRQMc0a-d0&hl=en&sa=X&ved=0CCoQ6AEwAmoVChMI_M7Rra-1xwIVwnM-Ch0ZZgL2#v=onepage&q=takimitlding&f=false.

17 American Indian Tradition & Continuity. *Cedar Plank House of the Northwest Coast*. Website: http://naxnox.weebly.com/plank-houses.html.

18 King, Anthony D. *The Bungalow: The Production of a Global Culture*. Oxford University Press (1995) New York. p. 141.

19 Floating Homes Association, Inc. *The History of Houseboats on Richardson's Bay*. Website: http://floatinghomes.org/about/community/.

20 Walker, Lester. Floating House. *American Shelter: An Illustrate Encyclopedia of the American Home*. The Overlook Press (1981) Woodstock, NY. pp. 280–282.

21 Scharmer, Roger P. Houseboats. *Home Sweet Home: American Domestic Vernacular Architecture*. Craft and Folk Art Museum, Rizolli (1983). New York. pp. 44–48.

22 Walker, Lester. Floating House. *American Shelter: An Illustrate Encyclopedia of the American Home*. The Overlook Press (1981) Woodstock, NY. pp. 280–282.

23 Western Wood Products Association. *Other Western Species*. Website: www.wwpa.org/SPECIES PRODUCTS/OtherSpecies/tabid/840/Default.aspx.

24 Anna Marie Erwert. *SFGate*. S.F. lots not the smallest in U.S., but still really small. (July 28, 2015). Website: http://blog.sfgate.com/ontheblock/2015/07/28/s-f-lots-not-the-smallest-in-the-u-s-but-still-really-small/.

25 Binney, Marcus. *Town Houses: Urban Houses from 1200 to the Present Day*. Whitney Library of Design (1998) New York. pp. 118–121.

26 Baer, Morley., Pomada, Elizabeth., and Michael Larson. *Painted Ladies*. E. P. Dutton (1978). New York.

27 Wikipedia. *Pacific Northwest*. Website: https://en.wikipedia.org/wiki/Pacific_Northwest.

28 Embassy of the United States in Japan. *About the USA*. Website: http://aboutusa.japan.usembassy.gov/e/jusa-geography-15.html.

29 National Park Service. *FAQ*. Website: www.nps.gov/redw/faqs.htm.

30 Big Sur Chamber of Commerce. *Ancient Redwoods Thrive Along The Big Sur Coast*. Website: www.bigsurcalifornia.org/redwoods.html.

31 Olson, David F., Roy, Douglas F. and Gerald A. Walters. *Redwood*. Website: www.na.fs.fed.us/pubs/silvics_manual/Volume_1/sequoia/sempervirens.htm.

32 Western Wood Products Association. *Douglas Fir and Western Larch*. Website: www.wwpa.org/SPECIESPRODUCTS/DouglasFir/tabid/405/Default.aspx.

33 Western Wood Products Association. *Hem-Fir*. Website: www.wwpa.org/SPECIESPRODUCTS/HemFir/tabid/299/Default.aspx.

34 NSDA. *Western Redcedar*. Website: www.na.fs.fed.us/pubs/silvics_manual/Volume_1/thuja/plicata.htm.

35 Melillo, Jerry M., Terese (T.C.) Richmond, and Gary W. Yohe, (Eds.). *2014: Climate Change Impacts in the United States: The Third National Climate Assessment*. U.S. Global Change Research Program. doi:10.7930/J0Z31WJ2. Website: http://s3.amazonaws.com/nca2014/high/NCA3_Climate_Change_Impacts_in_the_United%20States_HighRes.pdf.

36 University of Washington, College of the Environment. The Department of Atmospheric Science. *Northwest Windstorms*. Website: www.atmos.washington.edu/cliff/Wind.pdf.

37 Read, Wolf. *The Storm King: Some Historical Weather Events in the Pacific Northwest*. Office of the Washington State Climatologist. Website: www.climate.washington.edu/stormking/.

38 Schulz, Katheryn. The Really Big One: An Earthquake Will Destroy a Sizable Portion of the Costal Northwest. The question is when. *The New Yorker* (July 20, 2015).

39 *Dianne Rhem's Show*. 8/18/2015.

40 Embassy of the United States in Japan. *About the USA*. Website: http://aboutusa.japan.usembassy.gov/e/jusa-geography-15.html.

41 Foundation for Water & Energy Foundation. *Overview of Hydropower in the Northwest*. Website: http://fwee.org/education/the-nature-of-water-power/overview-of-hydropower-in-the-northwest/.

42 Embassy of the United States in Japan. *About the USA*. Website: http://aboutusa.japan.usembassy.gov/e/jusa-geography-15.html.

43 EPA. *Today in Energy*. Website: www.eia.gov/todayinenergy/detail.cfm?id=5070.

44 Western Wood Products Association. *Douglas Fir and Western Larch*. Website: www.wwpa.org/SPECIESPRODUCTS/DouglasFir/tabid/405/Default.aspx.

Chapter 9

Building a Sustainable Future Based on Vernacular Principles

Currently, a sustainable lifestyle is voluntary, an option that we can choose or not, and to many people, it is considered an inconvenient one. It requires us to drive less, turn the thermostat down in the winter, perspire in summer, put ugly solar panels on our roofs, . . . the list goes on and on. For the most part, we as a society have chosen not to make an all-out effort to resolve the earth's impending environmental problems because as Brian Edwards contends, "The problem is not a lack of knowledge but the reluctance of consumers to prioritise low energy design. Sustainable housing is constrained by consumer attitudes, not technical uncertainty. In fact, some have suggested that the resistance to sustainability is 80 percent cultural . . ."[1] Certainly, the changes anticipated in this book will only happen when we have little or no choice, as they seem to represent in the minds of the public a diminishment of convenience and by association—comfort. This perceived loss of comfort may be true to a certain extent, but there are tradeoffs that might make one's change of lifestyle much more palatable, maybe even more fulfilling than our present, more destructive and consuming one. Regardless of our desire to avoid these annoyances and retain the status quo in our lives, it is entirely likely that the timeframe that mankind can continue on its current destructive path will be shorter than many expect and may well be upon us by mid-century, if not sooner.

The solution commonly promoted to save the environment and allow us to continue our current lifestyle with only slight modifications and as little sacrifice as possible relies on the principle of sustainability. Somewhat ironically, "Reduce, Reuse and Recycle," the mantra of the sustainability movement, embodies the spirit of the vernacular. The vernacular teaches us how to live with less, conserve more, and work with renewable elements, which are the least detrimental to the planet. In many respects, a sustainable community is synonymous with those created using vernacular principles and values. In contrast with the popular perception of sacrifice, the vernacular can offer the possibility of a healthier, more pleasant, and fulfilling lives than in our current one, for a variety of reasons. When one links the best of the traditional with the best of the new, major strides can be made toward helping us reach the goal of a stronger society and healthier planet. Here are some aspects of the vernacular approach to building a sustainable future that demonstrate its virtues to future generations.

Vernacular and Economics

Some skeptics might argue that the use of seemingly outmoded, vernacular principles, technologies, and materials can never again affordably satisfy our needs. However, when one examines the choice of methods and materials the vernacular employs, it should be abundantly clear that from a purely economic perspective, these simpler means not only can pass that test, but will provide more worthwhile results than the steel and glass towers offer.

The vernacular has always been associated with an economy of means—thrift, practicality, and a judicious use of the available resources. The materials it employs are found locally, requiring minimal transportation, and little processing to make them useful— both of which save money. Construction with these materials is normally by way of simple, well-established methods that require little energy and are minimally polluting.

By its very nature, the vernacular depends on the efficiency of space, time, and materials. There is little waste of resources under these conditions. Unfortunately, we are currently living in the most wasteful and consumptive society ever to exist on the planet, which is leading us down a predictably self-destructive path. It is only through a more thoughtful and conservation-oriented approach that we can save for subsequent generations what we are in the process of destroying. The simple truth is that we cannot afford to continue in this mode indefinitely as our planet is priceless. The vernacular offers us an alternative that will pay off in more ways than immediate monetary ones can ever hope to do.

Vernacular and Nature

Beyond the economic benefits, the vernacular teaches us to live in harmony with climate, not try to overcome it by mechanical means. Passive strategies, when employed correctly, can be very effective and keep us reasonably comfortable when sun, rain, temperature, and humidity would make us feel otherwise. Under these circumstances, one might yet again perspire on hot summer days and need to add an extra layer of clothing on colder winter nights, but that may not be asking too much when our planet is at risk. The siesta may yet again find a place in southerners' lives. Sitting by a warming fireplace could have merit again in northern climates to relieve the chill. When temperatures allow, one may enjoy the pleasure of relaxing out of doors in the fresh air or on the porch. An outdoor lifestyle is easily equated to a healthy and vigorous one.

One of the major reasons for urban flight is that families simply want to have open space and fresh air, where kids can play and all can enjoy what nature has to offer. This is not to say that the city cannot give us these benefits as well, because it can with public parks. However, developers of future housing will also need to provide open spaces as an amenity, whether they be private on a balcony, a courtyard, or a yard at ground level. Common spaces where neighbors can congregate and socialize on rooftops or central courtyards can provide the community with that one special amenity—a natural setting.

Living with nature can give added value and meaning to our daily lives and begin to acknowledge our psychological and physical reliance on it for personal renewal. The ability to once again fully open our windows will give us the fresh air we have long traded for "conditioned air" made warm and cool by the burning of fossil fuels. We may end up sacrificing some of our comfort for a closer relationship with our surroundings, but it might turn out to be a bonus rather than a disadvantage.

Vernacular and Tradition

All too often, a desire for the *new* or the *modern* implies that one forgets the past and its ways. History to the modernist architects was a taboo subject. In 1938, when architect and educator Walter Gropius became the chairman of Department of Architecture at Harvard's Graduate School of Design, he removed the teaching of history from the curriculum. He wished to wipe the slate clean and start fresh. This movement sought to build a new form of architecture, without any trace of past concepts or techniques. Nor would these buildings have any relationship to climate, local resources, or tradition. The glass box was the result—a building that could be placed anywhere.

In a reaction against this attempt to erase history from our modern structures, the postmodernists of the early 1980s sought to promote its place in architecture, but they trivialized it through a pastiche of superficial historical references. They applied what could be referred to as cartoons of previously functional historical elements to their own modernist buildings. This distortion of tradition gave a meaninglessness to their work and was soon forgotten.

A society without a sense of history and place is one adrift without a context to learn from and build upon. Its buildings become generic in character—those of some other place and/or time with little or no local meaning. The vernacular bases its being on a respect for past ways and the natural growth that results from it. It gives a specific character to buildings that have been derived from these methods and takes pride in their differences from other places and cultures. It would be a shame to lose the special qualities of different countries and regions around the world as well as those of our own nation. This variety creates a richness that cannot be replaced solely by the modern. Without a past and a place, there can be little pride in who we are as a people or what our predecessors achieved. The vernacular celebrates one's uniqueness.

Vernacular and Aesthetics

Tall, glimmering modern buildings composed of steel or concrete structural frames and covered with a thin sheath of glass, metal panels, and veneers of various manufactured products have great allure, but the architects' goal here is to be unique and stand out on the city skyline. Each new building is vying for the position of most beautiful, unique, or spectacular. Tallest is the best, shiny is desirable, and the unusual is required to meet the challenge. The image projected by such powerful structures is designed to reflect the wealth and importance of the corporations that they represent.

By contrast, the aesthetics of the vernacular are found directly in an appreciation of the inherent beauty derived from the materials used, the details that resulted from their application and combination, as well as the visual pleasure resulting from the overall form. Vernacular builders were certainly aware of and worked in the style of the day, but their work was most closely tied to other fundamental, motivating forces. Their desire was not so much to invent, but to perfect. Time after time, the same basic form was constructed using the same methods with only small variations. However, even minor iteration had the potential to produce unique exemplars. We can now appreciate the overall collection of buildings that make up each type and produced in this evolution, as not only interesting or curious, but for their subtle refinements. Modest in scale and calm in nature, they have come to represent in their own way a uniqueness, but not one for the sake of being different, but one that displays a regional character.

Vernacular and Technology

The vernacular by its very nature is not static, but thrives on innovation. It embodies a process of growth, change, and development over time, which does not exclude new techniques, but thrives on them. More advanced, modern, methods, and processes that tend to save time, energy, and money, such as prefabrication and modulation, are easily integrated into the vernacular construction processes, making them more efficient and cost-effective, without sacrificing its integrity. The overall results of such inclusions allow us to build in the most practical manner, resulting in the best possible product at the lowest cost. This openness to the adoption of new ideas and technologies helps it grow and maintain a relevancy through time.

Similarly, its methods when linked with the best of modern, sustainable ones will tend to bring us a world that is less polluting and more harmonious with the natural one. Its integration of passive technologies to help heat, cool, and power our buildings bring us more in harmony with our surroundings. Favoring power generated from natural, unlimited, and nonpolluting sources such as wind, sun, water, and geothermal techniques and not a reliance on the earth's limited fossil fuels, the vernacular demonstrates its sustainability. The incorporation of these clean, safe energy techniques that limit negative climatic consequences are now an imperative.

Vernacular and Natural Resources

The vernacular teaches us to use those resources that are at hand, can be regenerated or are abundant, and require little refinement rather than search the globe for more exotic, limited, and potentially damaging ones. Steel, concrete, and aluminum make up some of the finite resources that we have become dependent on. Unfortunately, these materials are costly to produce, but they also come with a significant long-term environmental expense. Because of the need for enormous amounts of fossil fuels to transport and refine them into usable construction materials, they produce a large portion of the CO_2 in our atmosphere, thus contributing to global warming. It is said that the production of concrete alone is responsible for 5 percent of all greenhouse gases.[2] As a consequence, these manufactured materials may end up costing future generations much more than the generation that actually produced them. Their transportation and refinement processes cost money, beyond which the environmental degradation to our atmosphere and planet make any economic argument in their favor a short-term one at best. On the other hand, earth, brick, and wood are not only the cheapest materials that we have available to construct buildings and cities, but unlike popular ones today, they are benign and not harmful to the environment. They require less transportation, as they are found locally and there is little need to refine them further.

There is no doubt that in the future, we will continue to use steel, concrete, and aluminum for building construction, but it will be done much more sparingly and with greater thought. Concrete will be needed in foundations and slabs and to strengthen adobe brick and rammed earth. Steel will be needed as connectors for large timbers, wood to wood. Likewise, some materials made from petrochemicals will be of continued value. Insulation—foam (blown-in or ridged) and fiberglass, roofing membranes and the like will not disappear, but will continue to have a place in our future buildings.

By combining the vernacular approach of using sustainable materials with a more modest and appropriate use of modern ones, we will be able to build well into the distant future, without great harm to the environment.

Vernacular and the Urban Context

Even though the vernacular is most often focused on buildings more than on neighborhoods or cities, its lessons go well beyond those relating to simple structures. It can certainly be applied to the creation of better communities within the already existing framework of our nation's cities and towns.

Most communities that we can consider as vernacular were created before the automobile became ubiquitous, and consequently, these older places were where people actually lived and worked. Constrained by a lack of mobility, housing was located closer to the workplace, necessary goods, and civic purposes than we typically find in modern cities today. Cities were composed of single-family homes as well as a large percentage of multifamily buildings (townhouses and apartments) consolidated in low- to mid-rise buildings. Furthermore, these older buildings were designed and built long before air conditioning became a necessity and people lived out of doors more than we do today, providing greater social interaction among its citizens. People walked or biked more to get where they needed to go. These older cities were not always ideal places to live, as many people were relegated to unsanitary slums or ghettos, but when the best of the vernacular principles are merged with our highest social motivations, great cities can be achieved.

Figure 9.1
Soulless Apartment Blocks, Whether They Are Public Housing (On Left) In Cambridge, MA, Or Luxury Housing On Philadelphia's Society Hill (On Right), Vary Little In Concept. They Provide Shelter, And In Some Cases, Luxurious Amenities, But Lack Direct Connection To The Outside Or Sense Of Community

The Vernacular and a Better Style of Life

Most of the current solutions advanced to resolve our future problems are aimed primarily at sustaining our current lifestyle. All too often, these innovations are simply ways in which technology can help us save energy without changing our habits or downsizing. An energy-conserving approach is certainly advisable today and will be a requirement in the future. However, most Americans have reached a level of comfort and convenience that will be hard to give up. We actively seek ways to maintain it for ourselves and to pass it

along to generations to come. Unfortunately, by maintaining the status quo and simply reducing the amount of fossil fuels we use, we continue to destroy the planet and with it the very lifestyle that we are determined to keep.

Even though it may be true that a lifestyle based on vernacular methods will dictate certain tradeoffs, they could be for our own good. We might trade unhealthy buildings for fresh air. We may need to give up the thrill of speed that we find in powerboats, jet skis, snowmobiles, and other fast, motorized playthings and settle for paddling, sledding, walking, and biking for our excitement. We may need to put aside the daily commute and begin to interact with neighbors on an impromptu basis as we pass each other in the park or we walk by them as they sit on their porches or balconies. We may travel by air less and find our adventures closer to home as opposed to in other parts of the world. We may find that we shop more locally and our produce comes from farms nearby. We may give up going to the gym for integrating exercise into our daily lives as we propel ourselves between destinations. It could even signal an end to the so-called "obesity epidemic" and resolve other health problems associated with a sedentary life and polluted air. We may need to settle for one house, not two or more, and that one house may be smaller than our parents', but it may be more manageable and affordable. Convenience of mobility may not be the ability to drive anywhere at any time, but the ability to get there on foot, without the need to support a gas-consuming vehicle.

The benefits of working toward employing vernacular methods and adopting such attitudes that go along with it should now be clear. The list of advantages is a long one.

Figure 9.2
This Housing Focuses On Shared Outdoor Space Used For Social Gatherings And Recreation

The vernacular is basically a quieter, calmer, and simpler one. By adopting these principles as a way of life, the world and its people will be the overall beneficiaries.

However, little will change until society finally comes up against unavoidable challenges that require us to change our ways. Climate change with its assortment of unpleasant consequences and the depletion of petroleum and building materials will present these challenges. We can only hope that we do not wait too long to address them.

Each of us must do our part, but in the big picture, political action is what it will take to make the necessary legislation to bring all of the pieces together. Unfortunately, politicians are slow to act and seem to do so only in times of crisis or when their constituents demand it. Like voting for higher taxes, few politicians will dare risk re-election by voting for what might be perceived as reducing Americans' lifestyle or coming in conflict with corporate interests. We are in or will shortly be in crisis. It, therefore, is contingent upon American citizens to see into the future and require change for the sake of their children and grandchildren, if not for themselves.

Goals for Repopulating Cities

- Discourage tall buildings
- Discourage more highway building
- Change zoning to encourage more and denser family housing with other uses
- Build neighborhoods into communities by encouraging:

  - cultural and economic diversity
  - improved schools
  - shopping—food markets
  - cultural and religious facilities
  - indoor and outdoor recreational spaces

- We should not build in areas that are not sustainable or in harms way from storms and sea level rise
- Build near jobs
- Look to the past for advice
- Improve public mass transit
- Encourage walking and biking

Notes

1 Edwards, Brian, and David Turrent (Eds.). *Sustainable Housing: Principle & Practice*. Taylor & Francis (2000) London. p. 10.
2 Rubenstein, Madeleine. Emissions from the Concrete Industry. *State of the Planet: Earth Institute*. Columbia University (May 9, 2012). Website: http://blogs.ei.columbia.edu/2012/05/09/emissions-from-the-cement-industry/

Appendix

The following pages are intended to show the variety of building types that can be derived from the previously suggested regional design strategies and building components. They are not to be construed as definitive, only representative of the possibilities.

The Northeast

This prototype of a brick row house expresses its relationship to the northeastern tradition through the use of bay windows, the stoop (front steps), and sunken basement level with living space. Windows are designed to capture as much sunlight as possible and require minimal shading from the sun. The usable flat roof and rear porches provide fair weather outdoor space for occupants. Common rooms located on the roof give the occupants a place to socialize and relax.

Figure 10.1

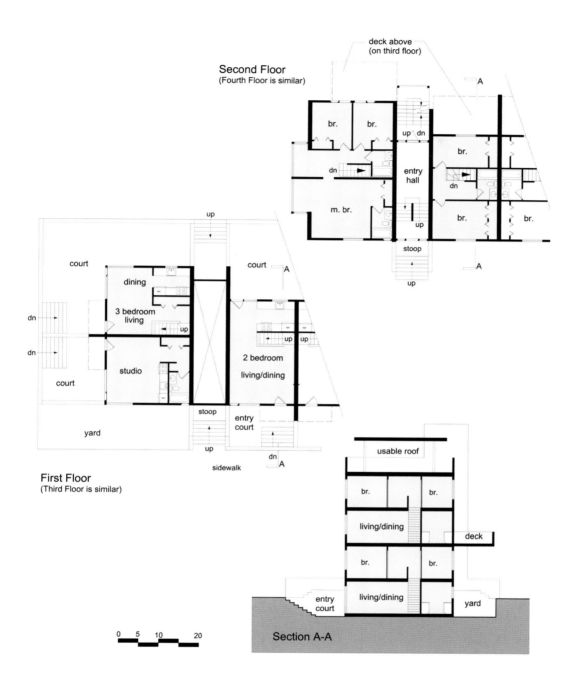

Second Floor
(Fourth Floor is similar)

deck above
(on third floor)

br.   br.

up dn

dn

entry
hall

br.

dn

m. br.

br.   br.

up

stoop

up

A

A

up

court

court   A

dining

dn

3 bedroom
living

up

dn

studio

2 bedroom

living/dining

up up

yard

stoop

entry
court

up

First Floor
(Third Floor is similar)

dn   A

sidewalk

usable roof

br.   br.

living/dining

deck

br.   br.

living/dining

entry
court

yard

Section A-A

0   5   10   20

Figure 10.2

The Midwest
The courtyard forms the core of this prototype, which not only serves as its focus, but provides outdoor social and recreational space in addition to the flat roofs and rear porches. Rather than bay windows, so typical in the northeast, it provides sunrooms that add a buffer from the cold and wind and make pleasant sunny sitting areas year round. Brick with stone detailing are the predominant exterior materials in this example.

Figure 10.3

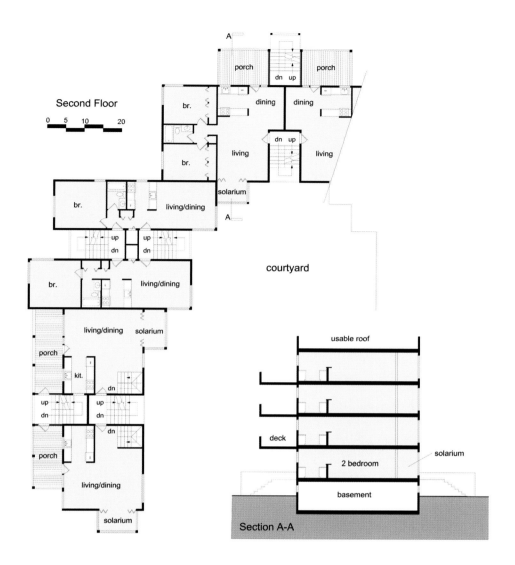

Second Floor

0 5 10 20

porch

dn up

porch

br.

dining

dining

br.

living

living

br.

living/dining

solarium

A

A

up
dn

up
dn

courtyard

br.

living/dining

living/dining

solarium

porch

kit.

dn

up
dn

up
dn

dn

porch

living/dining

porch

solarium

usable roof

deck

solarium

2 bedroom

basement

Section A-A

Figure 10.4

The South

Raised above the ground on piers, this southern prototype is made solely of wood with a heavy timber frame, board siding and shingle roofing. Whenever possible, it is configured to be only one room wide with large operable windows to facilitate cross ventilation. Shaded or screened porches, as well as roof decks provide opportunities to enjoy the outdoors. Pitched roofs not only shed rain efficiently, they provide a surface on which to install solar panels.

Figure 10.5

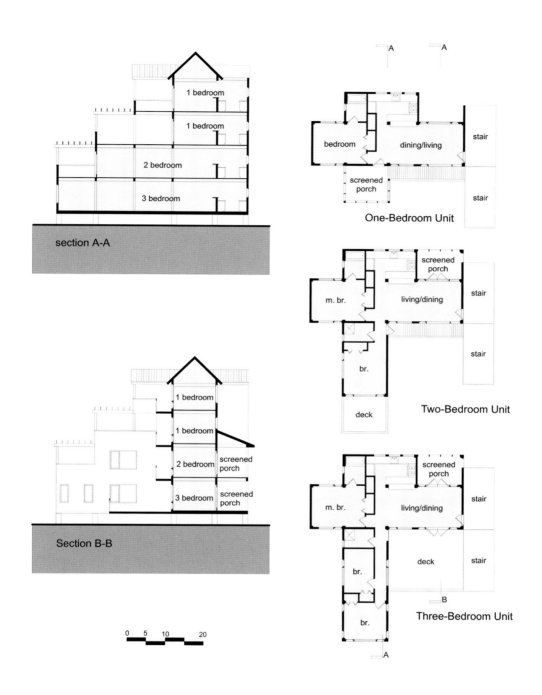

section A-A

One-Bedroom Unit

Section B-B

Two-Bedroom Unit

Three-Bedroom Unit

0 5 10 20

Figure 10.6

The Great Plains

This building's rounded ends, sunken first level along with earthen berms and evergreen windbreaks help protect the building from the brunt of frequent high winds - especially tornados. Thick earthen or concrete block walls buttressed by the stairs provide additional strength and rigidity to the overall structure. Shaded balconies give upper units private outdoor space, while lower ones benefit from ground floor courtyards.

Figure 10.7

REINVENTING AN URBAN VERNACULAR

4th

3rd

2nd

1st

Section

0 5 10 20

roof

roof

dn

br.

m. br.

roof

Fourh Floor

dn

dn

m. br.

br.

living/dining

up

dn

Third Floor

balcony

dn

roof

roof

up

dn

dn

dn

up

dn

dining/ living

living/dining

dining/ living

up

dn

dn

Second Floor

Figure 10.8

The West

Thick earthen or concrete block walls separate units and provide support for floors and roofs. The flat roof is designed for outdoor living under the shade of solar arrays reminiscent of *ramadas* of previous times. Courtyards on the ground floor provide spacious outdoor space for families while upper levels have deeply recessed balconies, which serve as shady courtyards.

Figure 10.9

REINVENTING AN URBAN VERNACULAR

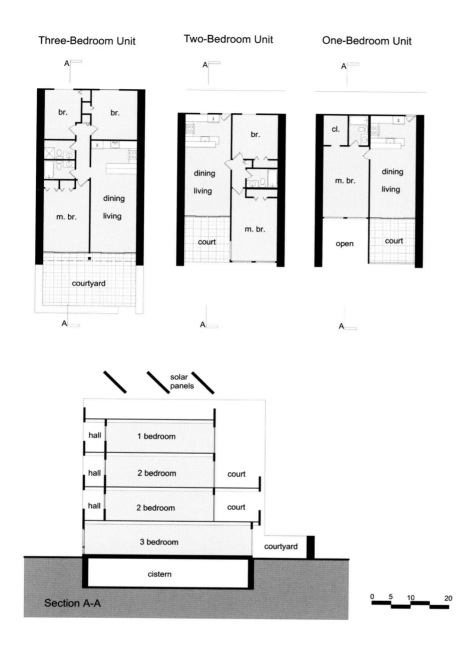

Three-Bedroom Unit

br. br.

m. br. dining living

courtyard

A

Two-Bedroom Unit

br.

dining living

m. br.

court

A

One-Bedroom Unit

cl.

m. br. dining living

open court

A

solar panels

hall 1 bedroom

hall 2 bedroom court

hall 2 bedroom court

3 bedroom courtyard

cistern

Section A-A

0 5 10 20

Figure 10.10

The Pacific Northwest

As buildings of the Northwest are obliged to conform to often steep contours, this prototype steps up and down with the roll of the land. In keeping with a vigorous outdoor lifestyle, stairs are open and inviting. All units are provided with large balconies on street side, some have them in the rear as well, while the ground floor units enjoy semi-private courtyards. The outside is brought inside by way of folding doors that allow the entire wall to open up. In order to get the maximum amount of illumination, light shelves reflect sunlight back into the deeper units while shading the glass below them from direct exposure.

Figure 10.11

REINVENTING AN URBAN VERNACULAR

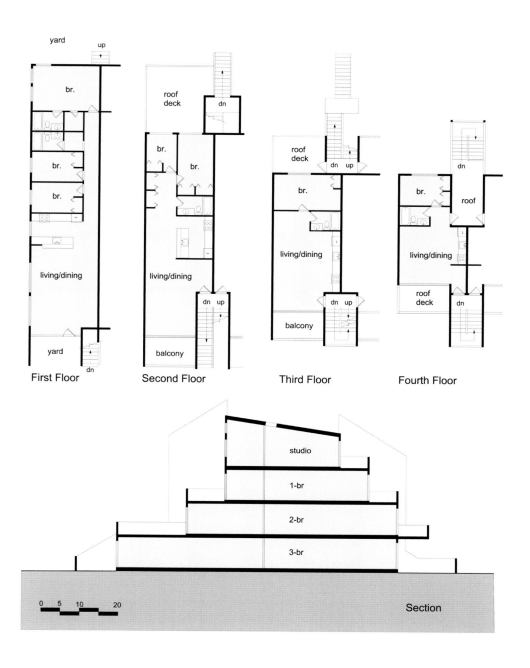

yard

up

br.

br.

br.

living/dining

yard

dn

First Floor

roof deck

dn

br.

br.

living/dining

balcony

dn   up

Second Floor

roof deck

dn   up

br.

living/dining

balcony

dn   up

Third Floor

dn

br.

roof

living/dining

roof deck

dn

Fourth Floor

studio

1-br

2-br

3-br

0   5   10   20

Section

Figure 10.12

Index

Note: Page numbers in *italic* refer to figures

Taylor & Francis eBooks

Helping you to choose the right eBooks for your Library

Add Routledge titles to your library's digital collection today. Taylor and Francis ebooks contains over 50,000 titles in the Humanities, Social Sciences, Behavioural Sciences, Built Environment and Law.

Choose from a range of subject packages or create your own!

Benefits for you

» Free MARC records
» COUNTER-compliant usage statistics
» Flexible purchase and pricing options
» All titles DRM-free.

Benefits for your user

» Off-site, anytime access via Athens or referring URL
» Print or copy pages or chapters
» Full content search
» Bookmark, highlight and annotate text
» Access to thousands of pages of quality research at the click of a button.

REQUEST YOUR
FREE
INSTITUTIONAL
TRIAL TODAY

Free Trials Available
We offer free trials to qualifying academic, corporate and government customers.

eCollections – Choose from over 30 subject eCollections, including:

Archaeology	Language Learning
Architecture	Law
Asian Studies	Literature
Business & Management	Media & Communication
Classical Studies	Middle East Studies
Construction	Music
Creative & Media Arts	Philosophy
Criminology & Criminal Justice	Planning
Economics	Politics
Education	Psychology & Mental Health
Energy	Religion
Engineering	Security
English Language & Linguistics	Social Work
Environment & Sustainability	Sociology
Geography	Sport
Health Studies	Theatre & Performance
History	Tourism, Hospitality & Events

For more information, pricing enquiries or to order a free trial, please contact your local sales team:
www.tandfebooks.com/page/sales